HOW TO CUSTOMIZE YOUR

SPORT TRUCK

A Complete
Guide to Interior, Exterior, and
Engine Modifications and Accessories

D1710091

Michael Bargo

Motorbooks International
Publishers & Wholesalers ®

First published in 1989 by Motorbooks International
Publishers & Wholesalers, P O Box 2, 729 Prospect
Avenue, Osceola, WI 54020 USA

Printed and bound in the United States of America

The information in this book is true and complete to
the best of our knowledge. All recommendations are
made without any guarantee on the part of the author
or publisher, who also disclaim any liability incurred in
connection with the use of this data or specific details

We recognize that some words, model names and
designations, for example, mentioned herein are the
property of the trademark holder. We use them for
identification purposes only. This is not an official
publication

Library of Congress Cataloging-in-Publication Data
Bargo, Michael.
    How to customize your sport truck / Michael
Bargo.
        p.   cm.
    Includes index.
    ISBN 0-87938-380-1
    1. Trucks—Customizing.   I. Title.
TL230.B2825 1989   89-33510
629.28'73—dc20   CIP

cover credit

On the front cover: Combining all the elements of
sport truck style—lowering, groundhugging bodywork,
low-profile tires on wide wheels, convertible top and
custom paint, graphics and interior—this 1989 Mazda
is the envy of all who see it. This truck was built by
HoTTops of Tucson. *HoTTops*

On the back cover: Another sport truck with
everything on it—including a color-matched sportbike!
This Chevy S-10 and matching Honda Hurricane were
built by Cars & Concepts Inc. *Cars & Concepts Inc.*

Contents

Acknowledgments

Many persons provided product information, suggestions, comments and other material useful to the creation of this book. These include (in no special order) Steve Stillwell, editor of *Truckin'* magazine, who provided many helpful comments on the history of lowrider pickups; Billy Christine (the "Kid") of Main Street Graphics in Indianapolis, who provided many helpful photo opportunities and references; Herb Martinez, a famous pinstriper who provided helpful comments on graphic art as applied to vehicles; Jim Piccolo and Les Jarvis of HoTTops, Inc. of Tempe, AZ, who provided photos, product information, and comments; Dave Russ of Goodyear; Tom and Debbie Dougherty; Len Manning, Dawn Manning and Tim Colbeck of Spring-Align of Palatine, IL; John and Garrett Kolf of Perfection Upholstery; Bushwacker and the Lou Frank Agency; Donna of Sanderson Headers; Chris Kuczynski of Holley Replacement Parts Div.; Ron Francis' Wire Works; Bill's Custom Louvering; Extang Corp.; Sharon Cornelius Iles of Paasche Airbrush Co.; Lowrider Hydraulics and Truck Accessories; Reinard Helder of Helder Mfg.; Roberts Motor Parts; Meridith and Seth Doulton of Golden State Pickup Parts; Tim Brackett of Bell Super Tech; Jim Shulman of The Eastwood Co.; Sherry and Chris Rubino of Mr. 50s Window Tinting in Harvey, IL; Craig Consumer Electronics; Mekler/Ansell Associates and Armstrong Tires; James Shreve of Conversion Components, Inc.; Randy Fritz; Michael Stevens of Performance Covers; Stillen Sportparts, Inc.; Pop Top Minis; Street Neon of Houston, TX; John Baker Performance of Webster, WI; Lester Orr of East Coast Customs in Maryville, TN; Hedman Headers; Julie Davis of Lund Industries; Doug Davis of Rugged Trail Suspensions; Bill Long of Rancho Suspension; Bruce Snyder of Trail Master Suspensions; Brenda of Freelance Lettering in Indianapolis, IN; W. Alex Cantrell of C&A Control Systems in Knoxville, TN; Dave Vranicar and Patty Volstad of MaxiGuard of America in Elk Grove, IL; Warn Industries; Edelbrock; Digital Fuel Injection; L.C. Engineering of La Verne, CA; Weiand Automotive Industries; Blower Drive Service; and Robert Morris & Gerry Rosenquist of Fel-Pro.

1

Choosing a sport truck

Not since the customized van craze of the 1970s has there been such a revolution in vehicle styling as there is in the field of sport trucks. The low-riding sport truck, or "slammer" as its Californian creators have called it, is gaining tremendous popularity in all parts of the country.

This 1983 Chevy S–10 Pro Street mini shows what you can do with a minipickup. It has ground effects, a lowered suspension, body graphics and a Chevy 350 engine with tunnel ram. The interior has also been customized.

The rear of the truck shows the body graphics, tinted rear window, tonneau cover and narrowed rear end with 33×19.5 Mickey Thompson tires.

This 1987 S-10 Blazer was dropped five inches in front and four inches in the rear. It has Center Line wheels. Body graphics by Billy the Kid of Indianapolis. Body moldings and emblems have been removed to smooth out the body lines.

And for good reason. They're more stylish, exciting, inexpensive and versatile than any other vehicle today. For $8,000 you can buy a new Chevy S-10 minipickup, add a couple of thousand dollars' worth of ground effects, suspension lowering hardware and customized paintwork, and you'll catch more eyes than any other new vehicle in the parking lot that costs twice as much!

Why the excitement over slammers? There are several good answers. Probably the most important reason is that American cars are so sterile, homogenized and difficult to modify that car buyers were just waiting for something to get their hands on and modify. There's nothing you can touch in the same price range as a minipickup that will give you as much style and excitement for your automotive dollar.

Since the late 1940s American car buyers have wanted an individual, not an assembly-line produced, vehicle. They've gone to great lengths to give their vehicle an identity, appearance, feel and style that's their own. And in the late 1980s the hottest thing to customize is the minipickup.

History of the slammer

For as long as custom cars have been made, they've been "slammed" to the ground. This was true of the 1929 Ford T-bucket, probably the earli- est vehicle to be slammed, to the hot rods of the 1950s, to the slammed full-size cars of the 1960s and 1970s created by Hispanics living in southern California and Arizona.

Although slamming minipickups is relatively new (since American-made minis are a recent phenomenon) there were slammed pickups in the early 1970s. Steve Stillwell, editor of *Truckin'* magazine, the bible of the lowrider pickup enthusiast, remembers the 1973 Chevy pickup as the start of slammer popularity. That year Chevy came out with the flat-nosed truck with a coil spring front suspension and leaf spring rear. It was instantly seized upon as a vehicle that could be easily lowered. And it was. The Ford F-100s were also lowered at about this time.

These lowered pickups were often used to tow lowered cars to the hydraulic slammer contests in southern California and Arizona. In fact, they were so popular that the very first issue of *Truckin'* magazine, which came out in the summer of 1975, contained a story on a lowered truck.

Although lowering the 1970s trucks was more work and required some custom suspension modifications, the trucks are now much easier to lower, thanks to the lowering kits sold by such national aftermarket suspension companies as Rugged

This 1985 C–10 Silverado shows what can be done with a full-size Chevy pickup. Lowered four inches, it has a 350 hp 355 ci turbocharged Chevy 350 engine, 12 bolt rear end and body graphics by Billy the Kid.

Another full-size lowered Chevy pickup with paint graphics and custom window tinting.

Trail, Trail Master and Rancho. These companies have caught on to the slammin' fad and have actually made it possible to lower a truck much more easily and safely than in the past.

Whereas ten years ago you had to find someone to cut your front coil springs and reverse the leaf springs, or install a lowering block, now you can buy a complete kit that makes the lowering

This 1969 was lowered five inches, has custom interior, tonneau cover, chromed engine accessories and pin- striping. Slamming cuts across all vehicle makes and years.

An unusual 1978 Chevy Luv dropped four inches. It has a custom metal tonneau cover, front spoiler, side dams and rear roll pan.

A 1967 GMC Stepside Pro Street pickup. It has a super-charged engine, Mickey Thompson Sportsman tires, custom wood and chrome bed and dozens of custom accessories.

project possible for anyone with a floor jack and a few wrenches. These companies have also made it possible to lower such vehicles as the Ford Ranger, which otherwise, because of their short front coil springs and independent axles, are impossible to lower properly.

But lowering the truck is only the beginning. A slammer is not complete without ground effects or Euro styling as it's often called. This is the aerodynamic fiberglass, plastic or urethane front air dam, side skirts and rear roll pan that not only give the slammer truck a lower, more European-style appearance, but also increase the vehicle's aerodynamic efficiency. For slammer owners, though, the styling alone is more than enough reason to make the change!

Finally, no slammer is complete without the unique brand of paint detailing or "body graphics," as it's called, painted on the sides of the truck. These often include waves, a different form of flames, neon tubes and traditional pinstriping, done with more style than ever before. There's a section on body graphics that gives a good idea of how to design and paint a truck in the slammer style.

Model choices

You can convert virtually any older full-size pickup or mini into a slammer, but for those who

are looking for new trucks, here's a list and description of the new 1989 models and the options available for them. Along with each truck model, a brief description will be given of the products on the market for converting it into a slammer. Some trucks are easier to lower than others. And for some trucks, there is an enormous variety of aftermarket products available such as ground effects, grilles, aero wings and so on. The truck you choose to buy will make a great difference when you go to modify it.

As far as lowering the truck goes, the Ford Ranger is the most expensive to lower due to the independent front axles. The Dodge Ram and Japanese trucks are the least expensive to lower, since these have torsion bar front ends and only require lowering blocks and new U-bolts for the rear ends. The Chevy/GMC trucks are about midway between the Ford Ranger and inexpensive trucks. They are easy to lower, but cost more to lower than the Japanese imports, since you need the front replacement spindles to do a proper job.

Imports

Imported minis are popular for several reasons. One is that their body styling looks great as a slammer. They also have better construction in the roof and roof support areas, so if you plan to make your mini into a convertible, the Japanese trucks

This lowered Nissan has custom tires and wheels and custom body graphics.

*A 1989 GMC lowered and customized for an auto show. It
has full ground effects, body graphics, tinted windows
and a smooth body without moldings or emblems.*

*The rear shows the custom taillights, roll pan and aero
wing.*

are better prospects. Lowering kits and ground effects are widely available. Many people also like the peppy engines and good price. Look for the Japanese to get on the slammer bandwagon and offer factory ground effects and convertible tops in future model years.

Ground effects and body graphics cost about the same for all minipickups. Not all full-size pickups can be lowered, but for those that can ground effects and body graphics cost the same. So if you're choosing a truck that you can do the major three modifications to—lowering, ground effects and body graphics—only the lowering costs will vary. The other expenses will be about the same.

Chevrolet S-10 pickup

If any sport truck can be called the favorite for lowering and ground effects, the S-10 is it. The S-10 has several good things going for it. It has a good price, good styling, is easily lowered (the best way to lower the front is with spindles) and there's an enormous number of mail-order accessories available, from ground effects to windjammers, to tonneau covers and aero wings. Standard equipment includes 2.5 liter Tech IV engine, optional 4.3 liter 160 hp Vortec V-6 with electronic fuel injection; five-speed manual transmission with overdrive; and optional trim levels beyond standard.

S-10 Blazer is not as popular, but two-wheel-drive models can be lowered. It's usually not preferred, though, because it's more expensive than the S-10 pickup.

Chevrolet full-size pickup

Available in thirty-six different models, but the ½ ton V-6 fleetside is the best for lowering, since it has the body styling, low cost and ability to be lowered. Right now there are some ground effects available, although more ground effects manufacturers are realizing that a lot of full-size truck owners want ground effects, and there will soon be more.

GMC S-15 pickup

This is not just the S-10 pickup with the GMC logo attached. It has the most powerful V-6 engine in its class, and is probably the biggest mini. Comes with regular cab or Club coupe cab for more inside room. It's an excellent choice for someone looking for a mini with more room, engine power and trailer towing capacity, while still keeping that slammer look.

GMC S-15 Jimmy

More expensive than the pickup, but has a great deal more inside room. Two-wheel-drive models can be lowered. Good choice for anyone

The Dodge Ram 50 is imported by Dodge as their entry into the mini market. It can be lowered and fully cus- *tomized with ground effects and accessories available from a number of aftermarket suppliers.*

14

The 1989 Dodge Sport Convertible is the only showroom pickup available as a convertible. Most other minis can be converted using conversion kits.

The Ranger GT package features a V–6 engine, front spoiler, side dams and trim extras for a factory-made slammer look.

*The basic Ranger can be lowered using re-arched
springs in the rear and replacement independent axles
up front.*

looking for a family-size vehicle with enough engine power and inside room for traveling.

GMC full-size pickup

The GMC Sierra is not as popular as a lowered truck, but it has sleek styling and is a good choice for big trailering and towing needs.

Dodge Ram 50

The Dodge Ram 50 is an import, but a popular truck since you can get lowering kits, ground effects and convertible top conversion kits for it. Inexpensive with a lot of potential, and there's a good number of aftermarket products available for customizing.

The Dodge Sport Convertible is the first and right now the only pickup with an optional convertible top. It's a good choice for anyone wishing to get a convertible pickup without the extra effort of getting the conversion done. Also, it has some powerful engine options.

Ford Ranger

The Ford Ranger is the best truck to buy if you want a factory-produced slammer with ground effects. The Ranger GT comes with ground effects for the slammer look, plus a 140 hp V-6 engine for great street performance. It also has a new instrument panel that deserves a close look. On the other hand, if you buy the basic Ranger, it's the most expensive to lower since it has the independent front axles, which must be replaced with after-market front axles. But this will only cost a few hundred dollars more than lowering a Chevy S-10, so if you buy the basic Ranger and have it lowered you'll still save money over the GT. The choice is yours.

Ford Bronco and full-size pickups

These trucks can also be lowered, but they are not as popular as slammers. However, as slammers become more popular around the country you'll see many people lowering their full-size Fords rather than giving them up. But there are no replacement axles for full-size Fords at this time, so anyone wishing to buy a full-size Ford to lower it is in for a tough decision.

Toyota 2WD trucks

The Long Bed Deluxe has a larger cab and front bench seat for extra passenger room. For even more room, Toyota offers the Xtracab SR5 V-6, with two rear jumpseats that face forward, allowing rear passengers to enjoy the view through tilt-out rear quarter windows. The Xtracab SR5 also has a powerful V-6 3.0 liter engine with 150 hp, which is available as an option in several truck

The Toyota Xtracab SR5 has more seating room and can be easily lowered by cranking down the front torsion bars and installing lowering blocks in the rear.

The Mitsubishi Mighty Max comes with a standard four-cylinder engine, five-speed manual transmission and

can be easily lowered with its front torsion bar suspension and rear leaf springs.

models. The Xtracab SR5 also can fit a HoTTops targa top, offering an exciting way to open the roof to sun and wind. Toyota's new one-ton trucks are larger and more powerful, with power-assisted steering and optional V-6 engine.

Mitsubishi

The Mighty Max comes with a 2.0 liter four-cylinder engine, five-speed manual overdrive transmission, optional four-speed automatic overdrive with column shift, sports bench, carpeting and other extras as standard equipment. It's easy to lower its torsion bar front end and add a lowering block to drop the rear. There's also a great number of ground effects kits and other slammer customizing accessories to make the Mitsubishi as hot as you want to make it.

Isuzu

The Isuzu pickup comes in standard bed, long bed, one-ton long bed or spacecab. The spacecab extended cab model features two jumpseats that face forward, and has reclining front seats to relieve that cramped feeling you can get with small minis. It comes with a five-speed transmission, double wall cargo bed and other accessories.

Optional trim packages are available, including the stand S, high-style XS or luxury LS trim.

Nissan

The Hardbody is Nissan's minipickup two-wheel-drive model. Powered by a fuel injected 2.4 liter, four-cylinder or 145 hp 3.0 liter V-6 engine, it's also available in the extended cab "king cab" model for extra cab space. The torsion bar front end makes it easy to lower, and lowering blocks are all you need to lower the rear. Easy to lower, with ground effects and other accessories widely available.

Overview

Now that you've seen the 1989 pickups that can be slammed, the rest of this book will tell you how to do it. The first step in creating a slammer is to lower the truck. Chapter 2 will cover all the basic front and rear ends found in pickups, old and new, and describe in detail how to lower them. A list of manufacturers can be found in the Appendix.

If you want to customize the tires and wheels, you'll find basic guidelines and some sample tire/wheel combinations in chapter 3. For those who want more horsepower, or who want to rebuild an engine in an older pickup, chapter 4 will cover engine modifications. These engine modifications cover popular imports as well as American-made trucks. You'll learn how to install a supercharger and swap a Firebird Formula 350 TPI (tuned port injection) engine (the same as the Corvette TPI) into a Chevy S-10. It does fit!

A slammer isn't a slammer without ground effects. Chapter 5 will describe these in detail and tell you how to install them. You'll be able to see how the ground effects from several different manufacturers actually look on trucks. The more radical exterior changes, including convertible tops and tilt beds, are covered in chapter 6. You'll see how to use a power steering pump to lift a bed for a more economical, custom installation.

No slammer is complete without the New Wave body graphics, neons and pinstriping. Chapter 7 will give some superb examples of vehicles painted in the new style, as well as step-by-step directions showing you how to do this type of paint work yourself. For those who wish a less expensive alternative to custom body graphics, vinyl graphics will be discussed, including where to buy them and how to apply them.

The cabs of newer trucks allow a lot of room for the new high-tech automotive electronics. The selection and installation of speakers, radios, cassette players, radar detectors and security systems will be discussed, including photos of installations.

Finally, for those who wish to select and restore an older pickup, 1940s to 1970s, the last chapter will talk about pickup restoration. Topics covered include bodywork, painting, frame rebuilding and a Pro Street race truck.

The Isuzu mini is a good choice since a number of aftermarket suppliers make lowering kits, ground effects, *convertible conversions, tonneau covers and so on for the Isuzu pickups.*

2

Lowering your truck

The lowrider pickups get their look by their low road-hugging profile. But this low profile isn't done only for looks. It's done because of the great difference it makes on the handling of the vehicle, particularly on the street. Highway driving characteristics are also greatly improved.

There are good, sound reasons why a lower truck handles better. These reasons have to do with the simple physics of the motion of a vehicle on a roadway.

In order to understand why a lowered pickup handles better, it's necessary to go over some of the basic concepts involved in handling. These concepts apply to all vehicles, no matter what their size. They are a good way to understand why a lowered vehicle, whether it be a pickup or sports car, handles better than one that is significantly higher.

Principles of handling and steering

For an automotive engineer the terms "ride" and "handling" refer to two very different things. For most pickup truck owners, the term ride refers to the amount of bumpiness or stiffness in the

Here's a line-up of vehicles with Trail Master lowering kits installed: a full-size Chevy pickup on the left, Chevy S-10 in center and Ford Ranger on the right. Trail *Master kits ensure excellent ride and handling characteristics.*

springs, while the term handling describes the way a vehicle takes turns: whether it sways too much, is difficult to keep straight on the highway and so on.

Chapter 5 will talk about "ground effects" and how they affect the performance of a vehicle. Since ground effects mainly make a difference at higher speeds, where the airflow around a vehicle is much greater, most ground effects kits installed on low-riding pickups are for style only. There are some aerodynamic advantages to using ground effects kits and these will be discussed in chapter 5, where you will also read about how to install them.

The principles discussed here apply to all vehicles, but they highlight the reasons why a lowered vehicle handles better. To understand how a lowering kit can improve handling, read these sections first, then move on to the sections that describe how to lower a pickup truck.

Handling

Any discussion of a vehicle's performance while in motion is really a discussion of how the different forces acting on a vehicle affect its center of gravity or CG. The center of gravity of a vehicle is that point about which the entire mass of the vehicle rotates in all three dimensions of space. For our purposes it's important to know that when a pickup is lowered the center of gravity becomes lower.

There are three terms that refer to the effects of motion on a vehicle's CG. These are "roll," "pitch" and "yaw." Most people have first seen these terms mentioned in regard to the space program. These terms are ways to describe how a vehicle moves, just as left and right describe two different directions.

Roll

Roll refers to the tendency of a vehicle to sway on a turn, especially a fast turn with a vehicle that has a high center of gravity. A high center of gravity will make your vehicle seem tipsy, but the "tipsiness" is just a common way to describe the rolling motion. All vehicles have roll forces acting on them, even if they're not noticeable, and the vehicle does not have a high center of gravity.

You sway just a little every time you make a turn. This has more of an effect on traction than just making the body tilt; it takes weight off one side of the vehicle and puts it on the other side. This shift of weight from the inside wheels to the outside wheels diminishes cornering ability by pushing the outside wheels to their limit of traction and lifting the inside tires off the ground, reducing their traction to virtually zero. A stiff suspension, such as that found on sports cars, offsets roll to some degree because it forces the inside tire to stay closer to the ground where it gets better traction. A sway bar kit can do the same thing.

Rancho suspension will soon have a lowering kit available for this vehicle, the mid-size Chevrolet Blazer.

The best way to reduce the roll of your truck is to lower the center of gravity. This is something to keep in mind if you find that your truck has an annoying tendency to tip on sharp turns. Installation of a lowering kit will then improve the roll characteristics of your pickup.

Pitch

Another type of movement your truck has is pitch. This is the tendency to dive, or rock front to back. Pitch is more obvious with a big, heavy car with a soft suspension, or any long wheelbase vehicle with soft springs. Also, the higher a vehicle is off the ground (thus the higher the center of gravity) the more pronounced the pitch will be. The best way to cure pitch on your pickup is to stiffen the shocks and lower the truck.

Yaw

Yaw is the third type of movement. It's the "fishtailing" action of a car or truck that is the result of rotation about a vertical axis through the center of gravity. You may have actually felt the effects of yaw when you did a donut or lost traction on all four wheels in a turn. Usually, yaw is not felt as much as pitch and roll but it is always there to some extent. Your center of gravity and type of suspension also have a great effect on the amount of yaw.

Steering

The forces already mentioned are all working together on your vehicle whenever it is moving. No matter what you do—drive straight, turn or brake—these three forces are acting to influence the motion of your vehicle. There are three additional concepts that help you understand how your steering is affected by these forces. These concepts will give you a better understanding of how your vehicle's suspension acts whenever it is modified, or even if it's not modified at all.

The terms used to describe a vehicle's steering characteristics are oversteer, understeer and neutral steer. These three actually refer to the rear wheels' ability to follow the front wheels through a turn.

Oversteer

Oversteer describes the tendency of your rear tires to want to jump ahead of your front tires in a turn. This may cause you to spin out, as the rear tires swing around to catch up to the front. Lightweight pickups with stiff suspensions often have this tendency.

Understeer

The second term understeer talks about the opposite: when the rear tires don't follow the front tires in a turn. This makes turning sluggish and slow. The rear tires just don't seem to respond to the turning of the front tires. You may have driven some old cars that seem to turn very slowly. Also, pickup trucks with extremely big tires are very bad at making slow turns. They have very bad understeer, and are best when driven in a straight line.

Neutral steer

Finally, the third term neutral steer refers to the ideal situation, when the rear tires don't jump ahead of the front and cause you to spin out, or turn so slowly that turns are sluggish. This is a more ideal situation. Most vehicles achieve neutral steer at about 30 mph, and seem to glide right along in gentle turns at this speed.

Keep in mind that no vehicle has neutral steer all the time. Since the center of gravity and the moment of inertia both affect handling, and these vary depending on the vehicle's weight, speed and balance, there is no vehicle that handles great all the time. The best you can do is find out what the problems are with your pickup's handling, if there are any, and correct them for the type of driving you do.

Some sports car owners find that their car handles great at high speeds, where it was designed to operate well, but is terrible on city streets at low speeds. This is because the vehicle was designed to achieve neutral steer at high highway speeds, not at slower city and town driving speeds.

Steering problems

One way to correct oversteer and understeer problems is by changing the camber of the wheels. Lowering your truck can change the camber, so if you lower your truck be sure to have the camber checked by a good alignment shop. But if the stock camber settings don't give good results, you can change the camber to help correct them.

There are two general terms for describing camber: positive camber and negative camber. Positive camber is when the wheel tilts outward from the center at the top. Negative camber refers to the opposite: an inward tilt of the wheel at the top. The old Volkswagen Beetles had strong negative camber on the rear wheels. You may have seen how these wheels seem to bend inward at the top. This was designed to help improve handling and traction.

If your pickup still has understeer-oversteer problems, use these general guidelines to help correct them.

This Quickor Performance truck features the Quickor lowering kit, available for installation on most minis. Warn Industries

Adjustment	To increase understeer	To increase oversteer
Front wheel camber	More positive	More negative
Rear wheel camber	More negative	More positive

Center of gravity

All of the material in this chapter so far has led up to one thing: lowering your pickup truck to lower its center of gravity and improve handling. These introductory pages may seem like a waste of time to someone who just wants a lowered truck so it looks great, but this discussion is helpful because it shows that lowering your truck not only looks good, but makes it handle a lot better, too. That's why large, heavy luxury cars of the 1960s and 1970s were close to the ground—to give them better handling.

A lower center of gravity has several good benefits. Since the center of gravity has a profound effect on roll, pitch and yaw, whenever it's lowered these motions are reduced. With a lower center of gravity you greatly improve handling on turns for several reasons. One is that the transfer of weight during turns is less severe, so the vehicle doesn't lift up the inside tire and press down harder on the outside tire as much as it used to. A vehicle with a lower center of gravity has a better weight distribution at all times on all four tires.

When the weight is more evenly distributed the other things you can do to affect the vehicle's performance, such as change shocks, springs, sway bars and so on, are more effective. It's easier to perfect the handling of a vehicle if its center of gravity is lowered.

The following how-to sections will give detailed descriptions and step-by-step instruction on how to install lowering kits in the popular makes of minipickups.

Lowering the front end

Pickup trucks made within the last twenty years have three basic types of front end suspensions. The most common is the coil spring. This is used by Chevrolet, Dodge, GMC and others. Another type of front end suspension, used mainly by Japanese trucks, is the torsion bar front end. These suspension systems use two torsion bars that can be adjusted to lower the front end. The third common type is used exclusively by Ford: the independent axles. The only safe way to lower Ford Rangers is by replacing the independent axles with aftermarket axles. At the present time there are only two national manufacturers that make replacement axles for Ford trucks—Rancho and Trail Master. You cannot lower a Ford with independent axles by cutting the coil springs. This will change the front end alignment severely, making the truck unsafe and difficult to drive.

Methods

There are two basic ways to lower the front end of a coil spring suspended vehicle. One way, described in the following section, is to install replacement spindles. This is mainly for the Chevy S-10 and other Chevy trucks, and El Camino. Another way is to remove the coil spring and either cut it down a wrap or replace it with a shorter coil spring purchased from an aftermarket suspension manufacturer.

A replacement spring that is shorter is the best way to go for a simple reason: it keeps the front end within factory engineered wheel travel and handling specifications. The coil spring on your pickup is designed to provide optimum performance over a wide range of load, speed and handling conditions. There are two basic principles used to design the spring: 1) the rate at which the spring compresses, that is, how quickly the spring is compressed when you hit a pothole or a bumper, and 2) how far the wheel is allowed to travel up into the wheelwell. For ninety-five percent of all bumps and common road hazards, the stock coil spring will allow you to maintain control over the vehicle with its stock coil springs.

In order to lower the front end you have to lower the height of the coil spring, since the coil spring literally holds the vehicle up over the wheels. The less the coil spring holds the vehicle up, the closer the vehicle is to the ground. The cheapest (but not the easiest) way to lower your vehicle is to simply remove the stock coil spring, cut a wrap out of it, and replace it into your vehicle.

This does not change the rate at which the spring compresses, but it does change the distance between the tire and the fender. It will also most likely change the alignment. So the vehicle will handle pretty much the same as before, but you have to be more careful of potholes and bumps since the wheel travel has been reduced by the same amount that you lowered the front end. For example, if you lowered the front end two inches, your tires are now two inches closer to the fenders. They may be cut or bruised if you hit a pothole that would not normally cause the tire to hit the fender.

Remember, this will happen because you have not changed the rate at which the spring compresses. But there is a way to change the coil spring and still keep from bumping your front tires on the fenders, and this is with replacement coil springs specifically designed for lowering. With these replacement springs, available from Rugged Trail, Trail Master, Rancho and other manufacturers, you can lower your vehicle, but still keep virtually all of the stock handling and wheel travel characteristics.

This is possible because the manufacturers have designed the replacement coil spring to do everything the stock spring does, only the new one is shorter. Being shorter, it keeps the vehicle closer to the ground. The new replacement spring is able to do this basically because it is stiffer. That is, it does not compress at the same rate as the taller and softer stock spring. The result is a spring that is stiffer and keeps nearly the same wheel rebound, while lowering the front end.

Manufacturer's warranty

Another consideration when deciding whether to cut down the stock coil spring or replace it with an aftermarket shorter spring is the manufacturer's warranty. Since so many modifications have been done to pickups and sport trucks in the last decade, manufacturers are wary of any changes that consumers make. If you cut the front coil springs you may void the manufacturer's warranty regarding your front end parts. Remember, the automotive engineers who designed your suspension designed it to handle virtually all common road hazards, handling conditions and loads. If you change the front coil springs by cutting them, to the manufacturer it's the same as overloading the bed with too much weight.

If something in the front end should break, in the steering system or suspension, and it is determined by a dealership that you have cut the coil springs down, they may use this as an excuse to void the warranty on the entire truck, as well as on the modified parts. Another consideration is insurance. Suppose you cut your front coil springs down and have an accident where you lost control (because of road conditions or someone cut you off). The insurance company may very well say that it was your unauthorized modification of the front end that contributed to the accident, and fail to cover the person you hit or your own vehicle.

Because many consumers are filing fraudulent and misleading claims to make more money from insurance companies, the companies are now investigating accidents more closely. These recommendations are not meant to provide specific advice, but merely to inform you of the potential situations that may arise after you extensively modify your vehicle.

However, you may wait until the manufacturer's warranty is up, and the vehicle is no longer warranted, before you change the coil springs.

There are several things to keep in mind in regard to the vehicle warranty. One is that changing the coil springs with an aftermarket replacement may not void the warranty, since these suspension companies are responsible and employ professional engineers to design their products. Also, the warranty issue is usually up to the individual dealership. You may or may not have a Ford dealer in your area who is bothered by suspension modifications. He may look at your vehicle and say that your lowered coil springs had nothing to do

with the suspension problem at hand. Or he may use it as an excuse to not repair or replace the defective part of the vehicle.

If you know your dealer well, you may want to discuss this before making any changes during the warranty period. If he says that he won't hold the suspension changes against you unless they are a direct cause of a problem, then the best thing to do is have him sign a written agreement. Or, have him approve of the spring changes when they're made. He may want a mechanic to check them over to be sure all bolts are tight and so forth.

Usually, sport truck owners do not have problems when they modify their suspensions, but there is still room for some controversy when dollars are involved.

Insurance considerations

The same advice is also good for your auto insurance. Call your agent and ask if he/she is aware of the lowered slammer trucks on the street, and mention that you plan to lower your truck. Ask if there will be any possible problems with that. Usually, auto insurance companies want to know if the vehicle has been modified only so they are not surprised when you make a $1,000 claim for a winch and bumper that have been damaged or stolen. In other words, they are interested in the replacement value of such items as radios, stereo systems, lights, bumpers and so on, and usually are not as concerned about items such as suspensions, which cannot be stolen and are usually not damaged in fender-bender type accidents.

The best thing to do is bring up the topic, discuss it with your agent and explain that the item cannot be stolen or removed, and that you will therefore not be making a separate claim for it in the future, the way you might with a winch or stereo.

The only other potential area for a problem is with the other person's insurance company. At this point, however, insurance companies usually do not make an issue of suspension changes, especially when vehicles are lowered, since there are so many low sports cars on the road and lowering doesn't create special hazards, such as the tip-over hazard you have with a sky-high four wheeler.

On the whole, auto insurance will not create problems the way warranties might. Unless of course the job was poorly done, and a bolt came loose and caused the front end to loosen up! When these replacement items are properly installed, there is little chance of major problems being caused by the hardware.

Probably the most risky suspension change you can make, and one that would be likely to cause trouble with the vehicle warranty and auto insurance companies, is when you cut the rear frame on Chevy trucks to raise the axle higher. I do not recommend this, since the new truck frames are made of carefully hardened steel and are engineered to provide strength and safely carry loads.

If you torch cut and weld these frames you weaken them. Frame cutting and welding can be done by repair shops when the truck is involved in an accident, and the frame has to be straightened, but this is pre-approved by the insurance company, and even then there are certain radical changes repair shops are not willing to make.

If you have an older pickup and you wish to radically cut and rebuild the frame for custom truck shows, this is a different story. These trucks are usually trailered to shows and are so carefully built that driving them may not be a hazard. But to take a brand-new pickup, cut off one third of the frame in the rear, and rebuild your own frame rails for everyday street use is not a good idea.

If you do choose to cut and rebuild a frame used in a truck you drive every day and have insured with a regular auto insurance policy, be sure the work is done by a reputable, competent frame shop experienced in frame repair and that has liability insurance coverage. Then, in the event that the frame breaks when the truck is carrying a

After truck is raised and supported by jack stands, loosen brake caliper retaining nuts with allen wrench.

lot of weight on the highway and an accident occurs, they are liable for the damage and will have the insurance to cover it. Also, make sure the frame

Brake caliper is now free from rotor, but don't let it hang by the brake line alone. Tie it up with a piece of wire to prevent damage to brake line.

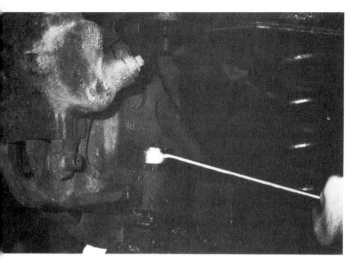

Remove the cotter pin from the steering arm castle nut, then loosen nut, as in this photo, and remove. Save for replacement later.

modification work is warranted by them for the period you own the vehicle.

Replacement spindles for GM trucks

The best way to lower the front end of your Chevy truck or El Camino is with replacement spindles. These spindles meet or exceed original factory specifications and are an ideal way to lower the front end, since only the spindle is at a new, lower location. The other components of the front end are not changed or altered in any way, so the front end keeps all of its handling characteristics. Since the stock coil springs and shocks are kept in place, spring travel and load carrying capacities are the same. There are some slight modifications you have to make when installing the kit and these are noted in the following sections.

Bell Super Tech replacement spindles

The Bell Super Tech spindle is widely used as a replacement spindle when lowering the front end of a Chevy/GMC pickup. This is because they are extremely well made and are relatively easy to install. The installation is the reverse of the removal of the old spindle. All the old parts such as the ball joints, tie-rods, brake caliper and so on remain exactly as they were. The location of the spindle is the only thing that is different, and this lower location enables the front tires to ride lower.

Follow these steps in installing the Bell Super Tech replacement spindles. However, be sure to consult the installation instructions with your spindles and note any changes that may have been

Knock the ball joints loose with a hammer and pickle fork. Be careful not to damage parts.

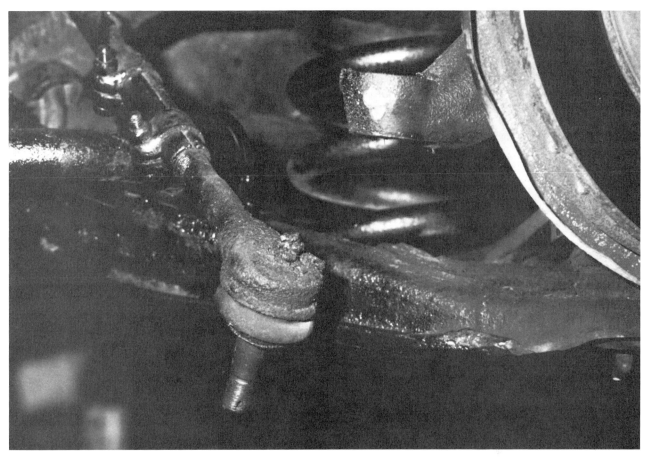

Now the ball joint is free of the wheelhousing.

made, since Chevrolet may change its front end design for future models.

1. Raise the front end high off the ground for the tires to be removed. Support the vehicle on both sides with jack stands, and lower the truck on the jack stands. Remove the jack.

2. Loosen and remove lug nuts and remove both front tires.

3. Remove brake caliper by loosening retaining nuts with L-shaped allen wrench. Pull brake caliper from rotor. Brake caliper is now held up by only the brake line. To prevent the brake line from breaking, use small pieces of wire to tie up the brake caliper to relieve the brake line of the caliper's weight.

4. Pry the dust cap from the rotor, remove cotter pin and remove rotor assembly from spindle. The bearings inside the rotor should be cleaned and repacked for reinstallation.

5. The next step is to remove the steering arm. This has a "castle" nut and a cotter pin. Pull out the cotter pin, loosen the castle nut and knock the steering arm loose with a lead hammer. Inspect for wear. Clean the steering arm end; you'll be able to grease it later.

This is how the rotor assembly will look when removed from the wheel.

The dust cover, on the left, is removed from the spindle by loosening the three bolts that hold the dust cover to the spindle. On the right is the rotor with bearings inside. Clean and repack bearings.

With dust cover on new spindle, replace spindle housing on ball joint and replace castle nut. Tighten to specs and lubricate ball joints.

6. Remove upper and lower ball joints. First remove cotter pin and castle nut, then force the ball joints apart. This can be done by either using a "pickle fork" type pry bar, or by knocking the control arms with a lead hammer. The safest way is to get a small crowbar, put some leverage on the control arm to hold it steady and knock the arm with the lead hammer. This will jar it loose.

7. Remove the three small bolts holding the dust cover onto the spindle. With the ball joints loose, the spindle can be removed.

8. Put the dust cover on the new Bell Super Tech spindle, and replace the three bolts.

9. Carefully clean the ball joints and inspect them for wear. Replace them into the new spindle, and replace the castle nuts and cotter pins of the ball joints. Use a new cotter pin. Torque ball joint castle nuts to 80-90 lb-ft, or per manufacturer's specifications if different.

10. Replace the rotor (with repacked bearings) and install retaining washer and nut. Tighten spindle nut to hand tight (or manufacturer's specs) and replace cotter pin.

11. Replace the brake caliper and tighten with allen wrench.

12. Replace wheels and tighten lug nuts. Lower the truck and try out brakes, then inspect.

13. After new spindles are installed, you must have the front end aligned. The original specifications for caster, camber and toe-in are the same as before.

Special modifications for light-duty trucks

After installing the rotor on the new lower spindle, spin it to see if it rubs on the backplate. If it does, spin it again and feel for the point where it rubs on the cast iron spindle housing. There is a small nub of cast iron that has to be ground off so

You can see the drop of four inches in this comparison photo. On the left is the new Bell Super Tech spindle, mounted, and on the right is the old spindle. The Bell Super Tech spindle is much higher, without altering the position of the springs or affecting spring performance.

that the backplate doesn't rub. This rubbing will occur on light-duty trucks with the one-inch-wide brake rotor. On heavy-duty pickups with a one and three-quarter inch rotor, you won't need to do any grinding. This is because the calipers are different.

Also, you usually have to use a spacer at least five-sixteenths-inch thick to space the wheel out farther from the rotor assembly. This is because the lower control arm will rub on the wheel in its stock position. Also keep in mind that you can't use stock Chevrolet rally wheels. They will not fit the new lowered spindle assembly.

Replace the castle nut on the upper ball joint, and lubricate with grease gun.

Replace rotor on the spindle, tighten bearing nut and replace brake caliper by tightening allen head bolts.

After new spindle is installed, and brake caliper is secured, clean rotor surface with brake cleaner. This is *because some grease will have gotten onto the rotor through handling.*

Applications for Bell Super Tech replacement spindles

Spindle lowering kits are available for the following vehicle models and years, with the indicated drop: Chevrolet and GMC ½ ton pickups, three inches of drop. Two-wheel-drive versions of GM's S

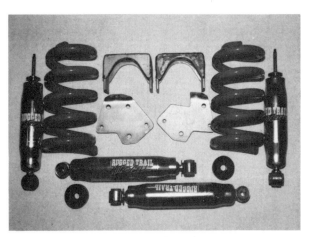

Here's the Rugged Trail kit for lowering a full-size Chevy, model years 1973 to 1987. Two-wheel drive only.

trucks, including S-10, S-15 Mini-Blazer and Jimmy, two inches of drop. The 1979 to 1986 Chevrolet El Camino, two-inch drop.

Aftermarket systems for GM trucks

The other recommended way to lower coil spring front suspensions is to replace the stock springs with shorter, stiffer springs from reputable aftermarket suspension manufacturers such as Rugged Trail, Rancho or Trail Master. Your truck will ride somewhat stiffer, but will retain much of the stock ride quality.

Rugged Trail front coil springs for GM pickups

The following instructions specifically cover installation of the Rugged Trail replacement springs on the front of GM full-size pickups. Later in the chapter I will cover rear end lowering.

1. Set parking brake and make sure wheels are pointed directly forward. Jack up the front of the vehicle and place jack stands under frame directly under doors. Remove tires, wheels and shocks. Remove sway bars (if so equipped) from the A-arms.

2. Place hydraulic jack under passenger side (over A-arm), but do not put pressure on arm. Remove cotter pin from lower ball joint and loosen

This full-size Chevy pickup uses the Trail Master lowering kit, part no. CL23. It features shorter replacement coil springs in the front and hardware for reversing the location of the leaf springs on the rear axle.

nut, but do not remove. Break lower ball joint using a pickle fork. Remove nut and allow A-arm to rest on jack. Slowly lower jack until vehicle's weight is entirely on jack stand.

3. Remove and discard stock coil spring. Remove stock rubber stops on lower A-arm. Place new RT polyorange bumpers on slot of lower A-arm where stock rubber bumpers were removed. Put inset hole in toward bumper and attach with ⅜×1¼ inch bolts, washers and lock nuts provided.

4. Install new Rugged Trail coil spring. Mate the small, straight section of coil with the indentation in lower A-arm and properly align. Raise jack under lower A-arm to hold coil into position, rein-

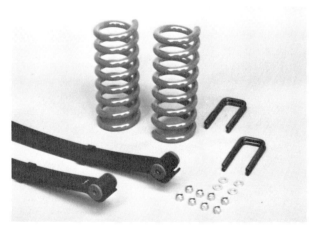

This Rancho kit will drop the full-size Chevy pickup 2½ inches in front and four in rear to make the entire truck look level. It'll fit the 1988 2WD C-1500 truck, 1973-87 2WD C-10 and 1983-88 S-10 and S-15. Rancho

This unusual Rancho kit will drop the 2WD Jeep Comanche two inches. It includes front coils, front limiting straps and rear blocks with new U-bolts. Rancho

If you have a Chevy S–10 pickup built from 1983 to now, this lowering kit, complete with front coils, rear lowering blocks and shocks, is available as a bolt-on project from Rugged Trail. Rugged Trail

stall nut on lower ball joint. Tighten nut and insert new cotter pin provided with Rugged Trail kit. Repeat steps 2 through 4 on other side of vehicle.

5. Place the driver's side shock bracket against the outside of the frame and align the two ¼ inch holes in bracket with the matching holes in the side of the frame rail. (Some vehicles may not have ¼ inch holes in the frame. If so, attach the shock to the bracket and position bracket so that shock has approximately ½ inch clearance at the rear of the upper A-arm.) The bracket fits around the outside of the dimple where the factory shock stud mounts through the clutch linkage when clutch pedal is depressed.

6. Mark the holes in the frame and drill a $^7/_{16}$ inch hole through frame that aligns with bracket. Install bracket using 2¼×1 inch hex bolts and nuts

and 1$^7/_{16}$ inch hex bolt and nut provided. Repeat steps 5 and 6 on other side of truck.

7. Attach shocks to new brackets at top and stock brackets at bottom. (*Note:* The speedometer cable bracket on driver's side firewall must be bent to the left so that upper stud on shock will have clearance.) Also, push driver's side shock upper mount all the way to the front of bracket when installing so that stud will not interfere with clutch linkage.

8. Remove sway bar brackets from frame and reinstall sway bar to lower A-arms. Check to see that sway bar extends through the bracket equally on both sides and tighten bolts on lower A-arm. Place jack under center of sway bar and raise up to the frame. Drill new holes and reinstall original bolts. Check that location on frame is the same on both sides.

9. Check all tightened nuts to see that they're tight to specs, and recheck after several miles to see that nothing has worked loose. Installation of the rear lowering kit (blocks) will be covered later.

Rugged Trail lowrider coils for 1982-86 S-10/S-15 2WD

The last section covered the front end coils of full-size GM trucks. This section covers the smaller S-10/S-15 replacement coils. The newer S-10s require the spindle already described.

Installation is as follows:

1. Set parking brake and make sure wheels are pointed directly forward. Jack up front of vehicle and place jack stands under frame directly under doors. Remove tires and wheels. Remove sway bar, if so equipped, from lower A-arms. Remove front shocks.

2. On driver's side, place jack under lower A-arm, leaving ½ inch gap between jack and arm. Remove cotter key from lower ball joint and loosen nut, but do not remove. Break lower ball joint loose

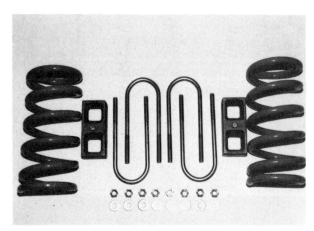

This S–10 lowering kit from Rugged Trail comes complete with lowering blocks, longer U–bolts and front coils. It's for 2WD S–10s built from 1983 to present. Rugged Trail

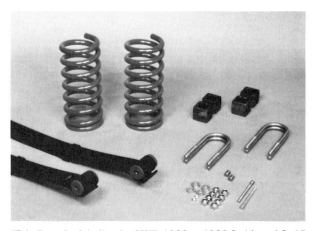

This Rancho kit fits the 2WD 1983 to 1988 S–10 and S–15 Chevy minipickup. It includes coils for the front plus replacement leaf springs and blocks for the rear. Rancho

with a pickle fork, remove ball joint and allow A-arm to rest on jack. Lower jack and A-arm down slowly.

3. Carefully remove stock coil spring. Make sure the rubber ring stays in the top of the spring tower. Coil springs are under tension, so use extreme caution when removing. Install new RT coil spring. Locate the spring properly in the spring tower, making sure the rubber ring is in position. Lower A-arm has a straight section which the coil fits into. Raise jack to apply pressure under lower A-arm and hold coil in position, while guiding ball joint into lower A-arm socket. Replace nut, tighten lower ball joint and install new Rugged Trail cotter key.

4. Replace shock and wheel, and repeat process on passenger's side. When both sides are complete, reinstall sway bar and remove jack stands. Lower vehicle.

Trail Master replacement A-arms

Trail Master makes a different type of lowering system for the 1982 through 1988 Chevy/GMC S-10/S-15 pickups. This system keeps the stock coils, and uses different A-arms. This is a radical change from the idea of cutting stock coils or installing shorter replacement coils. The advantages to this system are that you are able to retain the stock ride entirely, since you keep the stock coils. Trail Master recommends that you replace your shock absorbers with their N7 Invader high-performance gas shocks for a more controlled ride.

The A-arm replacement kit is Trail Master part no. CL26 and includes replacement A-arms, new anti-sway bar links, cast iron lowering blocks for the rear and anodized U-bolts and hardware. Everything but new shock absorbers is included. These can be purchased separately. These installation instructions are for the 1983-88 2WD Chevy and GMC S-10/S-15 pickups.

Upper A-arm

1. Block rear wheels and place floor jack under front and jack up.

2. Place jack stands under frame, remove wheels. Keep slight pressure on lower A-arm with floor jack.

3. Remove upper A-arm by removing the two bolts and nuts at cross-shaft. Be sure to keep shims in order so you can replace them in same location during reassembly.

4. Remove upper ball joint nut and cotter key. Remove upper A-arm. Remove ball joint rivets and bumper stop.

5. Reinstall ball joint and bumper stop into new upper A-arm. (*Note:* A-arms in kit are marked P for passenger side and D for driver's side.) Use ¼×1 inch bolts and lock nuts. Torque to 9 lb-ft.

6. Remove nuts and washers from each end of cross-shaft in old upper A-arm. Press out bushing from each end of cross-shaft. (*Note:* Use of new

bushings is recommended, since old ones are compressed and may not fit tightly. When pressing out old bushings and pressing in new bushings, be sure to support A-arm leg so it will not bend during pressing of bushings. Remove cross-shaft.

7. Install new bushing, GM part no. 473786. Be sure to press bushings down only to step bushing. Install cross-shaft and opposite end bushing. Reinstall nut and washer onto cross-shaft, but do not tighten at this time. Reinstall new upper control arm onto vehicle.

8. Reinstall shims in same order as removed.

9. Reinstall bolts and nuts and tighten. Reinstall ball joint nut and tighten. Reinstall cotter pin.

10. Repeat steps for opposite side of vehicle, but only after you have completed the first side.

Lower A-arm

1. Remove shock on either side.

2. Remove sway bar link bushings sleeve and nuts from lower A-arm.

3. Insert spring compressor onto coil spring and compress spring. If a spring compressor is not

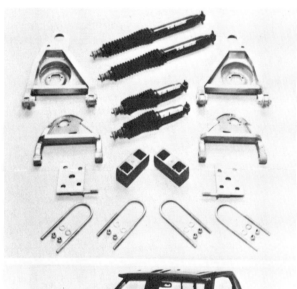

This Trail Master lowering kit for the 2WD Chevy/GMC S-10 and S-15 pickups features replacement front A-arms that use the stock coil springs, and rear lowering blocks with new U-bolts. Trail Master

Remove the coil spring from the vehicle, and place it on the floor. The smaller section is the bottom. Cut a wrap and a half from the top, as in this photo.

The easiest way to mark where the spring will be cut is to mark it right next to the end of the coil, as in this photo. This will ensure that both sides are even. This will lower the vehicle about two inches.

available, you can use a floor jack by placing a heavy chain around frame and tying to floor jack. Be sure jack is set under lower A-arm and jack up the floor jack slowly to release tension on coil spring so ball joint nut and cotter pin can be removed. Dislodge ball joint from spindle.

4. Lower floor jack slowly at this time, releasing tension on coil spring.

5. Remove coil and two remaining bolts and nuts in lower A-arm. Remove lower A-arm. Press out lower ball joint from old A-arm and press into new lower A-arm.

6. Remove shock nut clips from old A-arm and reinstall into new A-arm.

7. Press new bushings, GM part no. 1-14024143, into new lower A-arm and be sure to keep A-arm bushing ends supported while installing new bushings.

8. Reinstall lower A-arm and bushing nuts and bolts. Do not tighten at this time.

9. Using a spring compressor, install onto coil spring and compress spring. Reinstall coil spring into upper spring pocket, making sure rubber spring pad is in proper position. Install spring into lower spring pocket, making sure spring lower coil is sitting in lower A-arm pocket correctly.

10. Place floor jack under lower A-arm and jack up to reinstall ball joint into spindle.

11. Tighten lower A-arm bushing bolts and nuts at this time.

12. Remove floor jack and spring compressor. Install shock and tighten. Reinstall sway bar bushings, sleeve and nuts, and tighten.

Notes on A-arm lowering

1. Alignment will be needed after installation is complete.

2. Alignment settings are the same as stock specifications.

3. The front end will now be three inches lower.

4. Vehicle can still use stock sway bars if so equipped.

5. Installation of new A-arm bushings will make installation much easier.

Cutting your front coil springs

Warning: Cutting front coils can void manufacturer's warranty!

The least expensive way to lower your front end is to cut the coil springs down two inches or so in height and replace them in their stock position. This involves removing the spring, cutting it and reinstalling it. As noted earlier, this is not the best way to lower your front end, since the coil spring now has less height and will bottom out more easily. A better method is to replace the stock coils with lower, aftermarket coils, such as those offered by aftermarket suspension makers. These coils are carefully engineered to provide adequate handling and load carrying characteristics.

Use a torch to cut the spring steel where it has been marked. Cut quickly and do not heat up any adjacent areas of the coil springs. This will cause the flexible steel to lose its temper.

However, should you decide to cut your coil springs, this is the best method to follow:

1. Jack up front end, support by frame, loosen lower A-arm and remove coil spring as described earlier in this chapter. Use of a spring compressor is not essential but is preferred. If you do not have experience with removing and installing coil springs, have a spring shop do the lowering job.

2. After removing the coil spring, carefully measure off about a wrap and a half and mark it with welding chalk. Make sure both coils are marked precisely the same. You can use the end of the coil spring as a guide.

Grind the edges of the coil spring to remove any rough edges.

After cutting and grinding, this is how the coil will look.

3. Use an acetylene torch to carefully cut the spring at the position marked. A torch will not damage the coil, since you are heating up only a small portion of the coil spring near the end.

4. Carefully grind the edges of the coil spring with a hand or bench grinder.

5. The end of the coil spring will now stick up a little over the other side. This section must be flattened out for the spring to seat properly in the vehicle. Heat the spring at a point about three inches from the end and bend the spring with a one-inch inside diameter pipe, as shown. Do not

In order for the spring to seat properly in the vehicle, the end of the spring must be flat. Use a length of one-inch pipe to hold and bend the steel while it's being heated by a torch. Do not heat any adjacent coils. Heat the coil about four inches from the end, over a two-inch area, and bend it carefully.

heat any other part of the coil spring. This will cause the spring to lose its temper. Heating it at the end to bend it will not damage it.

6. Reinstall the coil spring in its stock position, lower the vehicle and carefully check the spring to make sure it's seated properly and all bolts are tight.

Other kits

Trail Master makes a kit that will lower the two-wheel-drive Chevrolet/GMC half-ton pickup from 1973 to 1988 by *four inches.* This is achieved with specially wound front coil springs, which lower the vehicle four inches while retaining full factory characteristics, lower front shock brackets, which enable shocks to be mounted in a new lower position, and lower rear leaf spring mounts. The coil springs will carry the same load as the original springs.

You can cut a wrap out of your stock coil spring and lower your front end two to three inches. Then you can install a replacement spindle, the front end will be lowered four, five inches or more. You could also install aftermarket springs with the spindle for similar lowering. Unless you

Trail Master also has a kit to lower the Ford Ranger 2WD, with replacement front axles. These axles allow you to use stock coil springs in the front. In the rear, spring perches are replaced so leaf springs can be reversed on the axle.

have the equipment to do this safely, have it done at a suspension shop. The shop also carries liability insurance to cover their work on the vehicle.

The specific lowering kits and methods already mentioned are not the only ones available. It pays to contact the manufacturers because they are creating new kits for new applications all the time. And, depending on how much you want to lower your truck, you can combine the lowering effects of two of the methods.

Other aftermarket systems

Trail Master for Ford Ranger

Trail Master makes a replacement axle pair for the front end of the 1983-88 Ford Ranger pickup. This will mechanically lower the front end a full three inches. The stock ball joints and brake parts are kept. The second part of the kit, covered in the sections on rear end lowering, includes new rear end spring locater pads to position the rear springs on the bottom of the rear axle, lowering the rear end four inches. New shocks are recommended and can be purchased separately.

The advantage of this kit is that it keeps the handling and suspension of the front end. The only thing that is changed is the height of the vehicle from the ground. While this may seem like a trivial advantage, the disadvantage of coil spring cutting or shorter coils on other vehicles is that they definitely change the handling of the vehicle and its "feel." This Trail Master kit does not.

Use the following steps to install the Trail Master kit.

1. Block rear wheels, jack up front end. Remove tires and shocks. Remove left and right side tie-rods.

2. Remove bottom ball joint nut and loosen top ball joint nut. Remove spindle from ball joints. (*Note:* After they are removed, the complete spindle assembly and brake assembly can be tied up to frame rail and out of the way. Do not let assembly dangle by the brake hose. It may kink and later cause brake failure.)

3. Remove coil spring lower retaining nut. Remove front sway bar if so equipped. Pull axle down and remove coil spring. Keep for reuse.

4. Remove radius rod to axle assembly bolt. Remove axle to frame assembly bolt. Remove stock axle. Repeat steps on opposite side.

5. Remove ball joints and upper ball joint snap ring from old axle and reinstall into same location in new axle. (*Note:* To reinstall bolt joint use Loctite part no. 680 or equivalent.)

6. Install bushings and sleeves (supplied in kit) into new axles. Install two orange bushings on outside with one black bushing in center. Install new axles. Reinstall axle to frame assembly bolt. Do not tighten at this time. Reinstall radius rod to axle assembly bolt and tighten. (*Note:* There may be ¼ to ⅜ inch gap between upper radius rod and upper

axle. When tightening bolt be sure to tighten so there isn't a gap remaining.)

7. Reinstall coil spring making sure coil is seated properly into pocket. (*Note:* For 1985 and older models, if stamped axles are being replaced, the lower cast iron spring seat must be modified for axle clearance. This involves removing the iron tab.) Reinstall coil spring lower nut and retainer.

8. Reinstall brake and spring assembly, making sure camber adjusting bushing is in place into upper ball joint of spindle. At this time it is very important that spindle be in its uppermost position on ball joints. This may be clamped or held in place until ball joint nuts are tightened. Reinstall lower ball joint cotter key. Repeat steps on opposite side. Tighten axle to frame assembly bolts. Install shocks and sway bar, if so equipped.

9. Attach tie-rods at this time but do not tighten. Loosen tie-rod adjusting sleeves. Shorten tie-rod approximately three to five turns for each side. Tighten tie-rods and sleeves. Reinstall cotter key. (*Note:* For 1985 and newer trucks with memory steering, tie-rod ends cannot be tightened until vehicle is sitting on tires. At this time, tire should be straight ahead and steering wheel straight. Then tighten nuts and install cotter keys on tie-rod ends. Align front end.)

Rancho kit for
Jeep 2WD Comanche

Rancho offers a lowering kit for the 1984-88 2WD XJ Jeep Comanche. This kit lowers both the front and rear two inches. The front is lowered through use of replacement coil springs which have an increased rate. The rear is lowered with blocks.

Rancho for Ford Ranger

Rancho makes a slightly different pair of replacement front axles for the 1983-89 Ford Ranger. This kit (#6450) includes a pair of dropped axle beams constructed of seamless tube and SAE high-strength alloy steel plate. The axle beams will accept factory ball joints and spindles. The beam pivots feature Rancho Duracush polyurethane bushings (better than original equipment bushings). This kit lowers the Rangers by three inches and improves handling with the lower center of gravity and the fact that the new axles are twenty-five percent lighter than the stock steel axles. The installation of the replacement front axles is similar to the Trail Master, but the complete Rancho installation instructions must be followed since there are some differences. The rear end is lowered through the use of axle relocation brackets and new U-bolts.

Import trucks

The front ends of most import trucks are held up by torsion bars. These torsion bars use the same principle as anti-sway bars: a bar made of spring steel is firmly held in place by the frame. When the

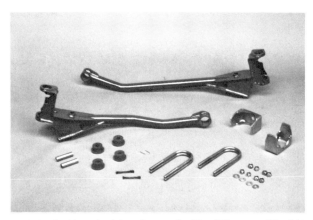

This is the Rancho kit to lower the Ford Ranger. The kit fits the 1983–88 Ford Ranger and features seamless steel tubing for light weight. It also includes replacement polyurethane bushings for the new axles and rear axle brackets to lower the rear. Rancho

vehicle hits a bump, a small "crank" on the wheel translates this up-and-down motion to a twisting motion of the torsion bar. The torsion bar resists twist (as a coil spring resists being compressed) but does have some give built into it. It twists a little bit, providing rebound, and at the same time it keeps the wheels firmly pressed to the ground for excellent handling and cornering.

Torsion bars can be adjusted. This is done by turning out a bolt that holds the opposite end of the torsion bar to a cross-member under the cab. To lower the front end of a two-wheel-drive vehicle equipped with a torsion bar suspension, follow these steps:

1. Place the transmission in park, and lock the rear wheels with the emergency brake. Block the rear wheels. If you wish to measure the height of

The Rancho Ford lowering system lowers the truck three inches. Rancho

To determine how far you want to lower your truck, first install the tires and wheels of your choice, then with the wheels resting normally on the ground, measure the distance from the ground to the top inside edge of the wheelwell. With this Toyota the distance was 28½ inches.

First use two wrenches to break loose the lock nut (the top nut) and back it off about two inches. Do not remove the bolt while you are lowering the truck. Then you can turn the bolt with an air or electric wrench. As the bolt head lowers, the front end will lower. The amount of thread showing above the cross-member will shorten as the truck is lowered.

the vehicle over the ground, do it now by measuring the distance between the center of the wheelwell over the tire to the ground. With the Toyota in the photos (a 1989 model) this was twenty-eight and a half inches, stock height.

2. Jack up the truck to a height of a foot and a half or more so you have enough room to get under

it and work under the cab. You do not need to remove the front wheels, although removing them may make it easier for you to get under the truck and work on the torsion bars.

3. Before you get under the truck, support it with jack stands, placed under the frame, in the middle area of the truck, under the cab. Place another jack stand on the front of the vehicle for extra protection.

Locate the torsion bar ends with their adjusting bolts. These are attached to the cross-member located in the center of the truck just behind the transmission.

This truck has been lowered as much as possible. The lock nut (top) is within a quarter inch of the end of the bolt. The lock nut must be completely threaded for safety reasons.

4. Locate the torsion bar adjusting bolt. With the Toyota in the photos, these are located on a cross-member under the cab. The bolt is located inside of the torsion bar, toward the center of the truck.

5. Use a suitable metric closed-end wrench and socket wrench. You must first use these two tools to loosen and back off the lock nut located on the adjusting bolt. Loosen the lock nut and back it off to where it is flush with the end of the bolt.

6. Use an electric torque wrench, air wrench or ½ inch drive long-handled wrench to back off the bolt on the cross-member. As you back it off (loosen it on the frame) you will notice the front end of the truck becoming lower. The maximum distance you can lower the truck is where the cross-member hits the lock nut. The lock nut must be filled with threads from the bolt. So at the maximum drop point, the lock nut will be flush with the end of the bolt.

7. Lower the right and left sides in a similar way. When you are finished with both sides, you can correct for the weight of the driver by measuring the height of the wheelwell to the ground with the driver in the vehicle. The vehicle will have to be lowered off the jack stands for this to be done. If the driver's side (with the driver seated) is lower than the passenger side, tighten the torsion bar adjusting bolt until both sides are even (that is, the distance from the wheelwell to the ground is the same when the vehicle is resting on its wheels with the driver seated in the cab). This will ensure that the vehicle rides level when the driver is seated.

8. To raise the vehicle (if you don't want the vehicle lowered to its maximum drop or if you want to raise the driver's side) you must have the vehicle jacked up and supported by jack stands. This must be done because the torsion bars support the weight of the front end. If you attempt to raise the truck while it's resting on its wheels, you will in effect be raising the weight of the front end by turning the torsion bar adjusting bolt. This bolt is not made to take the weight of the entire front end. You may strip the threads or break the bolt, making it impossible to drive the vehicle until it's repaired. So if you must raise the truck, be sure to raise both wheels off the ground first and support the truck with jack stands. This will take more time but will save you unnecessary repairs.

9. You should always use the wheelwell height as the best indication of how level the truck is. You could measure how much bolt is exposed over the lock nut, but this is not as accurate.

10. Remember that the front end will lower itself again when you and a passenger get in the truck. You may want to raise it a half-inch or so to counteract this.

11. If you install new tires and wheels check the front end height again.

This is the front end of the truck. The arm with two nuts is lowered as the torsion bar turns.

12. Remember, when you lower the front end, you shorten wheel travel. At its maximum drop (about three and one-half inches) the front end will bottom out much more quickly than at stock height. If this is a nuisance, raise the vehicle an inch or so and drive it around until you're satisfied with its height. You can always lower the front end more for custom truck shows.

13. When you have adjusted the torsion bar to your satisfaction, tighten the lock nut on top of the

Now with the torsion bar fully backed off, you can lower the truck to the ground and measure the distance the truck has dropped. The distance on this truck is now 25 inches, the truck has been lowered 3½ inches. In order to make the driver's side level, you can have the driver sit in the seat, measure how much his/her weight lowers the truck, then raise the truck so the side with the driver seated is the same height as the passenger side wheelwell.

bolt. This is very important. After driving the truck for the first time, tighten the lock nut again, and periodically inspect it for looseness. Record the height of the front end (measuring from center of wheel opening to ground) and keep this as a record of where it should be.

Lowering the rear end

Lowering the rear end is much different from lowering the front end. Front ends have coil springs, torsion bars and spindles to work with. With rear ends you only have the leaf springs, axle and U-bolts to work with.

There are four ways to lower the rear end. These can be done separately or in combination. The first is to simply reverse the location of the axle on the springs, placing the axle over the springs rather than under them. This can be done with most trucks. Many compact trucks already have the axle over the springs, however, and for these trucks this modification cannot be performed.

Reversing the location of the axle on the springs does change the angle of the drive shaft, so the drive shaft may have to be shortened. If so, have it shortened at a custom drive shaft shop. They can cut the splined piece down and then balance the drive shaft. You shouldn't just take a big hacksaw and cut a piece off of the splined section of the drive shaft, though. This is basically what the shop will do, but the drive shaft should be balanced afterwards for the job to be done properly.

The second method is to place a block or spacer between the axle and leaf springs. This is usually done after the axle is reversed (or, if your axle is already on the leaf springs, this is your first option) so the axle moves up even closer to the truck's bed, away from the ground. The net effect is to lower the truck the width of the block. After the axle is moved on top of the leaf springs, a one-inch spacer will lower the truck one inch more. A word of caution: Do *not* use homemade blocks. Always purchase a lowering block from a responsible national manufacturer. These manufacturers have done the engineering and manufacturing work needed to make sure the block is safe and will function permanently. Homemade blocks may crack, causing the axle to loosen on the springs, which may result in road accidents.

There is a limit to how much you can lower the rear end, just as there is a limit to lowering the front. Usually, use of a spacer block and reversing the springs on the axle will give you the maximum amount of drop, three or four inches, that your truck can handle.

If you want to drop your truck even more, there is the third method, re-arching the springs. What this involves is removing the leaf spring assemblies from the axle, taking them apart and then having them re-arched or straightened out by a suspension shop. These shops have the equip-ment needed to arch their own springs. Don't heat the spring with a torch to bend it, since this only weakens the temper of the spring and will cause it to break prematurely. Have a spring shop re-arch the spring and reinstall it.

The fourth method is the one that I do not recommend: cutting the frame of the new Chevy pickups and welding in a new section of frame with an arch or C-shape. This is not recommended for the safety and insurance reasons already discussed. There is only one set of circumstances where rebuilding the frame is okay, and that is where you're building a truck strictly for show, one that will not be driven on the street. Then you can do what you like with the frame since it will never be driven and subjected to any kind of stress.

In reality, most sport truck owners do two of these methods in combination, such as reversing the springs on the axle, and then installing a lowering block. This will give you all the drop your vehicle can take and still be street drivable.

The nice thing about the lowering block is that it's only held in place by U-bolts. You can install the lowering blocks for custom truck shows only, while in everyday use you can keep the truck lowered but leave out the extra drop you get with the blocks. So the blocks can be installed, taken out and reinstalled whenever you want to show the truck. And if you happen to sell it in the future, you can also reverse the springs and return the truck to its stock height.

If you have the springs re-arched, you are doing something that permanently changes the truck's ability to carry weight and respond to road bumps and hazards. This is okay if the truck is basically used to get you to work and for show. But this is not a good idea if you use your truck every day for hauling 500 pounds or more worth of building materials, tools and so on. The truck will still be able to carry as much weight, but it will bottom out more easily when it hits potholes or bumps.

Of course, the springs can be removed and replaced with stock springs at any time in the future, but this is not as easy as removing a drop block after a custom show. It's not something you'll want to do every other weekend, since there's a great deal of work involved.

The following sections describe how to do these kinds of drops to the rear end of a truck with leaf springs. Always be cautious when working with springs and be sure to replace the U-bolts with longer ones. If you purchase a lowering kit, such as the universal lowering kit offered by Rugged Trail, you will get longer U-bolts with the kit. This is important since the lowering block increases the distance between the axle and leaf spring, and therefore requires the use of a longer U-bolt.

Lowering using blocks

Most sport truck rear ends can be lowered by placing spacers or blocks between the axle and leaf spring. The following paragraphs contain specific instructions for lowering most of these trucks.

Rugged Trail for Chevy S-10/S-15 2WD

1. Raise rear of vehicle and place jack stands under frame, ahead of spring hanger. Release parking brake, and put transmission into neutral. Remove rear tires, wheels and shocks.

2. Place jack under rear differential, supporting axle, but do not raise. Remove stock U-bolts from axle. Jack axle up approximately three inches and place new Rugged Trail two-inch block between spring pad and leaf spring. Place block so that pin on top of block aligns with hole in spring pad, and center pin of spring goes into hole in block. Place smaller end of block toward the front of vehicle.

3. Install new Rugged Trail U-bolts down over axle and through U-bolt plates. Install new washers and lock nuts, and tighten. Torque all nuts to 75 lb-ft. Install shocks, wheels and tires, and lower vehicle.

4. Go back and check that all installation steps have been completed. Recheck all bolts for tightness. All bolts should be checked for tightness after every 100 miles, and after an off-road use during first 300 miles. Front end of vehicle must be aligned after installation. Use of 60 series tires is recommended.

Trail Master for Chevy/GMC S-10/S-15

If you have purchased the replacement A-arms for the front end of your S-10/S-15 (kit CL26), you also have the parts you need to lower the rear end. This involves installation of lowering blocks and new, longer U-bolts. Follow these simple steps:

1. Jack up vehicle and place jack stands under frame. Lower floor jack, but use jack to keep slight pressure on axle while you remove tires, shocks and U-bolts.

2. Raise floor jack and install three-inch block between axle and spring with tapered end toward transmission.

3. Lower floor jack, install new U-bolts with new U-bolt plate provided with kit. (Plate is marked D for driver's side, P for passenger side.) Tighten U-bolt nuts, install shocks and tires. Vehicle is now lowered three inches in the rear.

Toyota, Mitsubishi, Dodge, Isuzu and Nissan rear ends

The front end of all torsion bar suspended front ends can be lowered by modifying the position of the torsion bar. The rear ends of these vehicles can be easily modified by installing a lowering block between the axle and top of the leaf spring assembly. This in effect raises the height of the rear axle under the vehicle, lowering the wheels at the same time.

Rugged Trail makes a universal lowering block that will fit most application. If in doubt, check

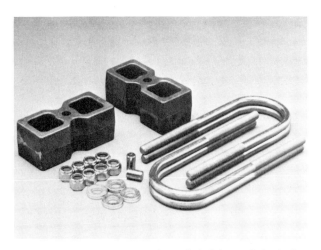

This Rancho kit is for lowering minipickups. It includes two-inch rear blocks, zinc–plated U–bolts and hardware. Instructions for lowering the front torsion suspension are included. Rancho

recent catalog listings. Rancho also makes lowering blocks with U-bolts specifically designed for your truck. You can also have a suspension shop make a custom lowering block for you. If a lowering block is fabricated, be sure that the hole and pin are the same size as stock, so the block will be securely anchored into the leaf spring and axle. Also make sure the U-bolts are of the proper length and stock thickness, so they're just as strong as the original U-bolts. The one nice thing about lowering blocks is that they can be installed just before a show, then removed for everyday street use, if you need your truck for everyday use.

Installation of Rugged Trail or Rancho lowering block kit

Rugged Trail sells a universal lowering block kit, which includes a block and parts for lowering the rear end on virtually any vehicle. Check the applications list in their current catalog, because size of U-bolts varies among vehicles.

Follow these steps:

1. Jack up vehicle, and place jack stands under both sides of frame, in front of front leaf spring mount.

2. Remove U-bolts, but only do one side at a time.

3. Using a hydraulic jack, slowly raise the axle (after both U-bolts have been loosened by removing nuts) and lift over leaf spring.

4. Carefully insert the lowering block between the axle housing and leaf spring.

5. Lower axle down so weight is on the lowering block, and install and tighten U-bolts to 45 lb-ft.

6. Repeat procedure for other side of vehicle.

Check bolts after 100 miles, and periodically thereafter. Consult with the manual that came with your lowering block kit for any variations.

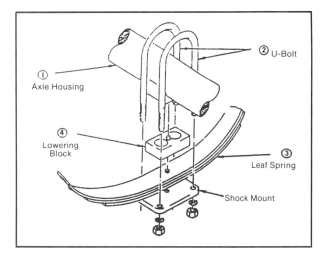

This universal lowering kit from Rugged Trail is for all minipickups. After adjusting the front torsion bars to lower the front end, install the lowering blocks as described in this diagram.

Lowering by putting axle over springs

Some trucks come stock with leaf springs mounted on top of the axles. The easiest way to lower these trucks is to mount the axles over the springs. This will lower the rear end the width of the axle housing. Several aftermarket companies make kits for this type of lowering. The following paragraphs give instructions for installing these kits and for putting the axle over the springs without a kit.

Rugged Trail for full-size GM trucks

1. Place jack under differential and raise rear of vehicle. Place jack stands under frame ahead of front spring hanger. Remove tires, wheels and shocks.

2. Place jack under differential but do not raise up. Loosen and remove U-bolts and axle plates from rear springs. Lower jack slowly about six inches so axle comes down away from springs. Place a jack stand under the drive shaft near the differential to prevent axle from rolling forward.

3. Remove bolts from spring hangers and remove springs. Remove rubber axle bumpers and their support brackets which are located on bottom of frame. (Rivets can be cut or ground off.) With springs removed, raise axle up next to frame. (Axle will now be located on top of springs.) Rebolt springs to shackles at top. Place clamps on one spring to hold the leaves together and remove stock center pin. Replace it with new center pin (included in kit) but reverse it so head is now on top of spring. Tighten center pin nut, release clamps and repeat on other spring.

4. Lower the rear axle down onto the springs and axle, making sure the brackets fit inside axle pads. Place the short side of the brackets forward,

which moves the axle to the rear to lengthen the drive shaft. Make sure center pin in spring is seated into hole in bracket. Reinstall shock U-bolts which now go from top of axle down through the axle plates, and tighten nuts.

5. Install rear shocks using new ½×2½ inch bolts, washers and nuts included in kit through the bottom mounts. You must use this shorter bolt to allow clearance past the U-bolts. Top mounts of shocks use a parts pack which bolts to the frame.

6. Replace tires and wheels and let vehicle down off jack stands. Go back and check that all installation steps have been completed. Recheck all bolts for tightness. All bolts should be checked for tightness after first 100 miles and after any severe use, during the first 300 miles. Vehicle alignment should be checked after installation. Retighten bolts after six months.

Trail Master for Ford Rangers

If you have purchased the Ford Ranger replacement axle kit, you also have a set of new axle positioning pads to install in order to lower the rear end. Use of these parts will lower the rear end about four inches. Follow these simple directions for lowering the Ford Ranger rear end:

1. Block front tires, jack up rear axle, place jack stands under frame just ahead of rear spring front shackle. Remove rear tires, shocks, remove U-bolts and springs.

2. Reverse spring center bolt. Hold the end of the center bolt with vise-grips while you loosen the nut. If the center bolt nut is frozen, you may have to grind it off and replace it.

3. Place axle spring pads (as supplied in Trail Master kit) on bottom of axle housing, placing tabs into original spring pad. Reinstall springs, with axle on top of springs. Reinstall stock U-bolts and tighten. Reinstall shock absorbers and tires. Tighten bolts to proper specifications.

Note: For proper shock clearance, rear sway bar may need adjustment. This is, of course, only for those vehicles with rear sway bars.

Ford, Chevy/GMC

There is only one easy way to lower the rear axles on newer Chevy trucks. This is to reverse the location of the leaf spring so that it's *under* rather than *over* the axle. To do this properly you have to weld new axle saddles (or axle pads) under the axle to hold the axle in place on the leaf spring. This is best done by a good suspension or axle shop.

In order to lower the Chevy axle, follow this procedure:

1. Jack up the truck so the rear tires clear the floor, and place jack stands under the frame. Lower the truck on the stands and let the truck be supported by the jack stands. It's much easier to use a garage hydraulic lift so you can work under the axle, but this may not always be possible.

2. Place another jack stand under the axle housing, near one side. Work with one side at a time.

3. Loosen and remove the U-bolts holding the axle to the leaf spring.

4. Loosen the bolt holding one side of the leaf spring to the frame. This is located at the end or "eye" of the leaf spring.

5. Remove the bolt at the other eye of the leaf spring and remove the leaf spring completely from the vehicle.

6. Remove the leaf spring from the other side of the vehicle, being sure to support the axle housing first.

7. Raise the axle up about four inches, and place the leaf spring *under* it. Replace and tighten eye bolts on both sides of the leaf spring. Then place a new leaf spring saddle under the axle housing.

8. Raise the axle on the other side, and replace the leaf spring *under* the axle as in step 7. Also place a new leaf spring saddle under the axle housing. Line up the center bolt on the spring saddle.

9. Replace the U-bolts and plate and snug up carefully, going from side to side on the U-bolt. At this point the axle should be supported by a jack or jack stand at the center of the axle, under the differential housing.

10. Replace the U-bolts and plate on the other leaf spring, and snug up. Do not tighten bolts to full torque.

11. Shorten the drive shaft about one inch. This may be done by cutting the splined end of the drive shaft with a hacksaw. Be sure to tape the ends smooth after cutting.

12. Check the position of the drive shaft to make sure the differential hasn't rotated and changed the drive shaft angle too much. At this point, you can straighten out the drive shaft angle to match the original angle.

13. The new leaf spring saddles or pads will permanently fix the axle's position in relation to the drive shaft. So make sure the pinion side of the differential housing is parallel to the ground.

14. Carefully weld the new leaf spring saddles to the axle housing. Do this on both sides, and then tighten up U-bolts to stock specifications.

15. Check to make sure all U-bolts are tight, then remove jack stands and lower vehicle. Take the truck for a test drive, then snug up the U-bolt nuts once again.

Re-arch springs

An inexpensive and relatively easy way to lower the rear suspension is to re-arch the springs. Springs are made of flexible spring steel, and like any piece of steel, they can be bent. A suspension shop can remove your new stock springs, bend them and replace them into the vehicle. This only involves some labor and use of a hydraulic ram.

To determine how much the spring should be re-arched, first place the spring upside down on the floor, and measure the distance from the floor to the topmost part of the spring (not including the center bolt).

Follow these steps to re-arch springs:

1. Jack up the rear end of the vehicle. Remove one leaf spring at a time by loosening the U-bolts, support the axle by a jack placed under the differential housing, then remove the leaf spring shackle bolts. Raise the axle enough so that its weight is no longer resting on the spring. Loosen and remove

This spring shop, Spring-Align of Palatine, Illinois, uses a 50 ton ram to bend the springs. Press each side of the spring two or three times.

After bending the spring, check it again by measuring the distance from the floor. This spring has been lowered from ten inches to eight inches, simply by pressing it in the ram.

the U-bolts from one side. Work on one side at a time.

2. Remove the leaf spring from the vehicle, place it on level ground upside down, and use a tape rule to measure the distance from the top to the floor. If the spring has a height of eight inches,

you want to bend the spring until it's six inches from the floor in order to lower the vehicle two inches. The height of the spring from the floor will give you exactly the amount of drop you're looking for, whether it's two or three inches.

3. Place the spring under a ram upside down, and use the ram to gently bend the spring. Try it a few times with each side, then place the spring on the floor to see how much it's been lowered. A little experience will tell you how much you need to bend the spring. If you bend the spring too much, you can bend it back.

4. Bend the spring until you have achieved the desired lowering height. Generally, you should bend the leaf spring only about two inches or so. Bend it about the same distance as you cut the front coil springs. If you want to lower the vehicle even further, install a lowering block or spacer. The spring still needs to be able to dampen most of the shocks the vehicle encounters on the highway, so you don't want to bend it to extreme proportions.

5. Replace the leaf spring and tighten the U-bolts (longer ones are not needed unless you install a block). Usually, you will need to use new U-bolts, especially if the vehicle is over a year old. Repeat this procedure on the other side of the vehicle. Generally, you should keep the driver's side about a half-inch or three-quarter-inch higher to compensate for the driver's weight. This will make the vehicle appear level when the driver is in the vehicle and will improve handling somewhat.

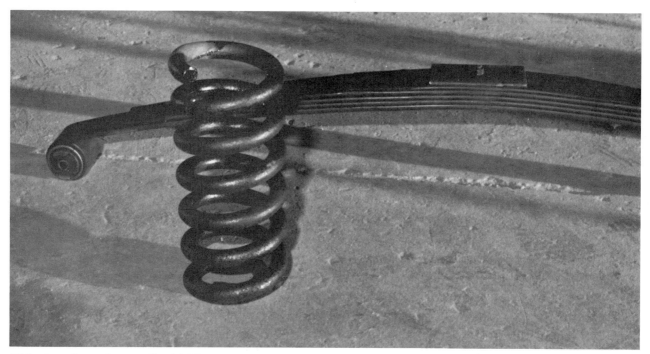

This photo shows the cut coil, which has been lowered two inches by cutting, and the lowered leaf spring, which has been de-arched to lower it two inches. No new springs or other parts had to be purchased.

This pickup's springs are already reversed. This sequence of photos will show how to lower it one inch more.

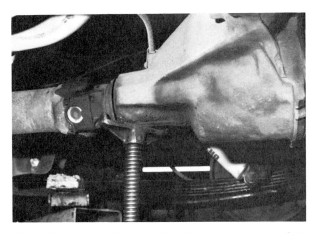

When the axle is loose on the U-bolts, it may tend to rotate. Place a jack under the pinion side of the housing and keep it level. You may also have to shorten the drive shaft a half inch or more. Take it to a drive shaft shop to be shortened.

Additional rear end lowering methods

You may be able to lower your truck an additional inch or more by placing either a block, or two short leaf springs under the leaf spring saddle. A lowering block should have a hole in the center for the center bolt line-up. The truck in these photos used two small pieces of leaf spring steel. Since this

Support the vehicle on a lift or on jack stands, and place a jack under the axle. Loosen and remove U-bolts.

Use a jack, such as this screw jack, to raise the axle over the springs. This gives you enough room to place spacers under the axle housing.

1. Jack up the truck and support it with jack stands. Place a jack and jack stand under the axle, so you can lower it and support it when necessary.

2. Unbolt the U-bolt nuts and remove the U-bolts. You will probably need longer U-bolts, since they'll need an extra inch of "reach" to bolt to the lower spring plate.

3. Jack up the axle to loosen it from the spring saddle. It should be jacked up about two inches for a one-inch block.

4. Place the spring block under the spring saddle, making sure the hole in the spring block lines up with the center bolt on the leaf spring.

5. Lower the axle housing on the spring saddle, checking to make sure the center bolt is in the hole in the spring block.

6. Snug up the U-bolt nuts, working one side of a U-bolt at a time, to make sure the nuts are evenly tightened.

7. Tighten U-bolts, remove jack and work on the other side of the axle.

8. Placing the spring block under the axle has the effect of lifting the wheel and tire higher into the wheelwell. You'll have the same amount of spring travel and load carrying capacity, but may scrape the tire against the wheelwell. Check for clearances and test drive to make sure no rubber is chafing against the sheet metal.

lowering was done at Spring-Align in Palatine, Illinois, the spring steel was readily available at the shop.

To install a lowering block, follow these guidelines:

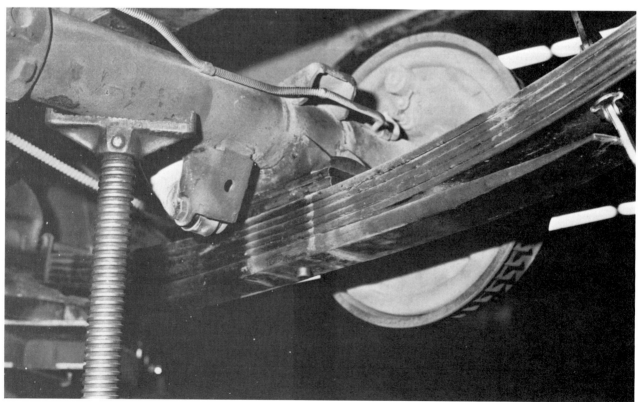

Two one-half inch pieces of steel are used as a spacer over the old leaf springs. They must be bolted to the leaf spring with a center bolt. This will also have to be longer than the original.

9. Tighten all U-bolts and give a visual check of the axle and leaf springs to make sure everything is lined up and tight.

Anti-sway bars

One useful accessory that helps improve handling is the anti-sway bar. The anti-sway bar is a torsion device that's actually a different kind of spring. It helps reduce sway on turns—but doesn't create a stiff ride the way stiff springs do—by doing the same thing stiff springs do but in a different way. An anti-sway bar is mounted to the frame by means of low-friction bushings, and its two bent ends are then firmly attached to some part of the suspension, such as a wishbone arm.

When both wheels rise or fall together, the anti-sway bar simply moves along with them without causing any springing effect. But when the vehicle is cornering, the anti-sway bar takes advantage of the weight transfer or roll that compresses the outside wheel's suspension and extends that to the inside wheel. The result is a torsioning of the anti-sway bar as its two bent ends move in opposite directions. This torsioning temporarily

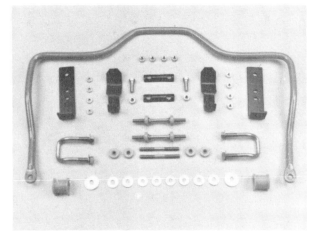

This sway bar kit is from Trail Master and will fit the rear suspensions of most pickups. Trail Master

increases the "stiffness" of the outside wheel's spring (makes it resist movement). So you can achieve a firm, controlled turning motion with an

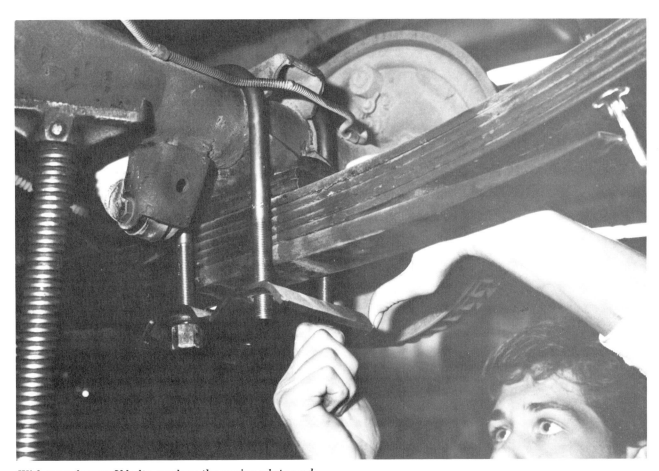

With new, longer U-bolts, replace the spring plate and tighten up, alternating between sides. Take it for a test drive to check for wheel travel.

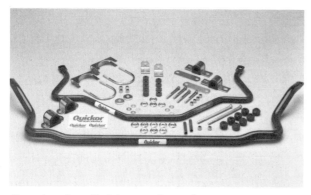

Sway bar from Quickor can be used on most minis. Warn Industries

anti-sway bar, without having to live with stiff springs 100 percent of the time.

An anti-sway bar kit is now available from Quickor, which can be installed on minipickups to improve the street handling of the vehicles. This is a better option for those who want to improve street handling, since it allows them to attain better performance in turns without suffering from stiff springs all the time.

If you want to greatly improve the handling of your minipickup, get the Quickor anti-sway bar kit and the spring lowering kit. You'll have the best of both worlds with a suspension that gives you a lower center of gravity plus anti-sway bar handling.

Trail Master also makes anti-sway bars. They can be installed on virtually every two-wheel-drive rear end, but for our purposes fit the front ends on Chevy full-size pickups, S-10 and S-15 Blazers and Jimmys, full-size Ford pickups, Ford F100s and F150s and full-size Dodge vehicles. They do not fit the front ends of Nissan and Toyota products, although an anti-sway bar is available for the rear of all Nissan and Toyota trucks.

Steering stabilizers

Lowering your truck will greatly improve handling, but there is still a need for a steering stabilizer, as there is with almost any vehicle of pickup size. Trail Master makes steering stabilizers for the Dodge pickup and Chevrolet/GMC pickups. This is a different type of installation than the four-wheel drive steering stabilizers, since the two-wheel-drive trucks have independent front suspensions.

Chevrolet/GMC

With some applications of GMC models the power steering or oil cooling lines may have to be rerouted to allow room for the stabilizer. The stabilizer must have unobstructed movement at both its far left and far right extensions. This is critical if a power steering hose is nearby, since a power steering hose breakage can cause loss of steering power.

To install the Trail Master steering stabilizer on a Chevy/GMC pickup, these directions should be followed:

1. Raise front end so tires are completely off the ground, and support the frame on both sides with jack stands. Remove jack and let vehicle rest on jack stands.

2. Turn wheels to straight forward position.

3. The steering column housing is bolted to the frame on the front left (driver's) side. Remove the lower bolt. The steering stabilizer bracket will

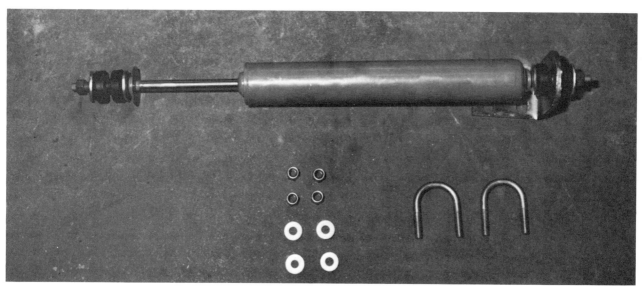

Here are the parts of a two-wheel drive steering stabilizer for Chevy and GMC pickups. It includes mounting brakes, stabilizer and hardware.

be bolted to the same hole as the lower steering bracket, using a longer bolt. Install the bracket, bolt and lock washer into the lower bolt hole.

4. Attach one side of the stabilizer to the bracket after you have first installed the rubber bushings and washers. Tighten nut on end of rod hand tight for now.

5. Attach the second bracket to the stabilizer rod, using the rubber bushings and washers included in the stabilizer kit.

6. Extend the end of the stabilizer four inches, and attach the second bracket against front face of the relay rod. Secure to relay rod with U-bolts and nuts.

7. Turns wheels to extreme left and right making sure that wheel stops are contacted. Be sure that the stabilizer is not hitting or rubbing against the frame rails, oil pan or anything else up front.

8. Tighten all nuts and pal nuts to make sure they're tight. Generally, about 40-50 lb-ft is adequate.

Note: Always consult manufacturer's instructions when installing any steering stabilizer. Instructions vary by manufacturer and model of truck.

This mounting bracket uses the bolt that secures the steering column housing to the frame. A longer bolt is furnished with kit. This will support the collapsible end of the stabilizer.

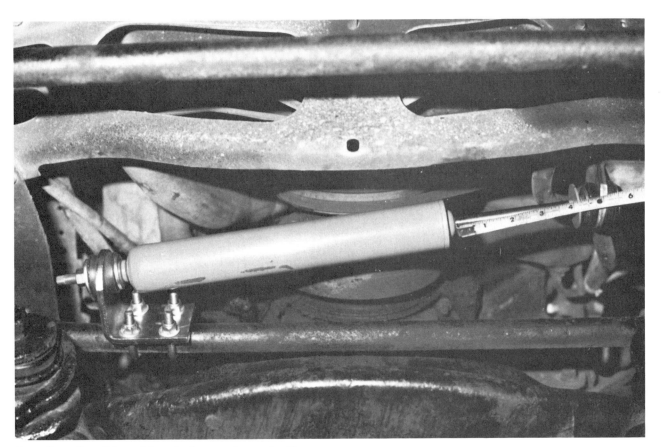

Open the collapsible end four inches, as shown, to allow complete movement of the stabilizer. The stabilizer must not interfere with steering, oil cooling lines and so forth.

3

Wheels and tires

Every type of customized vehicle seems to have its own special type of tire. And lowered trucks are no different. There are certain sizes and types of tires that are more popular than others with lowered pickups.

These tires and wheels are used in all models and years, from early 1940s restorations to brand-new truck models. This chapter will discuss what tires and wheels are being used on lowered sport trucks, and will show some specific examples of tire/wheel combinations used on trucks. There will also be some specific recommendations and cautions on using 50 and 60 series tires on lowered trucks. These precautions are intended to promote safety and prevent the hazards that can be found with extremely small tires.

Here's a low–profile 50 series BF Goodrich Radial T/A tire mounted on a chromed and painted steel wheel.

The stock wheels and tires were selected to provide the best balance of ride quality, handling, payload, gear ratio, and braking. Changing to a lower profile tire will shift this balance. The right choice of wheel and tire will improve the handling and appearance of your truck while only slightly decreasing payload and ride quality. The wrong choice could degrade the handling and ride quality of your truck to the point that it is no longer fun to drive and could be unsafe. The recommendations in this chapter will help you make the right choice.

Popular sizes

The most popular sizes actually used by slammer truck owners are the 50 and 60 series tires. The names 50 and 60 series refer to the "aspect ratio" and is a measure of the ratio between the height and width. For example, a 50 series tire has a height that is fifty percent of the width, a 60 series tire has a height sixty percent of the width and so forth. The smaller the aspect ratio number, the shorter the sidewall (for the same tire width) and the closer the wheel's rim is to the ground. Tires with low aspect ratios were first developed for racing cars and are now used on high-performance cars such as Corvettes, Porsches and Ferraris. When these high-performance tires are used on minipickups in conjunction with ground effects, suspension lowering and body graphics, they give the mini the sport truck look.

The popular size for 15 in. wheels is the 195/50-15. For 14 in. wheels the 60 series is more popular, or 195/60-14. The smaller 14 in. wheels work better with the slightly taller 60 series tires. Both of these tire sizes are commonly used with wheels seven inches wide. These low-profile tires mounted on wide rims add to the low and wide look of slammed trucks.

The lower section height found in 50 and 60 series tires have several characteristics that make them different from larger tires. The differences may not be important to the function of the tires on your truck, but you should still be aware of them before replacing your stock tires.

Payload

Low-profile tires cannot support as much weight, so your truck's payload will be reduced. If the load carrying capacity is important to you, check the load carrying capacity of the tire you intend to buy (it's molded into the sidewall of the tire) and also ask the dealer what the capacity is.

Usually, there is an operating range, about two thirds of maximum capacity, that is best for everyday use. Tires should not be driven near their maximum load carrying capacity, especially 50 and 60 series tires on a mini.

The lower section height already has a tendency to increase the operating temperature of the tire under normal conditions. When the load is increased, the temperature of the tire is increased. This is not dangerous in itself, but will cause the rubber compounds of the tire to soften and wear out more quickly. And keep in mind that the more expensive high-performance low-profile tires already have softer rubber compounds to promote traction on the pavement and will wear out very

A BF Goodrich Radial T/A tire mounted on a sawblade-style wheel by American Racing. The "sawblade" or directional wheel is the most popular with lowered trucks.

quickly if overloaded. You can maximize the load carrying capacity of a tire by inflating it to the maximum recommended tire pressure. Increasing the air pressure will also decrease the operating

Virtually any low-profile (50 or 60 series) tire can be fitted onto a lowered truck. Here's a selection of Good-year's high-performance tires designed for high speeds. Goodyear

temperature, but these advantages are realized at the cost of an even harsher ride.

Handling

The best reason (after improved looks) for changing to 50 or 60 series tires is the improved handling characteristics. Because they help lower the truck's center of gravity, sway or body roll during cornering is reduced. And the short sidewall flexes less, improving steering response. When low, wide tires are combined with a quality lowering kit, the improvement in handling can be quite dramatic; your truck may handle more like a sports car than a truck!

There is a price to pay for the improved handling that the low-profile tires give. Your truck will ride harsher, lose payload and ground clearance, and gas mileage may decrease.

Ride quality

The sidewalls of low-profile tires are shorter and thus must be stiffer to support the weight of the truck. These stiffer sidewalls absorb less of the shock from bumps and uneven pavement. The result is that every bump seems larger and you may find this to be unpleasant.

This can be a real nuisance if you have installed shorter, stiffer coil springs in the front to lower the front end. However, if you have a Ford Ranger or Chevy S-10 and replaced the independent axles in your Ford or replaced the spindles in your Chevy, the coil springs (and therefore the ride) will be the same as stock. This is another good reason why you

should lower your Ford or Chevy with this more expensive option rather than just cut down the coil springs. Your softer stock suspension will seem like a blessing.

When you drive the low-profile tires you also have to be more careful of road hazards that may damage the sidewalls. Shorter sidewalls are more delicate and prone to curb damage, damage from stones and so on. A sure sign that some damage has occurred is a slow leak. If you get the tire remounted, change the valve. And if the leak persists, it may be a damaged sidewall (even though there are no apparent cuts or bruises).

Low-profile tires on minipickups wear out much more quickly than stock-diameter tires. This is born out by the experience of slammer owners in California: their tires rarely last more than 25,000 miles. More typical is a tire life of 20,000 miles.

But there is a reason for this which may be unique to California. In that state, you cannot legally change the alignment specifications from those recommended by the manufacturer. The state is very strict about this, as strict as other states are about bumper height with jacked up four-wheel-drive vehicles.

If you go to a low-profile tire, have the alignment checked. It will need to be realigned, usually (especially with the small minis) to an extent

The Eagle ST is the most economical entry–level high–performance tire. It's available in 60 series sizes. Goodyear

The Goodyear Eagle GT+4 is available in 50 and 60 series sizes, offering excellent traction. Goodyear

exceeding stock specifications. If the front end is not aligned after installing low-profile tires, excessive tire wear will result. Don't expect the tires to last more than 25,000 miles if you don't have the alignment checked.

Effective gear ratio

Low-profile tires reduce the effective gear ratio of your truck. For any given speed your truck's engine will be working at a higher rpm. This will tend to make your truck feel like it has more power and it will accelerate faster. All this is great around town and at lower speeds, but the higher rpm operation may be annoying on the freeway and your gas mileage will probably decrease.

Also, you will have a tendency to take advantage of the increased acceleration and steering response (the truck will be more fun to drive) and drive more harshly. This will wear out the tires more quickly. And with high-performance tires that have softer compounds, the effect is even greater.

Tire fit

When you replace the stock tire with a low-profile tire, you create a number of tire fit or clearance problems just as you would if you installed huge tires on a four wheeler. With a four wheeler, the larger diameter tires create clearance problems because the fenders and wheelwells weren't

If you can fit this tire on your truck (here on a Corvette wheel) you'll have the widest tire available. It's the Goodyear ZR35 Gatorbacks, designed for good handling at high speeds. Goodyear

The front end of this lowered 1969 Chevy uses Firestone SS tires on Center Line Champ 500 polished aluminum wheels.

The rear tires are wider Firestone SS also mounted on Center Line Champ 500 polished aluminum wheels.

designed for them. With low-profile tires, the lower tires (and lowered suspension) create an identical set of problems but for a different reason: you lowered the truck twice, once when you lowered the suspension, and a second time when you installed a low-profile tire. Both of these changes brought the tire up closer into the wheelwell, and during turns, closer to the fender edges.

The only way to be sure of the tire fit is to mount the tires on the selected wheel, mount them on the vehicle, lower the truck down to the ground so the weight of the truck is on the tires, then turn the steering wheel to see if the tire rubs anywhere.

If the tire rubs when you turn, you must either lift the vehicle up an inch or so to get the fender away from the tire, or go to a smaller tire. A tire that rubs when turning is a safety hazard. You may have to turn sharply to avoid an accident someday, and the fender may cut into the tire, deflating it, leading to an accident.

The amount of clearance you have on the rear tires depends upon the degree to which the truck was lowered. Many truck owners lower their truck to its maximum by adding lowering blocks just before they drive to a truck show, drive-in or go cruising. Then for normal street driving during the week, to work and back, they take out the lowering block and raise the rear end an inch and a half or so when tire clearance is not a problem.

Wheel selection

Selecting wheels is a matter of choice that involves three things: 1) the size of the tire you have chosen (choose the tire first), 2) the style wheel you like the best and 3) the quality of wheel you like, whether steel, chrome plated, polished aluminum, powder coated, painted and so forth. This is more of a matter of expense than taste.

The most popular wheels on slammers are the "sawblade" wheels. These are also called "directional," "cookie cutter," or just "cool" wheels, depending on where you live. A number of manufacturers have them available and they vary in quality and price, just like other high-performance parts.

Wheel fit and clearance

Generally, the wheels you buy will have to be at least seven inches wide to accommodate the wide, low-profile tires. This means a wheel size of 15×7 or 14×7. The 15×7 will fit the 195/50-15 tires, and the 14×7 the 195/60-14 tires.

After selecting a proper wheel size the next important factors are bolt pattern, offset and backspacing. The bolt pattern is simply the correct number and pattern of holes in the wheel to fit the lug nuts on the wheel. For most applications, particularly newer trucks, the bolt pattern is a simple matter of knowing the make and model year of your sport truck. Then choose the wheel made for your truck's model and year. Most manufacturers keep the same bolt pattern year after year, and they are not significantly changed unless a major downsizing of the vehicles occurs.

The offset and backspacing are more important, and with these specifications wheels can differ greatly. Often, wheel salesmen will not know if a certain wheel will fit your truck, particularly if you go to a size that's unusual for your truck. The offset refers to the location of the wheel center section (the center part with the bolt pattern) in relation to the center of the wheel.

With some high-performance and front-wheel-drive cars, the offset is critical because it determines where the tire's tread pattern will be located relative to the vehicle's weight. Also, offset can affect whether or not the wheel fits over the disc brake caliper, drum and so on. Positive offset is a term used to describe a wheel that has the center section outside of the center of the rim, away from the axle. Negative offset is when the center section is located in toward the vehicle. What these terms mean in real terms, when you try to mount the wheel on your axle, is that a positive offset wheel will reach farther into your vehicle's wheelwell, while the negative will push the tire away from the vehicle.

A wheel with too much negative offset will push your tires toward the fender lips. A wheel with too much positive offset for your truck may scrape on the disc brake caliper.

Backspacing is another term that describes the amount of space between the center section and back rim flange. It also has an effect on whether or not a given wheel will fit on your axle. If the backspacing is too shallow, the rim will scrape on a disc brake caliper. If it's too deep, it will force the tire too far in toward the axle. This may cause different clearance problems.

The only way to see if the wheel and tire combination you have chosen will fit your truck is to mount the tire on the wheel and then mount the wheel on the vehicle. If there is a clearance problem with a disc brake caliper, you will notice this immediately. The center section of the wheel will not seat flush against the hub.

If you cannot center the wheel on the hub, try to see where the obstruction is occurring. If it's only a small part of the disc brake caliper that is scraping, you may be able to file or grind off a bit of the iron casting so the wheel will fit. Do this slowly, removing a little bit of casting at a time. Sometimes the casting foundry that makes the brake caliper leaves a rough edge on the casting, and doesn't smooth it all off. It's okay to remove an eighth of an inch or more if the obstruction is caused by a nonfunctional part of the disc brake caliper. Usually a little grinding will correct these problems.

If you do a fair amount of grinding and the wheel still scrapes, you can buy a spacer that will slip over the studs and in effect, move the wheel away from the disc brake caliper. Spacers are available in one-eighth inch thickness or more. Don't use more than one spacer. If there's still a problem, change the wheel.

In reality, if you lower your truck three or three and one-half inches, there's bound to be some tire clearance annoyance when you hit a large pothole. For most truck owners, this is something they can easily live with. This is a side effect of changing the stock tires dramatically. Your truck is not built like a sports car that's made to take wide low-profile tires.

What you want to do is get a tire and wheel combination that looks nice, rides and handles as comfortably as possible for your suspension and doesn't cause any major problems. The only time you may have a real problem is when you buy an off-brand of wheels mail order and can't return them.

If you're unsure of the fit on your tires and wheels, go to a tire and wheel shop that's done lowered trucks in the past. They will know from experience which tire and wheel combinations will work from their stock.

Small diameter tires

Caution: Custom tires may affect the anti-lock braking system (ABS) found on many new trucks.

For the 1989 model year, the following trucks have rear anti-lock braking systems:

• GMC: S-15 Jimmy, 2WD only, or 4X4 in 2WD; S-15 pickup

This Pro Stock Chevy S–10 has 15×3 weld wheels with 135/45–15 Michelin tires, requiring special suspension modifications.

• Ford: F-Series trucks except F superduty; Bronco and Bronco II in 2WD only; Ranger regular cab
• Dodge: Dakota S have ABS system
• Chevy: S-10 Blazer in 2WD; S-10 pickup in 2WD; full-size pickups in 2WD only

The problem with extremely small diameter tires and the ABS systems is that tires that vary from the stock size tire by more than fifteen percent can make the ABS system inoperative. The brakes will still work, but the ABS warning light on the dashboard will be lit.

There are two basic types of ABS systems. One senses the relative speed of all four tires and monitors the rotational speed of each in relation to the others. This is the type of system found on most cars with ABS. With this system, tire size does not affect the ABS because all four tires are being compared to each other. And as long as all four tires are the same size, the system is not given false or misleading readings.

The second type of system is found on sport trucks, as previously listed. As of now this list includes most new American light trucks but no Japanese trucks. The second system monitors only the speed of the rear axle and evaluates that against the vehicle's programmed rear axle data.

The vehicle's programming is made to accommodate the great majority of tire sizes sport truck owners may put on their vehicles. The truck manufacturers assume that tire sizes that differ no more than fifteen percent from the stock equipment will be used. However, if you change the tire size more than fifteen percent, the warning light on the dashboard for the ABS will appear, and unless you're aware that the tire size change has caused it, you will think the braking system doesn't operate

The rear tires on the Pro Street S–10 are mounted on a narrowed Ford rear axle. They're 15×15 weld wheels with 33×19.5 Mickey Thompson tires.

properly. Most of the time a truck with smaller tires will not cause a problem with the ABS. Larger diameter tires are much more likely to make the ABS inoperative.

Polished weld wheels are also used on this 1967 GMC Pro Street, using 50 series Mickey Thompson Sportsman tires up front . . .

If this is a problem with your truck, there are four things you can do: 1) ignore the light on the dashboard, 2) put the smaller tires on your truck only when you take it to custom car shows, 3) go to a larger size tire and 4) have the ABS recalibrated to account for the smaller tire size (with some trucks you can do this). This way, the ABS will remain perfectly functional and you can still keep the smaller tires.

If you choose to ignore the warning light telling you that the ABS is inoperative, the ABS will not work in conditions where you may skid or lock up your rear tires. Remember, sport trucks have anti-lock braking systems on the rear axle only. As of now there is no truck that has ABS for the front brakes. Your brakes will still work fine, they just won't have the ABS feature. You may have driven for many years without ABS and never had a problem.

But there is one problem. Your insurance company may not like the fact that you've made the ABS inoperative by going to small tires, and in certain accidents (for example, if you slide into another car or truck in the rain) they may blame the inoperative ABS for the accident, or see it as a contributing cause. Then they will not pay for the damages to your truck or the other person involved. The money will have to come out of your pocket.

It will take insurance companies some time before they catch up to this aspect of small tires on lowered trucks, but remember, with four-wheel-drive trucks the insurance rates greatly increased after there was a lot of publicity about the high center of gravity of jacked-up trucks.

In order to cover yourself, have the ABS recalibrated by a certified mechanic, and have proof of this in writing. The written document should specify the exact tire size and type and the vehicle the tires were mounted on. This way, if you're involved in an accident with another person, their insurance company cannot jump on the fact that you had small tires as an excuse to blame you for the accident. It happens.

Another option is to replace the computer chip that runs the ABS. This is possible with Chevy trucks. The dealer can sell you a replacement chip.

As lowered sport trucks become more widespread around the country, insurance companies and tire manufacturers will be spelling out the hazards of them, just as they eventually did with

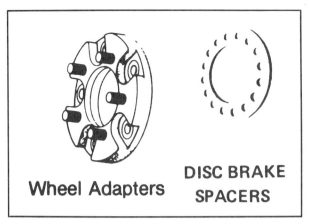

Wheel Adapters

DISC BRAKE SPACERS

Wheel adapters may be used in limited situations, such as on a show truck. Spacers are used when wheels rub against disc brake calipers to provide extra clearance.

sky-high four wheelers. Only this time it will be done more quickly since the insurance companies have the four-wheel-drive vehicles as a learning experience.

. . . and 60 series tires, Mickey Thompson Sportsmans, in the rear.

The compromise sport truck

The current trend for the sport truck is, by definition, without compromise. Build your own "slammer" and you know from the outset (and don't care)

A 1986½ Nissan Hardbody King Cab V6 SE two-wheel drive with Center Line Pro-truck wheel and Yokohama AVS Intermediate tire. Hidden are the Tokico gas shocks. Without lowering the suspension the wider wheel still has enough suspension travel without hitting the fender; ultimate cornering power may not be maximized but it's close behind on the street, and it's comfortable and tractible. These are 15 inch wheels with seven-inch rims, with 3½ inches of back spacing (the stock wheel is 14×6 with five inches of backspacing). The tires fitted are 225/60-15.

Center Line's Pro-truck wheel is a two-piece, riveted together. The rims are forged pieces and the rivets stainless steel. The "gap" is filled with silicone so that tubeless tires can be used. Note the rubber valves; used because they don't leak. Often steel or alloy bodied ones do. One locking wheel lug is used; an inexpensive deterrent to potential thieves. These wheels are supplied, normally, with center caps. Read the instructions that accompany the wheels regarding the specification of lug nut necessary; it may differ from OEM fitment.

that you can't carry anything in the pickup bed, and that the lack of suspension travel from your lowered chassis won't let you travel long distances. Couple this with 50 series tires and comfort is gone and fatigue has set in after 100 miles (maybe). Add stunning graphics to the bodywork and you are paranoid about letting anyone near it in case they even finger it. Your hobby vehicle is, without compromise, your hobby first, your get-to-work vehicle second.

There is help at hand for those enthusiasts who cannot indulge their hobby this way—they have to compromise. They, too, want a slammer but they have to haul weight in the bed, they have to drive 500 or more miles in a day, sometimes in the rain, and they have to face paint damage as an everyday consequence of just driving.

Take a look at this compromise sport truck. There are no apologies, it doesn't have any special paint, certainly no graphics. It does have stone chips on the hood and cab! Also, gearing and thus speedometers need to be close to stock.

Hidden from view are Tokico gas shocks all round, and it isn't lowered. The fresh shocks provide a compliant ride and allow for maximum cornering power without any harshness, whether the truck is loaded or not. Inside, add a Momo leather-covered

Many enthusiasts aren't aware that there may be local vehicle laws concerning wheels extending from fenders. Such an extension as this probably isn't anything to worry about in any state. Worth noting, however, is that water spray will be excessive in rain without fender flares.

Hardly subtle customizing, but still more functional than stylish. Cibie Oscar Plus driving lamps with PIAA foglamps under the bumper, in which are hidden Fiamm air horns, complete the visible and audible warning of this truck. Plexiglas side window shrouds allow for comfortable driving with the win- *dows wound down and a roof mounted antennae clears the hood. Add Recaro seats and a Momo leather steering wheel to the above, and the suspension and handling package, and the result is one person's best compromise sport truck.*

steering wheel, "standard" Recaro seats, a Sony stereo replacing the excellent Nissan OEM AM/FM radio and comfort is taken care of. The roof mounted antenna (as stock with various Audis and Volkswagens) works well, was inexpensive to fit and clears the front fender of the stock version. Inside the front bumper is a pair of Fiamm air horns! On the front are a pair of PIAA foglamps and another pair of Cibie Oscar Plus driving lamps—independently wired through relays and stock Nissan dash switches.

The stock Hardbody two-wheel-drive Nissan uses 14 in. wheels. This 1986½ Kingcab V-6 SE, with five-speed, was equipped with those seemingly solid "cross" alloys, 14×6 and all-weather 215/75-14 tires. A change to 225/70 Riken "street performance" radials provided much improvement but the truck felt heavy and seemed to bounce a little when unloaded. This required a switch to 15 in. wheels, and 7 in. rim width (much as the 4X4 Nissan V-6) and a calculated stick to a 225 width but 60 profile tire.

What was required was maximum street handling performance, perhaps with the occasional autocross, with some longevity and an ability to still haul maximum bed load. Using the workshop manual for the vehicle and the specifications published by both Center Line wheels and Yokohama tires, the follow-

ing fitment was suggested: Center Line Pro/Truck wheels of 15×7 with 3.5 in. backspacing.

This wheel uses two forged aluminum sections permanently mated with stainless steel rivets available in satin finish only. The Nissan, like Mazda, Isuzu and some Toyotas, uses a six-lug, 5.5 in. bolt circle. These 6061-T6 aluminum wheels have load limits, as do all wheels, which for the Pro/Truck series means 5,500 pounds gross vehicle weight. In reality this exceeds the specifications issued by Nissan for their truck at 4,290 pounds to include a 1,400 pound payload, including passengers.

The chosen tire was Yokohama's AVS Intermediate in 225/60-15. This is a high-performance street radial in a compound that is between their dry and wet models, as a suitable everyday compromise. Maximum load for this tire, as molded into the side casing, is 1,485 pounds. Multiply that by four and the tire capacity exceeds the maximum 5,500 pound gross vehicle weight. Perfect.

This truck now handles as well on the street as a stock chassis pickup can, unloaded or loaded, is comfortable, quiet, safe and good looking. Gearing is a fraction lower and the speedometer about seven percent faster. The perfect compromise—without the graphics, though.

4

Engine performance and economy

This Chevy 350 engine, bored to 355, uses a Dyer supercharger, two Holley polished aluminum 600 cfm carburetors, Holley fuel system and lines, is balanced and blueprinted and has Sanderson headers. Owned by Len Manning of Spring–Align in Palatine, Illinois.

The great beauty of the sport truck is that it defies any definition. While you can say very easily that a sport truck is *not* a car, it's almost impossible to pin down exactly what it *is.* Here's some examples of sport trucks: a 1940 Pro Street Chevy pickup, a 1988 Mitsubishi and a lowered 1972 Chevy Blazer. Each truck is very different from the others, yet they all fall into the category of sport truck.

This chapter has three sections to help cover most of the changes you might want to make to your engine. The first section will deal with the basic horsepower improvements. This includes replacement carburetors and manifolds for domestic and import vehicles. These replacement items are street-oriented, bolt-on types for ease of installation and virtually "instant" improvement in performance. If you have a Toyota or Mitsubishi, look for the special listings for high-performance parts covering these vehicles.

The second section covers several items that improve fuel economy. These include the Economaster carburetor and Z-series manifolds made by Holley, which can be installed in the same engine for both good economy and performance improvements.

The third section will deal with high-performance engine modifications—those that increase total horsepower and torque output. This section is intended for those who are building a Pro Street truck for either custom shows or competition. Featured in this section is the installation of the most effective high-performance modification—the blower or supercharger.

Making an engine run better

Whenever a mechanical engineer applies for a job with General Motors, he or she is asked a simple question: What is the limiting factor in the output of an internal combustion engine? For fifty years, the engineering department has heard every conceivable reply, from long theoretical discussions of the engineering concepts behind internal combustion engines, to simple answers such as displacement.

The engineer who applied for a job at GM and told me this story said that in fifty years no one has ever given the correct answer. (He didn't either.) The answer GM is looking for is a simple one: air. The amount of air entering any engine has more to do with its output in horsepower and torque than anything else. This is because you can dump all the fuel you want into a combustion chamber, but it must be mixed with the proper amount of air for combustion to take place.

All engine modifications have this goal in mind: to get more air (and secondarily, fuel) into the engine so its output is increased. The only way to dramatically increase an engine's output is to get more air into the cylinders.

Many people think that in a four-cycle engine, when the piston moves down and the intake valve opens, the air/fuel mixture is sucked down into the combustion chamber by the vacuum caused by the piston. This is not true. The piston doesn't *draw* in

Want to put a GM 350 Tuned Port Injected engine into a Chevy S-10 minipickup? This chapter will outline how it's done.

This supercharged small-block Chevy engine was put into a 1967 GMC dropped pickup, combining a late 1960s pickup body with pure Chevy power.

This is another Chevy 350 engine, bored to 355, with
Gurdy fuel injection and an Edelbrock tunnel ram.

Another small-block Chevy engine, this one installed in
a 1969 Chevy pickup that was also dropped by its owner.
All five of these engines were put in dropped pickups!

any air, the air is pushed down from the atmosphere above. And it does a poor job at that. Poorly designed, badly tuned engines can have the cylinders fill as little as fifty percent with ambient air pressure only.

To improve an engine's performance you have to either allow a clearer, cleaner "vent" for the air/fuel mixture to flow into the cylinders, or you have to force extra air in with some kind of air pump.

Aftermarket manifolds accomplish this: they allow more air to enter the combustion chambers by providing a better designed, clearer passage from the carburetor to the cylinders. You can make further improvements by installing a camshaft and lifters that do a better job of opening the valves long enough for them to fill to more efficient levels.

High-performance engine modifications do the same thing and more: they *pump* more air into the cylinders. Turbochargers do this, and blowers (superchargers) pump air even more effectively into the combustion chambers for a higher compression ratio.

Since the ideal air/fuel ratio is 14.7:1, the amount of *air* put into a combustion chamber is a greater limiting factor than the amount of fuel. You have to put more air into an engine before you can add more fuel.

This chapter will discuss some ways, both simple and complex, to regulate the amount of air and fuel in the combustion chamber. Since the air/fuel mixture is what produces horsepower, the result can be either greater performance or greater economy, depending on your goal.

Overcoming your engine's limitations

A quick look at the horsepower curve of an engine (a diagram of how the engine works as rpm increases) shows that the horsepower output of any engine increases with increased rpm. The problem is that stock engines cannot handle higher rpm without the addition of high-performance internal engine parts such as the distributor, main bearings, rocker arms, lifters, valve springs and so on. Stock engines simply don't have the high-performance parts necessary to achieve higher rpm without blowing apart.

Horsepower and torque?

Most people, if asked to define "horsepower," would say it's how powerful an engine is. Actually, the term has a precise definition: One horsepower is the amount of power it takes to lift 550 pounds one foot in one second. A ten horsepower engine could lift 550 pounds ten feet in one second, or 5,550 pounds one foot in one second. The distance and feet involved can be converted mathematically.

But you have to be careful when figuring out horsepower through your transmission. Remember, no matter how large a gear ratio your transmission and rear end have, you can never increase the total amount of horsepower produced by your engine with gearing alone. All the gearing can do is produce a larger effective amount of horsepower by trading off time or distance. You can have a greater amount of horsepower only if it's used in a shorter period of time or used over a much shorter distance.

Torque is also a measure of an engine's power output. Whereas horsepower is generally a matter of acceleration, torque is a matter of the actual rotating power of your engine. It's just like turning a nut on an engine: the more torque required to tighten the nut, the harder you have to pull on the torque wrench. This rotating or twisting force is torque. Engine torque is measured in pounds/foot, the same as the torque needed to tighten bolts. Edelbrock publishes the results of its Performer manifolds in torque because it feels that the torque measure is a more accurate and useful measure of

A blown Chevy engine equipped by Blower Drive Service. Blower kits are available from street to marine applications, with carburetors, fuel systems, distributors, bearings and other items you will need for a complete blower engine.

an engine's performance. Many manufacturers give both horsepower and torque ratings for their aftermarket products.

A high-horsepower engine can have low torque, and a high-torque engine can have only average horsepower. But usually, torque and horsepower increase together. You'll see later in this chapter how to make some modifications, such as the installation of Edelbrock's Performer manifolds, to improve overall engine performance.

Aftermarket distributor

There are several good reasons to replace your distributor. Some people don't like the uncertainty of an electronic ignition system, and prefer a mechanical set of points. Another reason is that the parts described here are of better quality than stock distributors. A third reason is that these distributors will give you a smoother running engine that is more reliable, particularly at high rpm.

All distributors are driven by a gear on the camshaft. This gear setup gives a mechanical linkage between the rotation of the engine, the opening and closing of valves, the compression and exhaust strokes and the firing of the spark plugs in the cylinders.

There are two basic ways to install a distributor, depending on whether the crankshaft is moved after the distributor is removed, or the crankshaft has not turned at all since the distributor was removed. If a replacement distributor is installed immediately after the stock distributor is removed, use this procedure: Park the vehicle on a firm, level surface, and block the tires to keep the vehicle from rolling. Remove the primary wire, vacuum advance and spark plug wires (noting the firing order) from the distributor cap. Remove the distributor cap and note the position of the rotor by marking the engine block under the exact position of the rotor. This is important since it will ensure that the new distributor is set up on the same cylinder. Loosen the hold-down bolt of the distributor and carefully remove the distributor. It will rotate slightly since the gears of the distributor and camshaft are cut at an angle.

With the new distributor in hand, rotate the drive gear assembly (rotor) until it lines up as closely as possible to the position of the previous distributor. While holding the rotor in place, carefully lower the distributor until it engages the camshaft teeth. As you lower the distributor, it will rotate a bit. Watch the rotation and be sure that the rotor ends up as close as possible to the position of the stock rotor. For example, if the rotor moves counterclockwise too much, pull the distributor out again, and replace it while moving the rotor about one-eighth turn *clockwise*. Lower the distributor into place and see how the rotor lines up. If you need to move clockwise another tooth, do so. It may not be possible to line it up exactly, but

you can use a timing light to straighten it out later. Another trick that may help is to install the distributor so the points are just about to open, but are not yet open.

Replace the distributor cap, spark plug wires, primary wire and other parts where they were originally. Use a timing light and crank the engine to check the engine's timing. If the engine is too far advanced, remove the distributor and turn it counterclockwise (or back, against the direction of rotation) one tooth. If too retarded, remove the distributor and rotate it clockwise one tooth (or one tooth in the direction of rotation) and replace. This procedure, along with turning the distributor cap as you do in normal engine timing, will give you the proper setup for your new distributor.

A different procedure is needed to install a distributor when the crankshaft has turned. If you rebuild your engine, or crank the engine a bit after the distributor is removed, you will no longer have the rotor at the same cylinder as before. What you need to do is establish a number one cylinder position again on the distributor.

In order to find the correct position for the firing of the number one cylinder, you have to first find the compression stroke of the first cylinder. Remove the spark plug from the number one cylinder. Have someone crank the engine while you place your finger over the spark plug hole of the first cylinder.

As the engine is cranked, the piston will come up toward the spark plug twice, once to compress the air/fuel mixture, the second time to force the exhaust gas out the exhaust manifold. What you want to find is the compression stroke, when the piston will force a jet of air out the spark plug hole. It may take a few revolutions of the crankshaft to find it exactly, but once you feel the air rush out of the spark plug hole, the next time around you can watch the piston come up with a flashlight. What you're looking for is the topmost position of the piston in the compression stroke of the first cylinder. When you've found this, note the position of the rotor on the distributor (the new distributor should be installed while you're doing this) and this is the position of your number one cylinder spark plug wire.

Replace the spark plug wires on the distributor cap clockwise, following the firing order of the cylinders. The firing order will be stamped on the intake manifold, or can be found in an automotive manual. You can also record the firing order while you're removing the original spark plugs. Once you've replaced all the wires in the proper firing order, check the engine timing using a timing light as above. Again, if the engine is too far advanced, remove the distributor and turn the distributor *counterclockwise* (counter to the direction of rotation) back one tooth and replace, and check the timing. This will give you the proper engine timing.

Distributor troubleshooting

If your engine will not run after installing the new distributor, you can check the following items to find the problem:

1. Be sure engine is timed properly. Refer to engine timing specifications and adjust distributor until timing is correct, using procedures outlined earlier.

2. If your distributor does not give a spark, first see if there is a spark from the coil. Remove coil to distributor wire and place it on top of the distributor cap. Crank engine. If coil doesn't spark, check that engine ground is good.

3. If engine is grounded properly and coil works but there is still no spark to the plugs, check the dwell to see if points are opening and closing. You can do this by cranking engine with dwell meter connected to obtain a dwell reading.

4. If there is a spark from coil and a good dwell reading (see tune-up specifications for your engine to check on dwell reading), the problem may be with a condenser. It may have been shorted while you were installing the new distributor and distributor wires.

These four items are the cause of virtually all ignition problems: the primary wire, engine ground, points and condenser.

Accel performance distributors

Accel distributors include 1) thirty-two-ounce spring tension competition points for up to 6500 rpm, 2) easily adjustable vacuum advance for exact timing calibration, 3) double thickness point plate to eliminate flex and stabilize dwell and 4) a close tolerance point cam for timing accuracy. For best results gap points at 0.018 to 0.020 in. Set dwell for each point at twenty-six degrees—total thirty-six degrees at 1000 (distributor) rpm. Optimum street advance is twelve degrees at 1400 (distributor) rpm.

Mechanical advance dual point distributors

These distributors are available for the following engines:
• Chevrolet (includes Chevy and GMC trucks) 1955-85: 265, 283, 302, 305, 327, 350, 396, 400, 402, 427, 454 V-8 engines. Also available in chromed models.
• Ford (includes Ford trucks) 1963-85: 221, 260, 289, 302 V-8 engines. Also available in chromed models.
• Chrysler 1965-85: 273, 318, 340, 360 V-8 engines.

Vacuum advance dual point distributors
• Chevrolet (includes Chevy and GMC trucks) 1955-85: 265, 283, 302, 305, 307, 327, 350, 396, 400, 402, 427, 454 V-8 engines.
• Ford (includes Ford trucks) 1963-85: 221, 260, 289, 302 V-8 engines.

• Chrysler (includes Plymouth Trailduster, Dodge trucks) 1965-85: 273, 318, 340, 360 V-8 engines.

Accel Unispark electronic distributors

These are available for most engines and provide a more maintenance-free system. They feature 1) encapsulated magnetic signal pickups, 2) close tolerance sintered iron reluctors, 3) adjustable vacuum advance controls and 4) bowl-mounted, solid state GM-style electronic control modules that require no additional external control box.

Mechanical advance electronic distributors
• Chevrolet (includes Chevy and GMC trucks) 1955-85: 265, 283, 302, 305, 307, 327, 350, 396, 400, 402, 427, 454 V-8 engines.
• Ford (includes Ford trucks) 1963-85: 221, 260, 289, 302 V-8 engines. 1969-81: 351C, 351M, 400, 429, 460 V-8 engines.
• Chrysler (includes Plymouth, Dodge trucks) 1965-85: 273, 318, 340, 360 V-8 engines.

Accel vacuum advance electronic distributors

These are a good choice for street machines. They have an infinite range of advance adjustment and zero maintenance for excellent razor-sharp accuracy in a Unispark.
• Chevrolet (includes Chevy and GMC trucks) 1955-85: 265, 283, 302, 305, 307, 327, 350, 396, 400, 402, 427, 454 V-8 engines.
• Ford (includes Ford trucks) 1963-85: 221, 260, 289, 302 V-8 engines. 1969-81: 351C, 351M, 400, 429, 460 V-8 engines.
• Chrysler (includes Dodge trucks) 1965-85: 273, 318, 340, 360 V-8 engines.

The Accel distributor listing is intended to give you an idea of the replacement distributors available for V-8 engines. This is not a complete listing of Accel products, by any means, but most V-8 American engines that have been used on pickups are listed here. For other distributors such as Mallory, please refer to their product catalogs. There may be a particular distributor you're looking for but is available from a different manufacturer than Accel.

Accel also makes an excellent line of spark plug wires and other ignition components.

Ballast resistor

Your new ignition system may require a new ballast. This is a resistor that keeps the voltage going to the coil down to six or eight volts. There are different types of ballast resistors, depending upon their resistance as measured in ohms. Use the type that's recommended for your new coil. Usually, aftermarket distributors and coils, such as those made by Mallory and Accel, have specific recommendations for a ballast resistor.

To install a ballast resistor, you will need some ordinary sixteen-gauge wire, wire strippers and wire connectors. First, run a wire from the I terminal of the starter to the positive side of the coil. Then, take the existing positive (+) coil wire and run it to the ballast resistor. Use another piece of

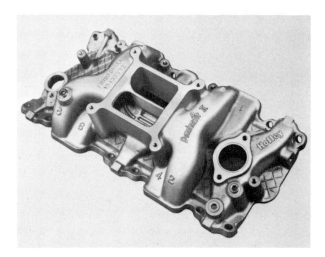

An excellent choice for improved street/strip performance in small-block Chevy engines is the Dominator II manifold. It is a high-rise dual plane design for all 1965–72 small-block Chevy engines without EGR. Holley

wire to go from the resistor to the positive side of the coil.

This new setup will run the coil on twelve volts when you are cranking engine, giving the spark plugs more voltage to start a cold engine, and will switch to about six volts once the engine is running. You should not run an ordinary engine on twelve for two reasons. First, you only need a full twelve volts when starting the engine; more voltage isn't necessary unless you're building a racing engine. Second, the full twelve volts will burn up the points and condenser unnecessarily.

Intake manifold

One of the easiest ways to improve the performance and economy of your stock engine is to replace the intake manifold and carburetor. Many different manufacturers offer products in this field, those by Edelbrock, Weiand and Holley being good choices for their quality, ease of installation and reliable results.

Edelbrock aluminum manifolds in the Performer series are easy to install, well designed and manufactured and yield reliable results. What these manifolds do is offer a bolt-on replacement for your stock manifold that's designed to give a cleaner, more homogeneous, more evenly distributed fuel mixture to all the engine's cylinders. Many of the problems stock engines have, such as poor acceleration, a "lag" when pressing the gas pedal, hesitation while passing, a sudden surge of power at part-throttle and a tendency to die out when cold are results of a power distribution of the air/fuel mixture to the cylinders.

The Edelbrock Performer manifolds give maximum results when used with the Performer-Plus camshafts and lifters. Edelbrock Performer manifolds and Performer-Plus cams and lifters are available for most AMC, Chevrolet, Ford, Chrysler and GMC engines. And while you're replacing the cam, it's a good time to replace the timing chain and gears with ones that are more reliable and accurate.

Another superb manifold for better street power is the 8000 series by Weiand. Available for most small- and big-block Chevy, Ford and Chrysler engines, this manifold should be used with Weiand camshafts and lifters for best results. Weiand

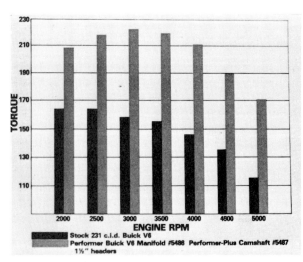

This graph shows the tremendous increase in torque you'll get with an Edelbrock Performer manifold, camshaft and headers. The results are for the Buick 231–252 ci V-6 engines, 1979 and later. These engines are ideal for engine swaps since they're compact, easy to install and have a lot of zip for their size.

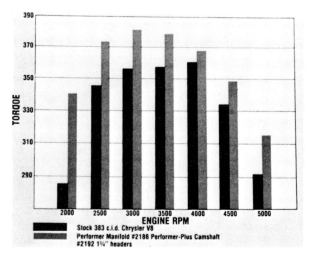

Here's another torque graph showing the dramatic increase in torque you'll get with an Edelbrock Performer manifold, Performer–Plus camshaft and headers with a Chrysler Mopar 383–400 ci V–8 engine. The increase at 2000 rpm, a good off-road operating range, is phenomenal.

manifolds tested by *Hot Rod* magazine outperformed all others in their category.

EGR replacement manifolds

Many of the aftermarket manifold models mentioned here can fit EGR or non-EGR engines. EGR refers to the Exhaust Gas Recirculation system installed to reduce the pollutants emitted by engines. All engines built in 1973 and later have an EGR system. You can buy a non-EGR manifold to replace your EGR manifold, but this will nullify the emissions control system that works off the EGR manifold.

If you're building a custom pickup for trailering to shows, this is okay. But you can find yourself with some legal problems later on if your state has an emissions testing program and your vehicle fails the test. In some areas you can be fined for removing the emissions control system. Either way, you alone are responsible for what you do to your vehicle and you should be aware that the best thing to do is replace an EGR manifold with another EGR manifold.

This is another reason why many truck builders and customizers build one vehicle for the street and another for shows. The show truck doesn't have to conform to state and federal emissions laws if it's displayed at exhibition halls and other shows that are located on private property, and if it's never driven on public roads.

Installation

Generally, installation of a replacement aftermarket manifold, such as those made by Holley, Weiand and Edelbrock, are bolt-on jobs. The only custom changes that have to be done are usually in the areas of rerouting a few vacuum hoses or reconnecting the fuel line. These are relatively easy and straightforward jobs.

Begin the installation by first removing the air filter, fuel line, throttle linkage, choke linkage and vacuum hoses from the carburetor. Carefully remove the carburetor from the manifold and be ready to install a new carburetor gasket if the old carburetor is going to be reused. If the carburetor has a lot of mileage on it, say 75,000 miles or more, have it tested at a carburetor specialty shop, if possible, or replace it with a rebuilt carb. Another option is to rebuild it yourself.

You can get some idea of how well the carburetor is working by testing it on the engine before you start the manifold swap. With the engine warm and at idle, turn the air/fuel mixture screws each one-quarter turn at a time, until the engine runs smoothly. Then turn them further until it runs too lean, and back them out several complete turns until the carburetor runs too rich. If a one-quarter turn on the air/fuel screws makes a difference in the engine's performance, then the carburetor is still in fairly good shape. If the carb is running so sloppily that a full turn or more doesn't make any difference, replace it or rebuild it.

You may also want to replace the carburetor with a four barrel at the time of the intake manifold swap. If so, be sure to get a carburetor recommended by the manifold manufacturer. You may end up with a carburetor that will deliver so much gas it'll hinder rather than help performance.

Loosen the radiator hose connections, PCV hose and so forth from the manifold, then loosen the manifold bolts and remove the old intake manifold from the engine. This should be done carefully, especially with large V-8 engines, since the cast iron manifold can have considerable weight and can scratch cylinder head surfaces if mishandled.

With the manifold removed, carefully remove the gasket pieces from the cylinder heads, using a putty knife and some gasket remover such as that made by Fel-Pro. Cleaning the gasket surfaces is a major part of the installation, so be sure to take your time and do a through job. A sloppy intake manifold gasket can cause vacuum leaks that will adversely affect performance.

With the old manifold off the engine you have a good opportunity to remove the water pipe, thermostat (if applicable), PCV fitting and other parts and replace on the new manifold. Most of these accessory items go into their stock positions on aftermarket manifolds. There may be some exceptions, but these will usually be pointed out in the installation instructions that come with the manifold. Be careful to use silicone or pipe thread sealant where needed.

Generally, intake manifold gaskets have two types of gaskets: two small, almost straight pieces that fit over each end, and the large pieces that match with the cylinder head. These pieces are pretty much self-sealing, but the four corners, where the intake manifold meets the engine block, must be filled in with a one-quarter- to one-half-inch long section of RTV silicone if it's to seal properly.

Careful installation of the new manifold on these gaskets is not easy, since the manifold may slip and ruin the seal on the silicone. Gently lower the new intake manifold onto the gaskets, and be sure that the end pieces haven't slipped out. Silicone rubber acts as a lubricant, and can cause the gaskets to slip out. Once the gaskets are aligned perfectly with the manifold on top, you can tighten the manifold-to-head bolts, starting at the centers of each side and working out toward the ends. Do not over-torque, especially with aluminum manifolds.

Installing a new carburetor may be somewhat difficult. First, connect up the choke linkage, throttle linkage, vacuum hoses and fuel line. Be careful not to overtighten brass fittings. A flare nut wrench is the best way to do a good job without tearing up soft brass threads. Once the carburetor is mounted on the engine, start the engine and get it running to where it's warm and idling. Usually the factory will have made all the necessary adjustments for the initial startup.

With a quality, factory new carburetor, such as Holley, you only have to adjust the air/fuel mixture and idle screws. You can use an off-the-engine tachometer such as those that come with tune-up kits to match the engine rpm to specs. To adjust the air/fuel screw, you may either do it by feel or use a vacuum gauge.

With the engine at a reasonable idle speed, such as 800 rpm (see your vehicle's engine specs), turn the air/fuel screws inward (clockwise) one-quarter turn at a time. With a two barrel, turn in one screw a quarter-turn, then the other and so on. Do this until the engine starts to lean out, that is, the engine rpm drops because it's not getting enough fuel.

To find where the engine's running too rich (too much fuel), turn the screws out (counterclockwise) until the engine starts to sputter. The ideal air/fuel mixture will be a little richer than the point where the engine starts to run too lean. At this point the engine will idle as smoothly as possible when it's warm. If the engine idles too high at the correct air/fuel mixture point, adjust the idle screw to where engine rpm is at factory specifications.

A more accurate way to determine the correct air/fuel mixture is to use a vacuum gauge. Connect it to a non-ported source of vacuum (not a vacuum source that has already run through the carburetor) and adjust the air/fuel mixture screws until

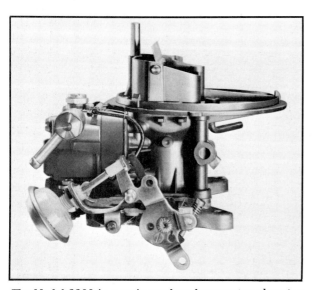

The Model 2300 is a universal replacement carburetor that fits a wide variety of engines. Available in two airflow sizes, 350 and 500 cfm, they feature a race–type fuel bowl with adjustable needle and seat, universal throttle linkage and manual choke with fast idle cam. Holley

the gauge reads about seventeen inches of vacuum. Anywhere from sixteen to twenty-one inches is okay, but seventeen is ideal.

If you have trouble making these adjustments, don't try to get the engine running properly by changing the jet size, choke or float setting. These are usually set at the factory, where they should be. If there's a problem it'll usually be a vacuum leak where a gasket isn't sealed properly.

Aftermarket manifolds improve performance because they route the air/fuel mixture of the carburetor more directly to the combustion chambers than does the stock manifold. Remember, the only thing pushing the air/fuel mixture into a cylinder is atmospheric pressure. Cylinders in poorly designed engines can be as little as half full when combustion takes place. The aftermarket manifold cures this factory defect and can improve mileage, horsepower, idling and acceleration.

Carburetor

The best way to choose a carburetor for a rebuilt engine is to estimate the capacity you need based on the engine's size and volumetric efficiency. Volumetric efficiency can be estimated using the table included here. Volumetric efficiency is an indicator of how an engine can "breathe." As noted earlier, the amount of air entering an engine is the limiting factor in its output.

Volumetric efficiency or VE is measured as a ratio of the actual mass (weight) of air taken into the engine compared to the mass which the engine displacement would theoretically take in if there were no losses. The ratio is expressed as a percentage. It is low at idle and low speeds and varies with engine speed. So it should be computed at the expected operating rpm of the engine.

To use the chart here, first estimate the volumetric efficiency of your engine. These three categories can help you make an estimate: 1) An ordinary low-performance street engine has a VE of eighty percent at maximum torque, 2) a high-performance engine has a VE of about eighty-five percent at maximum torque and 3) an all-out racing engine has a volumetric efficiency of about ninety-five percent at maximum torque.

The graph is based on 100 percent volumetric efficiency, so to find the VE of your particular engine you have to multiply by 0.80 or 0.85, depending upon whether or not you have a high-performance engine. For example, say your engine is a 300 cubic inch V-8 with a maximum rpm limit of 8000. It's been estimated that this engine has a volumetric efficiency of eighty-five percent. According to the chart, the engine's airflow requirement is 700 cfm (cubic feet per minute) at 100 percent volumetric efficiency. At eighty-five percent, the cfm requirement is 595. This engine would need a 600 cfm carburetor. Any one of several Holley universal carburetors could do the job. The majority of engines would fall into the eighty percent category and could get by with a 550 cfm carburetor.

Holley Model 5200

Few aftermarket items are available to improve the performance of small imported vehicle engines. However, Holley has a Model 5200 carburetor that will fit several import engines. These carburetors feature precise metering, an optimum booster configuration and balanced staging between the primary and secondary throttle bores.

They fit the 2.0 liter engine of the 1970s Datsuns (now Nissan), the 1976-78 1.8 liter Chevy Luv truck, the 1979-81 Chevy Luv 1.8 liter engine and the 1978-80 Ford Courier 2.3 liter engines.

The 5200 model carburetor, when installed in these engines, will improve the performance of the engine and were used as original equipment on Ford Pinto 2.0 liter engines.

Electronic fuel injection system

New engines have electronic fuel injection or EFI systems that not only use fuel injection to get a more precise metering of fuel into the combustion chambers, but have "computers" that monitor the amount of air entering the engine, the temperature of the air and engine, and fuel pressure to the injectors to achieve maximum efficiency and horsepower at any point in the rpm range.

The main reason auto makers went to electronic fuel injection systems is that the emissions systems of the 1970s and early 1980s choked off too much of an engine's power. The old mechanical carburetors were just too inefficient to both produce horsepower and have clean emissions. There were some quick fixes done to improve emissions, such as the 1970s air pump, but these were just afterthoughts. The air pump actually pumped air into the exhaust system, thereby decreasing the amount of pollutants in parts per million of exhaust gases.

A better way had to be found. EPA standards were getting tighter and tighter, and engines were losing power as the emissions systems gradually strangled the horsepower out of them. The only real solution was to use fuel injection, which Toyota did with its minipickups. Fuel injection made it

These two Holley carburetors are the new polished aluminum high–performance and street carbs from Holley. They are 4010 series, 600 cfm, square flange, with either vacuum or mechanical secondaries. The air horn acts as a cover, so all adjustments can be made without having to remove a float bowl. Jets and other parts can be changed from the top.

possible to produce an engine with more zip and less emissions problems.

Now American-made pickups also have fuel injection. But it's possible, if you have a carbureted engine, to go back and add an electronic fuel injection system. This is done by installing one of the aftermarket fuel injection kits now made by several manufacturers. And new ones are being introduced all the time.

When you go to shop for an electronic fuel injection system to replace your carburetor, keep in mind that there are two basic types of systems. One is the throttle body injection (TBI) type, and the other is the multi-point fuel injection design (MFI), or the tuned port injection (TPI) system. This is the system used by Chevrolet and Ford.

The difference between the two is how the fuel is delivered. With the throttle body design, the fuel injectors inject fuel into the main throttle body. The amount of fuel is what counts. This is determined by air sensors, which measure the amount of air coming into the engine (remember that air is the limiting factor).

The system computer or electronic control module (ECM) then processes the information from the sensors and sends an electrical impulse to the injectors, which opens them up to deliver the precise measure of fuel at the throttle body.

The multi-point fuel injection or MFI design does the same thing in a different way. It uses a larger number of fuel injectors, usually one for each cylinder, to inject fuel slightly upstream of the cylinder head intake port. This way, a precise amount is delivered to each cylinder.

The only other difference between electronic fuel injection systems is how the airflow is measured by the computer. Here again, there are two primary types of systems. One type, the mass airflow (MAF) system, physically measures the amount of air entering the engine. This can be seen in the photos for the Chevy 350 TPI engine swap in this chapter. The sensor, an expensive little item, is located in the air duct.

The other type calculates or estimates the airflow, rather than directly measuring it. This is the speed density system. The basic difference between these two systems, for practical purposes, is that the speed density system is somewhat easier to install, and is cheaper, since it doesn't include a mass airflow sensor in the kit. The MAF sensor is expensive to replace. You'll find this out if you own a Corvette TPI engine and the sensor is defective or becomes inoperative.

However, the MAF sensor, since it measures the flow of air directly, is more accurate. So for more money an MAF-based system gives slightly better performance. For most purposes, speed density systems work excellently, and are easier to install and dial-in.

Aftermarket systems

There are several makers of aftermarket systems, using the different types of technology. With some of these systems you can actually hook the system's control module to a laptop or IBM-compatible computer and get a visual graph of the fuel curve on the screen! Quite a change from the days when you revved the engine to see how it ran when the secondaries kicked in. You can then use the computer to "program" the fuel injection system to work at an optimum fuel curve for the rpm you desire.

One of the most versatile of the TBI (throttle body injection) systems is the Holley Pro-Jection fuel injection system, which can be installed on virtually any engine with a four-barrel manifold. A universal mounting flange permits installation to both square and spread bore flanges. Currently, the engines that can use the Pro-Jection system include the GM 305 and 350 engines. It replaces the Rochester Quadra-jet carburetor on these engines. Also, Ford 302 and 351, and Chrysler 318 and 360 engines can use the Pro-Jection EFI.

Because the carburetor delivers up to 670 cfm of airflow at one and one-half inches of manifold vacuum, it is a high-performance carburetor and is not legal in California. However, this is true of other high-performance aftermarket carburetors.

The Pro-Jection system uses two Holley high-flow injectors. Through use of a pressure regulator, these low-pressure injectors have an adjustable fuel pressure range of 11 to 17 psi. Both injectors are calibrated at 15 psi at the factory. Each can flow up to eighty pounds of fuel an hour, producing up to 320 hp.

The Holley Pro-Jection system is tall, so hood clearance should be checked before installation. Also, it's a good idea to install a performance intake manifold at the same time. If there's plenty of hood clearance, it's definitely the way to go. Any one of a number of aftermarket performance manifolds can be used, since the Pro-Jection fuel injection system will fit most four-barrel flanges.

The kit comes with fuel fittings, throttle position sensor, engine temperature sensor, flange adapter, fuel filter, fast-idle solenoid, throttle linkage and complete wiring harness. Provisions for PCV, timed distributor spark, manifold vacuum and EGR are provided.

One of the biggest changes that will have to be made to your vehicle is installation of a fuel line return. This can be done at any radiator repair shop, however. They can install the fuel line and return for you. All you'll have to do is hook the fuel lines up to the carburetor. After that, you can get the carburetor running with factory adjustments.

If you want to change some adjustments, the following section tells you how to dial-in the Holley Pro-Jection system. Other systems will differ.

Holley Pro-Jection

The great advantage of an electronic fuel injection system is that changes can be made without making jet, power valve, pump cam and secondary spring changes. With the old mechanical carburetors these required partial disassembly of the carburetor in order to change the hardware.

With an electronic fuel injection system, these changes are made through the system computer, which is mounted under the vehicle dashboard. A small screwdriver and turn of a screw is all that's needed to make necessary adjustments. You then dial-in the desired fuel curve characteristics using the external adjustments on the computer. Fuel delivery is then matched accurately to the engine's requirements based on input from the throttle position sensor, temperature sensor and tachometer signal, while engine rpm is picked up from the ignition coil. All the sensors of the system are connected to the computer with a prefabricated wiring harness that is insulated from moisture and dust.

When the Pro-Jection system is properly installed the engine will be able to run on the factory adjustments. However, you may wish to change some of these. To adjust the computer, first bring the engine up to operating temperature, from 180 to 200 degrees F. You can use a screwdriver to change any or all of five adjustments including Mid Range, Idle, Power, Accelerator Pump and Choke. Three quarters of a turn of any of these functions is all that's needed to obtain the adjustment you want.

These adjustments must be made in sequence. Mid Range is the first adjustment that should be made. This calibrates the fuel delivery for part throttle conditions. Begin by placing the vehicle in Neutral and bringing the engine speed up to about 3000 rpm, using a tachometer. Then, while watching the tachometer, turn the knob clockwise (increasing the fuel richness) until the rpm increases and levels off. Then, turn the knob counterclockwise until the engine speed just starts to decrease. This will be the optimum setting.

With your foot off the gas, repeat the above steps with the Idle adjustment. This is similar to setting the idle mixture adjustment screws on a carburetor. To change the Power setting, a 0-60 test could be run. Depending on your engine's size, alteration of this adjustment will vary. If responsiveness is low, increase the richness of the fuel by approximately a one-eighth turn clockwise. Conversely, if the engine feels sluggish, lean it out by turning slightly counterclockwise. Either way, the best technique is to dial rich first to locate the best "wide open throttle" setting and adjust accordingly.

If a bog is evident, this is eliminated by changing the Accelerator Pump adjustment. Like in the Power setting, turn the knob rich (clockwise) or lean (counterclockwise) to meet your engine's

acceptable level of performance. Generally, intakes with open plenums need a larger shot of fuel; those with divided plenums require less. To check the Choke setting, cold start your vehicle a few times to determine if it is running rich or lean. Should you need to make a change in the amount of cold fuel enrichment, follow the same procedure: try richer (clockwise) or leaner (counterclockwise) and see how the engine runs when cold again. This is much like setting the electric choke on a carburetor.

Test run the vehicle after adjustments at part throttle and wide-open throttle to make sure everything is operating correctly. A carbon monoxide meter is the best way to check on emissions. The computer can then be adjusted, if necessary, to minimize emissions. Of course, a computer is the best way to maximize fuel efficiency and power.

The following chart lists the applications for the Holley Pro-Jection injection system.

Make	Engine cid	Pro-Jection part no.	Holley manifold
AMC			
w/Ford transmission	304-401	502-2	300-31
w/Chrysler transmission	304-401	502-1*	300-31
Buick	300-400	502-1	——
Chevrolet	302-400	502-1	300-38
Chevrolet truck	305-400	502-1	300-38
Chrysler	318-400	502-1*	300-29, 300-10
Dodge	318-400	502-1*	300-29, 300-10
Dodge truck	318-400	502-1*	300-29, 300-10
Ford	302-400	502-2	300-29, 300-20
Ford truck	302-400	502-2	300-39, 300-20
GMC truck	302-400	502-2	300-29, 300-20
Jeep			
w/Ford transmission	304-401	502-2	300-31
w/Chrysler transmission	304-401	502-1	300-31

* Requires throttle lever extension part no. 20-7.

These manifolds are not essential to installation. However, they will improve performance if used. Be sure to check hood clearance before adding a high-rise manifold.

General Systems Research

General Systems Research, a company located in Dearborn, Michigan, has a console with eight knobs that control eight functions of the computer. These include idle mixture, idle speed, accelerator pump shot, accelerator pump duration, wide-open throttle mixture, "high load," part-throttle enrichment and choke enrichment. General Systems Research plans to include this console with a wiring harness and electronic control module.

Air Sensors

Another system is being planned by Air Sensors of Seattle, Washington. This will use a mass airflow (MAF) sensor. Air Sensors already has accessories that include larger mass airflow sensors, camshafts and some high-performance parts of the Chevrolet TPI manifold. They plan to make a com-

The Holley Pro–Jection fuel injection system is a throttle body type that can replace virtually any four barrel on a small–block engine. All adjustments when dialing in are made on the dashboard–mounted computer.

plete tuned port injection manifold similar to Chevy's with much larger runners and plenum that will increase airflow.

Before purchasing any electronic fuel injection system, carefully examine the system to check for compatibility with your manifold. Some injectors can be adapted to existing manifolds; with others you will have to purchase a new manifold that will match the EFI system to your engine. Keep in mind that all EFI systems have cfm requirements and limitations, just as carburetors do, and they should be chosen carefully.

Digital Fuel Injection

A company called Digital Fuel Injection, or DFI, makes a fuel injection system that offers another interesting possibility. With their system, you swap a Corvette, Camaro or Firebird TPI system onto your small-block Chevy engine, and then use their control module and other components to achieve high-performance results. The TPI systems must come from the 1985 to present Corvette, 1986 to present Camaro or 1986 to present Firebird.

With the DFI system you can use the TPI from one of these engines either obtained from a wrecking yard, purchased from GM (a costly alternative) or purchased from Leigenfelter Racing of Decatur, IN. Leigenfelter Racing is the best choice for high-performance engines, since they modify the GM TPI to flow better and move more air. The other systems are good, but DFI cautions that whatever year TPI system you use, it must be complete. Don't swap parts between a 1985 and a 1988 Corvette, for example. There are slight differences in the parts which will definitely cause regrets.

This chapter also features a Firebird TPI engine swapped into a Chevy S-10. Why can't you then just take the TPI system out with its wiring harness and computer and swap it onto a small-block Chevy engine? The reason is that the engine you will get with the TPI and small-block engine will not run well, if at all. This is because the TPI's computer (which is stock on the Corvette, Firebird or Camaro) was specifically programmed to run on that engine. It was designed for that engine's camshaft, manifold size and so forth. There are many small ways that engines differ from each other. You need the DFI electronic control unit (ECU) to fine-tune your small-block Chevy to work with the TPI taken from the GM engine.

DFI has their own recommended camshaft, which you can purchase from them if required. They also sell many other parts, and give a complete list of GM part numbers if there are parts missing from the TPI you intend to use. The best thing to do, if you plan to install a TPI system on your engine, is find the most complete TPI you can, then buy the missing parts from GM for the model and year of the TPI. This will ensure that the TPI's parts are compatible.

The Digital Fuel Injection system will then supply the extra parts, including sensors, fuel injectors and computer, that you need to adapt the TPI to your small-block Chevy engine. Additionally, you can buy software from DFI that will enable you to fine-tune your fuel curve. You can hook up a laptop or personal computer to your engine and actually see the fuel curve on the screen, and see the changes that occur as you dial it in. For high-performance engines, this is a real plus.

Keep in mind that the DFI system is not limited to Chevrolet small-block calibration. You can also do this with Ford and other injection systems. You can remove the fuel injection system from a Ford engine, and place it on another. However, the DFI parts and computer are needed to set it up properly. Contact DFI for details.

Computer chips for better performance

With the introduction of computer-controlled engines it's become possible to control the aspiration of an engine electronically, whereas the changes mentioned up to now only change the mechanical function of the valves with camshafts that change the duration the valves are left open, and so on.

Several companies make replacement chips that "reprogram" your engine to perform better. Most of these replacement chips are for cars, not pickup trucks. However, several companies do make chips for engines found on pickup trucks. Turbo City makes one for the 2.8 liter V-6 engine, and the price is about $125. The chip is designed to improve low-end throttle response.

Holley economy carburetors

There aren't as many options available for general improvements in economy, since most people who modify engines want better performance, not economy, and it takes gasoline to produce horsepower. Inevitably, any high-performance engine has low gas mileage!

But there are two bolt-on type items available from Holley that contribute to better performance and economy. I did a magazine article featuring the installation of a Holley Economaster carburetor and Z-manifold in a Plymouth Trailduster with a V-8 engine, and the engine actually got better gas mileage while having better performance on the street. It had better acceleration, was peppier and started easier. It all goes to show that routing the air/fuel mixture to the combustion chambers more efficiently is the only way to improve performance.

Replacement economy carburetors from Holley are available for these engines. Not all of these engines are standard equipment on pickups, but they may be used in engine swaps so they're included here:

- Chevrolet
  - 1977-78   305 engine, 2 bbl
  - 1975-76   350 engine, 2 bbl
  - 1973-74   400, 350 engine, 2 bbl
  - 1970-71   400, 350 engine, 2 bbl
  - 1966-69   327, 307, 283 engine, 2 bbl
- Chevrolet/GMC truck
  - 1977-78   305 engine, 2 bbl
  - 1975-76   350 engine, 2 bbl
- Dodge/Plymouth
  - 1977   318 engine, 2 bbl
  - 1975-77   400, 360 engine, 2 bbl
  - 1975-76   318 engine, 2 bbl
  - 1974   400, 360 engine, 2 bbl
               318 engine, 2 bbl
  - 1973   400, 360 engine, 2 bbl
               318 engine, 2 bbl
  - 1970-72   318 engine, 2 bbl
  - 1966-69   318 engine, 2 bbl
- Dodge truck
  - 1975-77   225 engine, 1 bbl
  - 1974-78   318 engine, 2 bbl
  - 1973   318-1 engine, 2 bbl
  - 1970-72   318 engine, 2 bbl
  - 1966-69   318 engine, 2 bbl
- Ford truck
  - 1979   302 engine, 2 bbl
  - 1977-79   351-M, 2 bbl; ½, ¾ ton
  - 1975-78   300 engine, 1 bbl; all models with Carter No. 7051 carb
  - 1970-72   390, 360, 302 engine, 2 bbl

Obviously, these engines are all two barrels and won't deliver the performance of a four barrel, but these replacement carburetors are for economy, not performance.

Z-series manifolds by Holley

The Z-series are an extension of the Holley street manifolds, but have many differences. There's a divider that splits the plenum in half. And at the rear of the manifold a unique "resonating channel" connects the back two runners. This design helps them work in harmony with the divider to increase operating efficiency. Powerful pulsations are created in the resonating channel which increases the charge density of the air/fuel mixture. This increased efficiency results from better distribution between cylinders and more uniform cylinder charging, which is what efficiency is all about. Fuel economy may be improved, especially if you use the economy carburetors listed above. A list of Z-series applications follows.

- American Motors
1970-79: 304, 343, 360, 390, 401 V-8 engines. Designed for use on 1970-79 AMC V-8 engines with or without EGR. Features square flange to accept the standard Holley bolt pattern carburetors.
- Chevrolet trucks
1971-81: 267, 305, 307, 350, 400 V-8 engines with or without EGR. Will fit vehicles originally equipped with four-barrel carburetor with an extra installation kit.

Additional information is available from Holley distributors. When choosing any manifold, be sure it fits the year and carburetor you already have, and be prepared to change choke or throttle linkage as required. Many times you have to try to put the manifold on before you know what you'll need.

Toyota modifications

There's a company called L.C. Engineering that has done some unique work with 20 and 22R Toyota engines. L.C. has complete Stage II and Stage III engines available. These complete street engines include L.C. Engineering Pro cylinder head with:
- valve seats machined for oversize valves
- oversize stainless steel exhaust and intake valves
- 8 large-diameter dual valve springs with chrome-moly dual valve spring retainers
- head and manifold ported and polished
- combustion chambers reshaped and polished
- 3-angle valve job
- gold erodite studs for intake and exhaust mounting
- all surfaces milled
- Teflon valve seats
- L.C. Pro new billet camshaft
- 2 pre-jetted 44 mm sidedraft Mikuni carburetors
- ported aluminum manifold
- complete throttle linkage
- 2 K&N chrome reusable air filters
- chrome pro flange header
- L.C.'s own 22R block, bored and honed
- choice of either L.C. Pro big bore 10.5:1 pistons or factory cast pistons
- L.C. Engineering custom ground and micro polished crankshaft
- L.C. Engineering connecting rods with silicon bronze bushings
- L.C. Pro clutch and pressure plate

- C-P main bearing, rod bearings and thrust bearings
- new oil pump
- double roller timing chain kit, timing cover
- oil pan
- complete gasket set
- precision computer engine balancing
- blueprinting and assembly

You can also add Weber carburetors, lightened flywheel, titanium valve spring retainers and other high-performance extras. Virtually all of these L.C. Engineering high-performance Toyota items can be purchased separately for a do-it-yourself high-performance street engine.

Items that can be bought individually include:
- L.C. top end kit, featuring the L.C. cylinder head and valve components
- bottom end kits, including the block, pistons, crankshaft, clutch, pressure plate, pilot bearing, rod bearings, main bearings, rocker arm assembly, gaskets and timing chain parts. With the bottom and top end kits you have a complete engine. However, either one will improve horsepower
- Pro Street cylinder heads, for 20/22R engines, from Stage II to Stage V, ported or unported. Also available for nitrous oxide
- chrome header for 20/22R engines, and exhaust manifold stud kit
- L.C. Pro billet camshafts, ground on new billets, from Stage II EFI cam, to Stage V 0.550 lift and 312 degree duration
- L.C. nitrous oxide kits
- dual Mikuni carburetors
- dual Weber carburetors
- Weber manifold kits
- Holley fuel pump

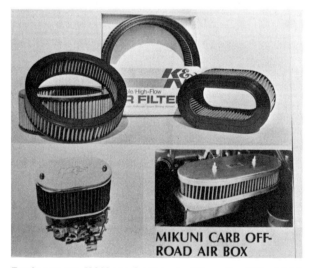

Replacement K&N washable air filters for Mitsubishi and most other engines. Also shown is a carburetor box for off-road running of Mitsubishis. John Baker Performance

- L.C. Engineering fuel pump kit
- K&N air filters for all 40-44-45 Weber and Mikuni carburetors, and oil breather for 20/22R engines

Other parts for your Toyota engine available from L.C. Engineering include:
- carburetor synchronizer for dual carburetors
- intake manifold stud kit
- Weber carburetor red caps for 40-45 mm Weber
- Terrycable throttle cable end for dual carburetors
- Oberg oil filter kits
- L.C. Pro 20/22R blocks
- L.C. Pro crankshafts, recommended for Stage II engines, a must for Stage IV and V engines when using nitrous oxide
- stock replacement crankshafts for 20/22R engines
- crankshaft pilot bearing
- L.C. Pro rods for 20/22R engines
- L.C. factory replacement rods
- L.C. stock piston set
- L.C. Pro piston rings
- stainless steel valves, titanium valves
- L.C. silicon bronze valve guides
- Teflon valve stem seals
- Pro dual valve springs
- brass freeze plugs, heavy-duty timing chain kit, high-volume oil pump, pro clutch kit, lightweight flywheel, main and rod bearings

Many of these parts are specially engineered by L.C. Engineering and are available nowhere else. For anyone interested in getting more horsepower out of the Toyota 20/22R engines, L.C. is a must as a source of parts and high-performance engine rebuilding kits. Catalog is $3.

Mitsubishi high-performance engine parts

John Baker Performance specializes in Mitsubishi parts and offers a wide variety of high-performance engine components specifically for Mitsubishis. These include:
- Perma Spark ignition coil and cables
- NGK spark plugs
- K&N air filters for Weber carburetors
- Weber carburetor kits, and jet kits
- Mikuni carburetors and Mikuni jet kits. Carbs are dual sidedraft, in 40 mm for 2.0 liter engines and 44 mm for the 2.6 liter engines. Jet kits for both 40 mm and 44 mm carburetors
- performance camshaft for 2.6 liter engine, with 0.327 in. lift and 262 degree duration
- camshaft blanks for you to do your own camshaft grinding
- performance headers for all 2.6 liter and most 2.0 liter engines
- 2.6 liter Baja engine kits, including 38 mm or 32/36 mm Weber downdraft carburetor, John Baker performance header and accessories. Increases horsepower by 25 percent.

Please consult latest John Baker Performance catalog for specific applications and details.

Headers

As you saw from the diagram on volumetric efficiency, the better an engine breathes the more horsepower it produces. But breathing doesn't only refer to what goes down the carburetor into the combustion chamber; it's also affected by what comes out the combustion chamber.

Your engine is a little like a water pipe: there's only a flow through it if it is also *emptied* at the same rate. What this means is that the combustion chambers are only going to be filled to their most efficient levels if the exhaust gases leave the exhaust valves efficiently. This is particularly important for street-machine modifications which don't employ blowers to force gases down into the combustion chambers. But any engine has to have a free-flowing exhaust system to work properly, whether it is turbocharged, blown or stock. Turbochargers are also sensitive to inefficient exhaust systems.

This is because an inefficient exhaust system causes *backpressure*, a subtle but very real problem, like vacuum leaks, that can affect an engine's performance. The reason is very simple: when an engine is running at only 2000 rpm, each cylinder is firing at $33\frac{1}{3}$ times per second. Each intake and exhaust valve must do its job $33\frac{1}{3}$ times per second.

For the exhaust gases to be removed from the combustion chamber completely, there must be a clear, unobstructed exit for the exhaust gases. Hairpin turns in an exhaust pipe and standard cast iron manifolds hamper the easy flow of exhaust gases and cause unwanted backpressure. The backpressure is so real it can be measured on machines and it has a direct effect on compression.

The best way to allow your engine to breathe is with straight, short pipes like those found on high-performance competition engines. But these are illegal and too noisy for street use, so you have to go the next best route, and that is using headers and a flow-through type of muffler, one that gives you the least backpressure. You're never going to eliminate all backpressure with an exhaust pipe that's over ten feet long and has a muffler, but it's the best you can do and remain street legal.

Installation

Installation of a header to replace your stock exhaust manifold is a simple bolt-on job. The more complicated and difficult part is taking off the alternator, air conditioning and whatever else may be in the way of the header.

Start by having a look at the stock exhaust manifold to see if it and the new header have the

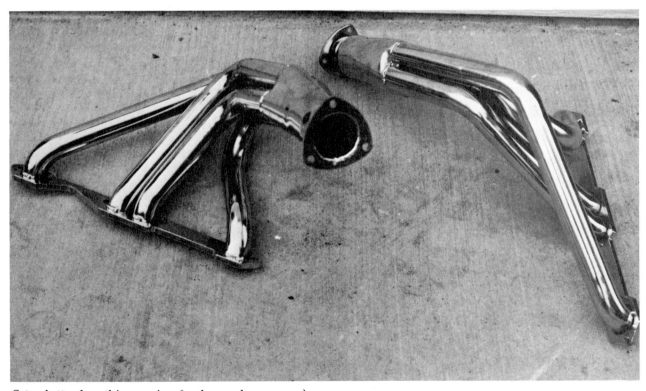

Get a better breathing engine (and more horsepower) through the use of headers such as these chromed headers from Advance Adapters. Fit most engines.

same type of exhaust pipe flange. Usually there's a three-bolt flange that connects the header to your exhaust pipe. If these don't match you'll have to take the vehicle to a custom muffler shop and have a new exhaust pipe put on or a modification made. You may be able to clamp a new piece of exhaust pipe with a flange onto the old exhaust pipe, then bolt these together.

After seeing how the header is going to mesh with the exhaust pipe, you can loosen up the old exhaust manifold (work on one side at a time). Your biggest problem is going to be rust. The flange bolts, if several years old, may be rusted solid. You'll have to grind or cut them off. Also, the stock manifold bolts may also be rusted, but these usually yield to some forceful wrench work.

As the manifold gets loose, you can wriggle it around and see if it'll come off the engine without too much hassle. You may have to loosen or remove an alternator or anything else in the way. Pull it up and out of the way; usually pulling it out at an angle does the trick. Replace the new one in much the same way, using a new manifold gasket.

At this time you may want to go to a dual exhaust system, which is worthwhile whenever headers are installed. This can again be easily done by a muffler shop or by you. If you do it yourself you can buy a dual exhaust kit for most recent domestic vehicles that's a bolt-on job. Or you can have it done at a shop. They have the advantage of using a torch to cut off old rusted pieces and possibly have a tube bender they can use to make custom parts.

How to rebuild your stock engine

Whether your vehicle's engine has 120,000 miles on it and is worn out, or you want to rebuild the engine to add high-performance parts, most of the work can be done by you, saving you thousands of dollars in labor costs that you otherwise pay to a mechanic. Reading this section cannot make you a mechanic, only good working habits and experience can do that. But if you can remove a transmission, take off a cylinder head, and have done lots of work on engines such as replacing a carburetor, alternator, radiator and other accessory components, you can go a step further and remove the engine.

The greatest amount of work in rebuilding an engine is in removing the engine from the vehicle. To remove an engine, use a suitable place such as a garage with an overhead beam that will take the weight of the engine—up to 500 lb. Park the vehicle with enough space in the rear so you can roll it back when the engine is removed, and block the wheels.

Start disassembling the engine by draining the radiator and removing fuel lines, vacuum lines and so on from the carburetor. Next, work on the wiring that goes to the carburetor, alternator and starter. To keep these from getting damaged while re-

moving the engine, use masking tape to tape them to the inner fenders or frame. You may want to tape labels or numbers on the wires so you can identify them later.

Start removing engine accessories such as the alternator, water pump, fuel pump, power steering pump, starter and other components. Unbolt the exhaust pipe from the exhaust manifolds, then remove the manifolds from the engine. Be careful to keep parts and their bolts together. This is easily done by taping the bolts together or keeping the parts in cardboard boxes along with their mounting hardware.

While you have the alternator and starter off the engine, it's a good opportunity to take these parts in to an automotive electrical repair shop and have them tested. The bushings in the alternator may be worn out, and the starter will probably need new brushes. A power steering pump can be replaced inexpensively and so can the fuel pump.

You can, of course, remove the engine with all of these pieces attached to it, but it's lighter and easier to remove if the exhaust manifolds and other attached parts are first removed. The final step is to remove the carburetor, then the transmission to engine bolts. Finally, when the engine has been freed from the transmission, you can start loosening up the engine mounting bolts. Then install a come-along or chain lift to the beam above the engine, and attach the cable or chain to the engine. This is easier if you use an engine lifting tool that allows you to tilt the engine.

With the engine firmly attached to the cable, put some tension on the cable, enough to support the engine. You don't want to put too much strain on the transmission and possibly damage the input shaft. The engine has to be first pulled forward so as to clear the transmission shaft, then it can be tilted upward and removed from the vehicle. An easier way is to remove the transmission first. If this is done, be sure to support the rear of the engine block with a jack stand. The transmission may hold up the rear of the engine.

With the engine lifted high enough to clear the front of the vehicle, roll the vehicle backwards, from under the engine, then lower the engine so you can remove the flywheel.

At this point you can make a decision on how you want the engine rebuilt. You can have a machine shop rebuild the engine, from oil pan to valve covers, or you can replace the internal parts yourself. If you decide to have an engine rebuilder do the job, you can either take the engine in yourself, or if possible, have them pick it up and rebuild it entirely, replacing all internal parts. A high-performance shop can do the work, or you can keep it stock and have a regular engine rebuilder do the job. If you're going to rebuild the engine yourself, the next few pages tell you how to remove and replace internal engine parts.

If you are going to rebuild the engine you should mount it on an engine stand. Carefully bolt the engine stand to the rear of the engine so you can remove the rest of the engine components such as the intake manifold, cylinder heads and oil pan.

This is best done by starting with the top of the engine. Remove the intake manifold and carburetor if this hasn't been done, then remove the valve covers. Loosen the rocker arm mounting bolts and remove the rocker arms. Take out the pushrods and lifters. They may be frozen in by oil sludge and require some effort. Loosen the cylinder head bolts, working from the outside first, toward the inside, alternating from side to side as you go. For example, first loosen the bottom left head bolt, then the top right, then the top left, then bottom right, until you reach the middle. This is to prevent head warpage by relieving stress on the sides of the head first.

With both cylinder heads removed, you can remove the crankshaft hub, harmonic balancer and timing gear cover. The timing gears need to be pulled off with a suitable gear puller. Then pry off the crankshaft seal, and remove the camshaft hold-down bolts or screws. Different engines have different ways of holding in the camshaft.

Once this has been done, you can flip the engine over, remove the oil pan, the oil pump and main bearings, and lift out the crankshaft. When removing the bearing caps, note their orientation on the crankshaft; they must be installed in the same order, facing the same direction. The easiest way is to place the main bearing caps on a piece of cardboard, exactly the way they came out the engine.

The pushrods and lifters can be reused, but with a complete engine overhaul these should be replaced with new ones. Buy new pushrods, not reconditioned ones, since reconditioned ones tend to bend easier than new ones. Depending on your ambitions, the pushrods and lifters may be replaced with high-performance ones.

With the crankshaft removed and bearings taken out, you should remove the camshaft, which pulls out the front, and the block is ready to be cleaned, pistons removed and cylinders rebored. A machine shop can remove the pistons, since this requires a ridge reamer that removes the built-up deposits on the walls of the cylinder. You can also have them remove the camshaft bearings.

At this point the engine is almost completely disassembled, and you can take the head(s) and

When the camshaft bearings are installed, use a flashlight to check if the oil hole is centered. If it is, you can see the light shining through the hole.

When rebuilding your own engine you may want the machine shop to install the camshaft bearings. A special camshaft bearing installer is used to insert the new camshaft bearings in the block. Bearings must be installed carefully so the oil feed holes are lined up. Usually when a block is rebuilt the machine shop rebores the cylinders, replaces the freeze plugs and installs new cam bearings. The other parts you can replace yourself.

Here's what you'll need to install your crankshaft: main bearings, bearing caps and connecting rod bearings to install the new pistons.

block to a machine shop. What they'll do is rebuild the cylinder heads, installing new high-performance valve springs if you wish, but they'll at least check out the valves, replace any that need replacing and grind the valves and seats for a tight seal. If you want to run the engine at higher rpm than

Close-up photo of new valves in cylinder head. Head must be carefully cleaned, seats reground and polished and new valves and springs installed. This work can be done by a machine shop and you can replace the cylinder head on the engine yourself.

stock, you'll need high-performance valves, springs, pushrods and lifters. The valves and springs should be installed by a machine shop. A high-performance shop should be used for high-performance work, since the work is more detailed and precise than simply reinstalling stock parts.

As far as the block and crankshaft, the block is completely hot-tanked to clean it, the water and oil passages cleared and checked and the cylinders rebored 0.030 in. or more, whatever is needed, to smooth them out and seal the new pistons and rings. The old crankshaft can be reground, magnafluxed to check for cracks and reinstalled with new, slightly oversized main bearings. If the crankshaft is in good condition, it may only need to be polished. But if it has a good number of miles on it, it will usually need some regrinding.

The connecting rods also need to be checked for out-of-roundness and straightness. This must be done by a machine shop that has the machine tools necessary to accurately calibrate and regrind the rod bearing journals.

When you replace the internal parts yourself, you can purchase a complete rebuilding kit, which will supply you with everything including camshaft, crankshaft, camshaft bearings, main bearings, piston rings, gaskets and so on. Before you buy the new main bearings and rings, however, you'll

On the left side of this photo are Manley Pro-Flo racing valves and springs, while the right side has the stock valves. There are many brands of high-performance valves and valve springs that can be used for performance engine rebuilding.

This high-performance aluminum piston is fly cut and gas ported for greater efficiency and durability at high engine rpm.

need to talk to the machine shop and find out how much they had to rebore the cylinders. It may or may not be cheaper to regrind the crankshaft rather than buy it in a kit. Usually, kits are the cheapest way to go, and the parts dealer will ask you for the old crankshaft on an exchange basis.

In addition to the internal engine parts, you'll probably have to buy a new water pump, fuel pump, carburetor and miscellaneous small items like a thermostat, radiator hoses and throttle linkage. At this point it's the best time to dress up the engine with chrome-plated parts like water pumps, alternators, water pipes, Russell Performance or Earl's stainless steel braided lines. There is almost no limit to the amount of money and time you can spend customizing an engine. Photos of some of the chromed parts you can buy are included here.

Gaskets

Believe it or not, most of the annoying problems you'll have with a rebuilt engine won't be that it doesn't run (providing it's put together properly!) but that it may develop little leaks of water, oil and vacuum that create performance and economy problems. It's also pretty aggravating to have spent a lot of time and money rebuilding an engine only to find that it's leaking oil all over the garage floor.

The next few sections will cover the basic areas of gasket installation needed for a clean, well-sealed engine.

Cylinder head gasket

The most critical gasket in your engine is the cylinder head gasket. This gasket must withstand enormous pressures. Jerry Rosenquist, Product Development Engineer at Fel-Pro, a top maker of gaskets, points out that with a small- or large-block Chevy—with the head bolts properly torqued—the total pressure on each head gasket is from 160,000 to 170,000 pounds, eighty to eighty-five tons! And engines are being designed to fit into ever-smaller vehicles, so engine designers make the cylinders closer together all the time. Often one-quarter inch of metal is all that separates one cylinder from another. With maximum cylinder pressures of 800-

This extra-capacity oil pan has a deep sump for extra quarts of oil, necessary to keep high-performance engines cool and well lubricated.

Here's some of the chrome accessories you can use to dress up your engine. You can get chromed alternators, alternator brackets, timing covers, carburetors, water pipes, hubs, intake manifolds and air cleaners, just about anything that can be taken off the engine and chrome plated.

1,000 psi, a head gasket has to seal the cylinder head with less than one-quarter inch of material!

It's not surprising that subject to these pressures, head gaskets can easily fail. You can be sure that if you've made the slightest mistake while installing a head gasket, it'll cause problems later on. For example, if the cylinder head is scratched while it's being replaced on the engine, the scratch will create a microscopic "tunnel" allowing combustion gases at high pressure to escape out the side. These gases will quickly corrode the metal around the cylinder, widen the tunnel and soon cause the cylinder to lose pressure.

To avoid this problem, treat the head very carefully. Carefully scrape and clean off the old head gasket, and handle the head very carefully while you're working on the engine. Place it on cardboard and newspaper so it doesn't touch the concrete floor or a metal shop bench. The worst thing you can do is treat the head like another piece of steel, and put it anywhere on the garage floor, on top of tools and so forth. It must be placed on a flat, horizontal surface.

While having the head machined, cylinder head and engine block surfaces must be flat to within 0.0025 in. in any direction. Try to remove as little material as possible from cylinder head and block to extend their usefulness.

Carefully place the new gasket on the cylinder block. Then lower the head carefully to the engine block, being careful not to scratch it or scrape it against anything on the block. Torquing down the head is the most critical part of installation. It requires more care and precision than anything else on the engine. Use hardened washers under the bolt heads.

Some mechanics act as if they have a feel for the torque required and start torquing the bolts by hand. Nothing could have more potential for disaster. With the head already under eighty tons of pressure, incorrect torquing can easily warp it and damage it permanently. Do the job properly, use a new torque wrench that is accurate and carefully torque the bolts down, following the torquing pattern recommended by the gasket maker or engine manufacturer. Fel-Pro has the torquing sequence enclosed with their head gaskets.

Generally, to avoid warpage you must torque down the middle bolts first, moving from left to right, up and down, out toward the ends of the head. You should coat the bolts with oil, since the torque values (such as 110 lb-ft) are for lubricated threads, not dry ones. Dry ones don't torque properly and can bind.

With performance aluminum heads, the head gasket (such as the Fel-Pro Performance head gaskets) may contain steel wire combustion seals which can indent the softer aluminum head. With most small-block Chevrolet V-8 engines, use Fel-Pro head gasket part no. 1010. It has copper wire that is softer and won't indent the head. Other Fel-Pro Performance head gaskets may contain steel wire which will indent the head but won't hurt the seal. In this case, retorque the head after warm-up. One alternative is to have the cylinders O-ringed and use a regular Permatorque blue gasket. This will work in all but high-performance competition engines.

If you have trouble finding a replacement head gasket (never reuse one that has been torqued down before) you can get a Fel-Pro at an auto parts dealer. Fel-Pro has gaskets for every engine ever made. The Fel-Pro Permatorque Blue high-performance gasket is an exceptionally well made gasket that will last a very long time when properly installed.

Intake manifold gasket

The intake manifold gasket seals the intake manifold to the cylinder head. Its critical function is to seal engine vacuum. Tiny vacuum leaks can cause mysterious engine problems and lack of performance. The intake manifold, usually made of cast iron, can be a heavy, hard-to-handle item on an engine, especially on big-block V-8s. It's a good idea to remove the carburetor from the intake

A high output, 114 gallon per hour mechanical fuel pump from Holley for mud bogging and sand drags. Holley

81

manifold whenever handling it, both when taking it off the engine and when replacing it. Aftermarket high-performance manifolds are usually made of aluminum and are much lighter and easier to handle.

Start the installation by first making sure that the manifold and cylinder head surfaces are clean and dry. Wipe them with a solvent and a soft, clean rag. Placing the intake manifold on properly involves two critical steps: 1) use of a high-quality gasket, and 2) preparation of the gasket with proper sealants. High-quality gaskets are embossed. That is, there are ridges around the ports of the gasket to create a better seal once the manifold is torqued down.

With V-8 engines and aftermarket aluminum intake manifolds, the embossed gasket may not form a tight seal if the manifold has slight imperfections. The embossed, stiff type of gasket may prove to be too stiff for these applications. To correct this problem and still get a tight seal, use Fel-Pro Printoseal gaskets. They're made to be forgiving of slight manifold imperfections.

Fel-Pro has a line of Performance intake manifolds that are an excellent choice for high-performance applications. When installing intake manifold gaskets, elimination of the exhaust crossover increases the top-end performance (but at the expense of low-end performance). So you don't want to do this for off-road use, just high-performance, mud bogging competition. If you install a manifold gasket on an engine that has an exhaust gas crossover, the port should be cut in the gasket with a sharp knife, such as a razor-sharp utility knife.

Most aftermarket manifolds do not require "bathtub" valley pan gaskets, as were installed as original equipment to prevent oil splash from hitting the hot underside of the exhaust crossover. Also, when assembling new or newly machined heads or manifold on an engine, manifold alignment and end rail gaps should be checked before permanent manifold installation. This may be slightly misaligned and cause vacuum leaks.

Fel-Pro's Fel-Cobond 205 quick-drying adhesive can be used on the head side to hold the gasket in place while installing the manifold. This is a sticky adhesive that will keep the gasket from slipping. To finish the installation, carefully place the

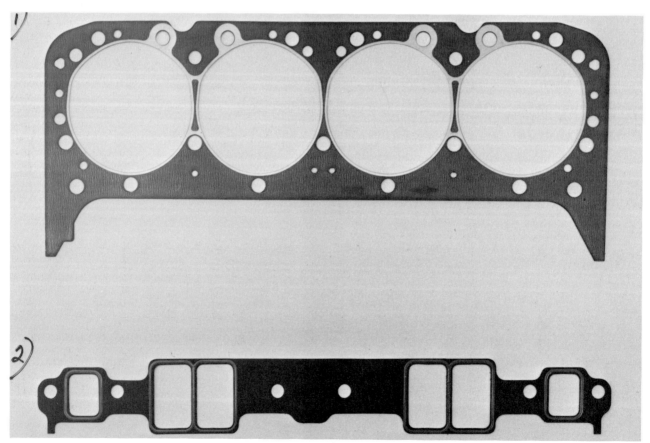

Both the Permatorque blue cylinder head gasket on top and the Printoseal intake manifold gasket on bottom are excellent choices for engine rebuilding. Both provide racing durability to street and competition engines. Fel-Pro Inc.

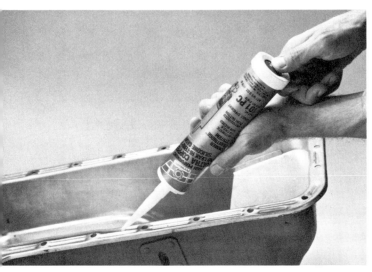

The new Permatex Ultra Copper silicone sealant is an excellent choice for high-temperature silicone applications. It can seal vacuum, oil and water up to an incredible 650 degrees F. Here it's used to coat an oil pan before the gasket is applied. Loctite Corp.

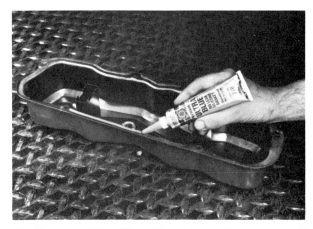

The Permatex Ultra Blue silicone is excellent for overall engine gasket applications. Loctite Corp.

end seals on the engine, and place a bead of RTV silicone at the corners.

The most crucial part is lowering the manifold onto the engine. You must be careful not to push the seals out of the way or break the solid bead of silicone. This is not as easy as it sounds, and may require several attempts, particularly with a large-block V-8 with a heavy cast iron manifold.

Once you're sure the manifold is lowered down and the seals haven't slipped out, the intake manifold bolts should be cleaned, coated with a high-temperature anti-seize compound and carefully torqued down. Use hardened washers under the manifold bolt heads. Careful installation of this gasket will avoid those vacuum leaks that hurt both performance and economy.

Valve cover and oil pan gasket

Valve cover and oil pan gaskets are so simple to install they're often done improperly. These gaskets often develop slow, oozing oil leaks that may not affect performance, but create a mess on garage floors and make the engine look like it's ready for the boneyard.

Valve covers usually leak because they've been warped. This happens after the bolts have been torqued down repeatedly, and is common with the garden-variety stamped sheet metal valve cover. The metal in these valve covers is so thin it easily bends under bolt pressure. To see if this may be your problem, remove the valve cover, clean off the gasket and sealant and check for bulging out at the valve cover holes. If the metal is bulged out under the bolt heads, straighten out the valve cover edge by pounding it on a flat metal surface with a punch. If this doesn't do the job, buy a new valve cover or

better yet, get an aftermarket aluminum or heavy steel valve cover. These have thicker rims that keep a straighter edge.

One way to avoid valve cover distortion is to use load spreader washers. These are available from high-performance shops or dealerships. They work by spreading out the bolt pressure over a wider area and can significantly reduce distortion.

Once the valve cover and head are clean and dry, the new gasket can be installed. These are usually made of rubber or a cork and rubber combination. Avoid cheap paper valve cover gaskets. Before installing the new valve cover or oil pan gasket, make sure every bit of oil film is removed. This can be done by spraying the surface with a spray solvent and wiping it clean with a soft clean rag. Under the engine, spraying upward will rinse away most of the oil and you can finish cleaning it up with a rag.

Chrome valve covers, also from Holley, are good for dressing up a street engine. Holley

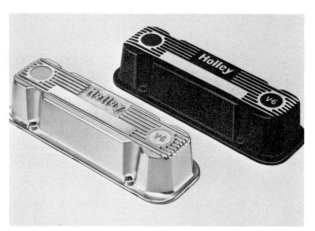

Holley replacement valve covers are available in either black matte or polished aluminum finish. They have a wider, stiffer flange for better sealing and repeated disassembly. Available for many American engines. Holley

Installing valve cover and oil pan gaskets so they'll seal is a two-stage process that involves two kinds of sealants. First, seal the gasket to the sheet metal valve cover and oil pan by applying quick-drying adhesive such as weatherstrip adhesive or Fel-Pro's Fel-Cobond to both the gasket and sheet metal. After the adhesive is dry, attach the gasket to the sheet metal. It will stick on permanently and form a tight seal.

The engine side of the gasket should be sealed with high-performance engine silicone. To install the valve cover back on the cylinder head, carefully apply a bead of silicone to the head only. Leave the gasket, which is now stuck to the valve cover, dry. Then carefully place the valve cover on the cylinder head, position the holes over the tapped holes in the head and install the bolts. The bolts should first be carefully cleaned until they're dry and free of oil, then coated with some silicone. This will help keep them tight and form a good seal.

Installation of the oil pan gasket is the same. Use quick-drying weatherstrip adhesive to attach the gasket to the oil pan, then apply silicone to the engine. Wait a few minutes, then apply the oil pan to the engine, keeping a bolt in hand so it can be held up to the engine by a bolt. Quickly grab a bolt and bolt another end of the oil pan to the engine. Replace all the bolts (they should also be cleaned first and coated with a little silicone) and make them only finger tight.

To tighten the bolts on the valve cover and oil pan, first install them finger tight, then carefully go around and gradually torque them to the same tightness. These bolts only need to hold the sheet metal to the engine, so make them only firm, not real tight. Tightening them too much will cause the valve cover to warp, and the silicone will ooze out before it fully cures.

This method of painstaking cleaning, applying

sealants and installing the valve cover and oil pan are more time consuming than simply slapping them on, but it will virtually guarantee a leak-free installation. I had an oil pan gasket that leaked for years, and I gave up on it—until I tried this method. Afterwards, it didn't leak a drop.

Engine swap in an older vehicle

If your vehicle suffers from an underpowered engine, a better alternative than installing high-performance parts may be to install an entirely different engine. Advance Adapters makes conversion kits so you can put a Buick V-6 into a Toyota pickup or Chevy S-10, or put a Chevy V-8 into any of a number of vehicles. Contact Advance Adapters to see if there's an engine conversion kit available for the swap project you have in mind.

In the area of engine swaps, it's best to start with what's available as a kit, rather than find an engine in a junkyard and force it to fit your vehicle. This is because there are small details involved in an engine swap that can create great headaches for you if you haven't planned for them in advance. Here are some of the clearances that have to be considered if you plan to swap an engine: Is there enough room in front of the engine for the radiator? Will the oil pan and harmonic balancer hit the front axle housing? In the rear of the vehicle, is there enough room at the firewall for the valve covers and distributor? What will the new height of the engine be? Will it hit the hood and make it impossible to close the hood? Is there a cross-member in the way of the oil pan, or will that have to be replaced or modified? Is the front cross-member in the way of the oil pan and/or harmonic balancer?

In the area of the headers and exhaust manifold, is there enough room in the engine compartment, or will the fenders need to be modified? Will the headers clear the fenders, starter and tires?

In the transmission and drive shaft areas, is there enough room for the new transmission and transfer case? Will a new cross-member need to be installed, or drive shafts shortened? Is there enough room for the steering gear to work properly (if not, you may have to go to Saginaw steering gear) and other engine accessories?

To highlight some of the work involved in swapping an engine, the following section describes how to put a Chevy 350 TPI engine in a Chevy S-10 pickup, a great way to get tremendous horsepower out of an S-10 without rebuilding the engine. This swap used the stock 350 TPI, which was taken out of a Pontiac Firebird Formula 350 that had been wrecked in an accident. The engine had only 18,000 miles on it and was in perfect condition, down to being as clean as the day it was made! The wiring harness was also retrieved from the wrecked car, since it was installed in the S-10 complete with the computerized dashboard!

This GM 350 TPI engine was obtained from a Formula 350 Firebird that had been totaled in an accident. It has only 18,000 miles on it, and is an excellent choice for "bolt on" horsepower.

Putting a Chevrolet 350 TPI engine in a Chevy S-10 2WD

The Chevrolet tuned port injected 350 engine is an excellent choice for an engine swap for several reasons. The major reason is that it allows you to swap a complete, high-horsepower street engine directly into your pickup without having to do your own dialing-in. This engine is stock and will deliver well over 200 hp as it is. You can also keep the air conditioning, computerized dashboard and other engine accessories. (Installing the dashboard is a lot more work, so be sure to have a wiring diagram of the vehicle before attempting it.)

The first part of the job is complete removal of the old engine and transmission. The stock transmission cross-member was kept, since it was found that this cross-member fit the transmission that came with the engine. You can change the transmission, but this is not required.

Remove the engine by first disconnecting the fuel line, control cables for the accelerator, air conditioning lines, radiator hoses and so forth. Loosen the steering column to allow more room for engine removal. If the S-10 already has air conditioning (the one featured in this swap did) it can be kept. Keep the air conditioning condenser and radiator

The four-speed overdrive transmission from the Firebird was kept for the Chevy S-10 swap.

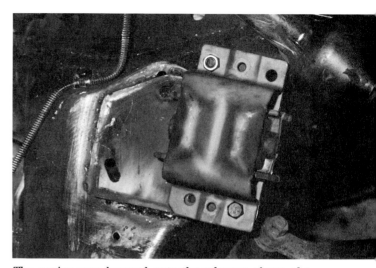

These motor mount adapter plates from Hooker Headers enabled the standard Chevy motor mounts to be installed on the S–10 cross-member.

The engine was lowered onto the adapter plates, the adapter plates were tack welded, then the Chevy motor mounts were bolted on.

from the Pontiac Firebird. This will fit with some modifications, which are outlined here and are shown in the photos.

Before installing the engine, it's a good idea to make sure all accessory items, such as alternator, water pump and so forth, are installed on the

This is how the engine support cross-member looks with motor mounts in position.

engine and that the drive belt for the engine is connected to all of these accessories. This is to ensure that the engine with all of its accessories will fit properly in the truck's engine compartment.

With this Chevy 350 TPI engine, there was no problem fitting the engine in, as can be seen in the photos. First, the engine mounting plates for the engine mounts were installed. These should be the beginning point of most engine installations. The adapter plates for this engine swap were purchased from Hooker Headers.

In order to find the proper location, the engine and transmission were suspended from a portable engine crane over the chassis, then carefully lowered to a spot that cleared the firewall and allowed enough room for the radiator and air conditioning condenser combined.

After the engine (with transmission attached) was lowered into the engine compartment, the proper position for the engine mounts was found and marked on the frame cross-member. Then the adapter plate was tack welded and the standard Chevy engine mounts were checked for fit. After

the proper fit was found, the plates were solidly welded to the engine support cross-member. Fortunately, the Chevy 350 TPI engine fit nicely in the S-10's engine compartment without any modifications being made to the engine mounts.

The adapter plates can also be bolted down. However, welding is usually a better way to secure the adapter plates. The Chevy engine mounts were later bolted to the adapter plates. The transmission also fit on the stock S-10 transmission support cross-member, another piece of luck. However, in order for the transmission to fit under the cab of the S-10, the hump on the S-10's cab floor had to be cut away. After the transmission was installed, the cab floor was welded back in place.

It is not essential to cut away the hump on the S-10 floor if the S-10 body is lifted, with a lift kit available from off-road suspension makers. But if you wish to lower the truck and keep the bigger transmission that comes with the 350 TPI engine, you must cut away the hump from the center of the cab floor. Since the owner of this S-10 wanted to lower the truck, he opted to cut away the floor.

The transmission can be kept, but the center of the cab floor had to be cut out to allow for the greater height of the transmission. Later the floor was welded back in place.

This photo shows the underside of the transmission, where it's held up by the stock S–10 cross-member. The cross-member fit with little modification.

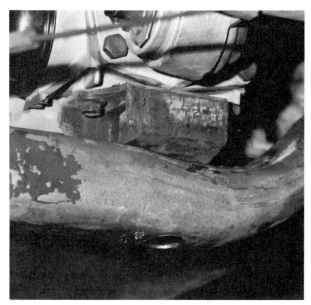

This rubber block in the center of the photo replaced the S–10 transmission mount. This was all that was needed to install the four-speed from the Firebird into the S–10. The cross-member was not modified.

The other changes that have to be made to the transmission include the mounting bracket. Cut off the old transmission support bracket (it's located on the center of the transmission support cross-member) and instead, drill two large holes, about one inch in diameter, to fit the rubber transmission mount from the Firebird. (This may or may not be identical to the Corvette transmission mount. If using a Corvette engine, check out this detail before installation of transmission.)

Another stroke of luck is that the standard drive shaft off the S-10 fits perfectly, and doesn't have to be altered. Of course, with different vehicles this may not be the case. If the transmission is too long, have it cut and balanced at a drive shaft shop. It it's too short, extend the drive shaft on the yoke an inch or two, but be sure to keep at least two inches of drive shaft in the yoke, more for high-performance driving. A new, longer yoke can easily be custom made at a drive shaft shop.

The fuel line from the Chevy 350 TPI engine has to be installed into the S-10 fuel tank with both of its lines, since one is a return line for the fuel

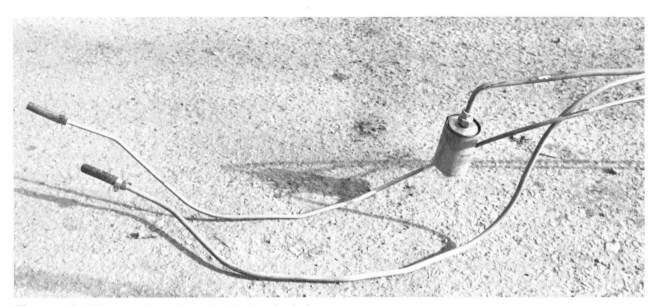

These two fuel lines ran from the engine back to the fuel tank. They had to be carefully routed.

injection pump. This again turned out to be easy, since the gas tank cover is the same diameter on both the Firebird and the S-10. However, the cen- tering tabs on the Firebird's fuel tank cover have to be removed (cut or ground off) so it can be oriented properly onto the S-10 fuel tank.

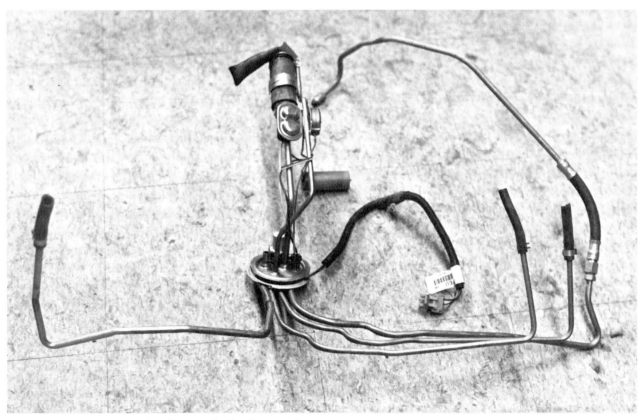

This is the fuel assembly that fits into the S-10 gas tank. Fortunately, it fit with little modification.

The S-10 fuel tank with fuel lines installed.

Be sure to route the fuel lines along the frame where they are clear of interference, and use mounting brackets and nylon ties to secure them.

Back to the engine. The major work involved in installing the engine, after the engine and transmission are in place, and the fuel lines are installed, is modifying the air conditioning condenser and radiator locations, modifying the air duct and reconnecting the lines for the air conditioning. New solid lines will have to be made for the air conditioning system.

To install the air duct, be sure to replace the solid piece of duct with another solid piece welded together, as shown in the photo. This is essential

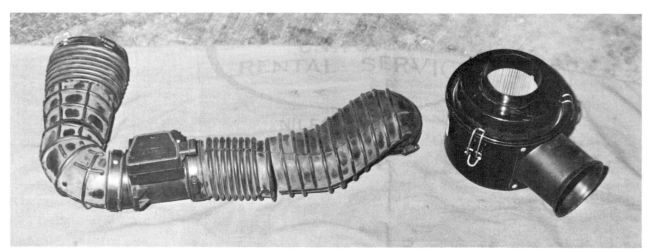

The 350 TPI engine uses a MAF (mass airflow) sensor located in the box on the right. It senses the amount of air flowing through the air duct into the engine. It must be adapted to the S-10 installation perfectly for the engine to work properly.

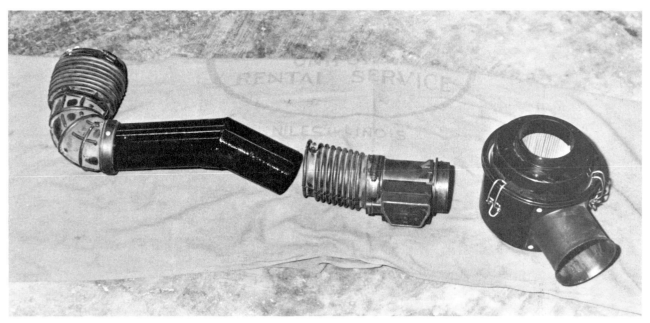

This is how the duct was modified to fit the S–10. A solid piece of duct must be used. Flexible duct will disrupt the airflow.

because the mass airflow sensor, a critical part of the fuel injection system, will not work with a flexible piece of duct. If a flexible duct is used to make the job easier, the air will not flow as easily and the mass flow sensor will give the engine's computer deceptive readings. The engine will not run properly and you won't be able to determine why. So be sure to use a solid metal duct, as shown in the photo, to connect up the air duct to the engine.

This duct work will require some time and custom work, but attention to detail at this part of the installation is essential. Another problem area, or at least a part that will require some time, is the mounts for the air conditioning condenser and radiator. The photos show the proper way to fabricate and install these mounts. Don't allow the mounts to be constructed in a loose or shabby way. Later on this will cause problems with the engine.

Also, don't use a smaller radiator than the stock radiator. You'll have overheating problems in warm temperatures which will cause the engine to have performance problems. Use the stock radiator and mount it solidly in the front of the engine, as close to stock position as possible. This radiator has been carefully engineered to provide the cooling capacity needed by this engine.

The only other major area of careful work is the wiring harness. In this S-10 swap, the wiring harness from the Formula 350 was completely removed from the car, and reinstalled in the S-10 to give it a computerized dashboard. This is a great deal of work, but ensures that the engine's computer and gauges will work properly. If you cannot use

the computerized dashboard, you can have an experienced mechanic connect the engine's wiring system to your S-10 dashboard. The computer, sensors and other components of the electronic fuel injection system must be kept.

Rebuilding an engine for high performance

The best way to rebuild an engine for high performance is to have it rebuilt by a high-performance shop. They know which pistons, bearings,

This bracket had to be made to support the air conditioning condenser and radiator. Rubber mounts are kept.

*These two cooling fans barely fit inside the S–10 grille,
but are important for proper engine cooling.*

*The 350 TPI engine in the S–10 with radiator installed. It
was a tight fit, but it did work with only minor
modifications.*

valves, carburetor, camshaft and so on to use. In engine building, like other things, there are no sure-fire "formulas," only individuals who know what they're doing. When championship racing teams want to rebuild engines, they either go with a well-known, proven "wrench" that they hire as part of their team, or buy engines from people like Arias, Rick Kippley and other well-known builders of proven engines. There are so many minute adjustments, precision parts and possible combinations of parts that go into an engine that it is more of an art than something you can put together following a recipe.

You can get hundreds of additional horsepower out of an engine by yourself, it's only that the experts know how to get that extra five or ten percent into a durable engine. That's what makes them experts: doing it consistently with an engine that will live, and knowing how to dial-in the engine, once it's built, to make it perform to its maximum.

Installing a supercharger (blower)

Since this book is about high-performance equipment, the recommended high-performance modification for the ultimate in performance is the blower or supercharger. Blowers have been used for many years on big trucks, since they are more reliable, more durable, simpler and easier to install than turbochargers. Whereas turbochargers came from the aircraft industry, which needed more compression to make up for the losses in compression due to high altitude, blowers came primarily from the heavy-truck industry, which needed the power and durability only blowers can provide.

There is disagreement, as with everything else, on whether blowers or turbos are better. But there are several advantages to blowers that make them better for racing. One major one is that they provide much more low-rpm torque than turbos, which have to use exhaust gases to build up pressure. A blower provides straight power from the word go. Second, blowers are more of a straight bolt-on procedure. Turbos work great from the factory, but few people know how to install them properly.

Blowers are not that much more expensive than a properly installed turbo, even though there's a myth that says they are. But there are

The engine installation is just about complete. The air conditioning was kept, as well as the computerized dashboard.

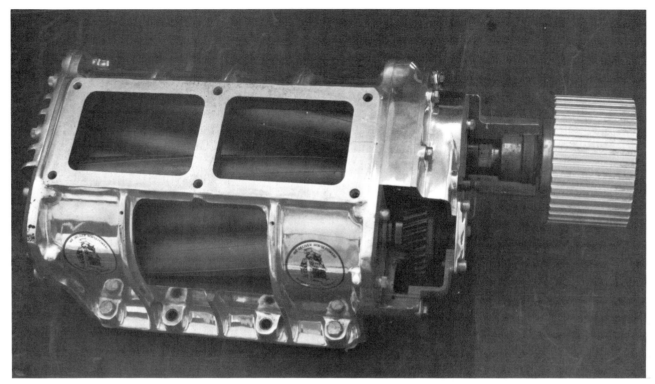

Cutaway views of a BDS blower show how the belt pulley drives the blower gears. The blower acts like a horizontally mounted fan, pumping the air/fuel mixture into the cylinders for much higher compression and greatly increased horsepower. An engine with over 500 hp is easily obtained with a properly installed blower.

several qualifications to this. Many people who sell turbo kits don't include all the parts you need to have. These are added on later and can add another $2,000. Second, used turbos don't have much resale value, whereas a blower, or blown engine, can always be sold to someone looking for one, and there are many machine shops and blower makers (such as Blower Drive Service, or BDS) that will gladly recondition a used blower and check it out. It's much more difficult to send off a turbo to have it checked out. Usually they want you to buy a new one.

The two rotors of a blower are precision machined to make it into an efficient air pump, pumping air downward into the cylinders for greater compression.

The front end cutaway shows how the rotor gears turn the two rotors. This simple belt-driven setup makes the blower an extremely simple and reliable method for increasing engine compression and horsepower.

How much does a blower installation cost? The blower itself is about $2,500 to $3,000, depending on size and whether it's polished and so on. Plus you need to beef up your engine with such items as a steel crankshaft, forged pistons and high-performance rings that add another thousand or so to the price. Plan on spending at least $4,000 on a first-rate job, usually $4,500 for first-rate parts. And this is if you do most of the labor yourself.

Another myth about blowers is that they use tremendous amounts of gas. A blower properly installed and carefully driven on the street will get reasonably good gas mileage, 10-12 mpg or more. Of course, when a blower is first installed the tendency is to put the gas pedal to the floor and enjoy the extra horsepower. But once a blower owner gets used to the extra horsepower and takes it easy on the gas pedal, driving normally, the mileage will greatly increase.

The blower shown in these photographs is a Dyer 671 installed in a Chevy 350 engine, a typical installation. With this installation the engine should produce 500-550 hp.

Installing a blower in a Chevy 350 engine

The engine should be mounted on a stand and be clean and ready for work. Some of the internal engine modifications that need to be done first are the installation of four-bolt main bearings; heavy-duty main bearings such as Clevite 77; high-performance steel crankshaft; roller timing chain; steel connecting rods; forged pistons with 7.5-8:1 compression ratio with Moly piston rings, or for high-boost applications stainless piston rings; stock heads with a standard three-angle valve job; dual point mechanical advance distributor such as Mallory or Accel; and a blower camshaft. Weiand suggests that with more than ten pounds of boost, you should O-ring the block and use a 0.043 dead soft copper head gasket. With ten pounds of boost or less, use Fel-Pro's high-performance head gasket with its built-in stainless steel O-ring.

A blower camshaft has a very low, almost negative overlap to allow the valves to open for just a very short time. This is because the blower is constantly pumping a great deal of air/fuel, and the valves don't need to be open long for them to fill. In a normally aspirated engine, the valves are filled by atmospheric pressure, so must be held open much longer. With a blower, there's always a lot of air behind the intake valves. For street blown engines, Weiand suggests a camshaft with a 240 to 300 degree advertised duration with a lift of 0.450 to 0.500 inch. For street systems a camshaft in the 260 to 280 degree range works well. For competition camshafts, check to see what the manufacturer recommends in a blower system.

A blower fuel system should have a minimum of ⅜ inch lines, half-inch is better, with an electric pump near the tank and a mechanical pump at the

This right-angle distributor from BDS is necessary when using a blower on some Chevy applications. The distributor will not fit under the blower case and must be bent out of the way.

block. Fuel pressure should be regulated to run at four pumps idle, six to seven at high rpm. A fuel regulator should be used since too much fuel pressure can leak fuel past the needle and seat into the blower, causing it to backfire.

Chevy block used for blower installation is stock except for four-bolt main bearings, steel crankshaft and forged pistons. Valves and rocker arms are standard street quality. At this point, intake manifold gaskets have been installed and silicone has been applied to front and rear corners of cork gasket strips.

The exhaust system should be as open as possible, since a backpressure of four pounds, for example, will reduce blower boost by four pounds. Use large tube headers with low restriction mufflers. For street machines, avoid hairpin bends in the exhaust pipe and keep the bends to a minimum.

With the crankshaft installed and a new crankshaft seal in place, install the steel crank hub. Heating it will make it easier. Next, you can install the space, vee pulleys (used for accessories such as air conditioning, alternator, water pump and so on) and tighten bolts. Next, install the crankshaft hub retainer bolt to standard torque specs.

With the new pushrods and rocker arms in place, install the intake manifold gaskets, placing silicone at the corners first. Then install blower intake manifold, carefully following manufacturer's bolt torquing pattern. This usually requires the center bolts to be torqued first, working outward toward the front and back alternately. The Dyer intake manifold shown here has a built-in airplane thermostat to save space. Next, place the blower case on a bench and install upper drive assembly on blower, following manufacturer's torque specs. Place blower on intake manifold and tighten bolts to proper specs. Turn blower snout by hand. It should turn freely and not bind.

With the blower properly installed, the idler pulley can be installed on engine. Next, the carburetor mounting adapter is placed on top of the blower, with screened side facing down, and bolts carefully torqued. Carburetors (two Holley 650s are used on this installation) are put in place and nuts tightened. You can now install the fuel lines and vacuum lines. Fuel lines should be braided stainless steel (available as a kit with carbs from blower maker) and vacuum lines must be con-

Before installing intake manifold, use silicone around ports to make sure air leaks don't occur. Then carefully torque down the manifold bolts. The Dyer intake manifold shown here is low profile, to help keep hood clearance when engine is installed in vehicle.

Carefully lower blower case onto aluminum manifold. It's held down by bolts on side and back.

After hold-down bolts are installed, you can install carburetor adapter plate and valve covers.

Carburetor adapter plate is aluminum and must be carefully torqued down.

The hub, belt and idler pulley can be installed. Be sure they turn freely and don't bind.

nected above blower only. Plug any vacuum connections that are not used. Also, on intake manifold, the manifold gasket covers up the heat riser passages.

Finally, install the blower drive belt with ¾ inch free play, spark plugs, distributor and other accessories. After installing the engine on the vehicle, you must do the initial settings to get the engine to start. If you have purchased the carburetors as a kit from a blower manufacturer, they'll be set for starting. The distributor should be advanced thirty degrees or more until detonation occurs at full throttle, then back off about five degrees or so.

Dialing-in the blower is the most difficult part of installation. Purchasing a brand-name blower with carb kit and so forth will usually ensure a good-running blower, but it must be properly adjusted to gain full horsepower output. Generally, blown engines run too lean, and this can be corrected with larger carburetor jets until it runs well at higher rpm.

Adjusting blower overdrive

As this table indicates, you can adjust the amount of boost you get from a blower by adjusting the overdrive.

	Engine size (cu. in.)					
Drive ratio	289	327	350	400	427	454
-20	10	8	6	4	3	2
-15	12	10	8	6	5	3
-10	16	12	10	8	7	5
-5	18	14	12	9	8	7
1	22	16	14	11	10	9
+5	24	17	16	13	12	11
+10	NA	19	18	15	14	13
+15	NA	22	20	17	16	15
+20	NA	24	23	20	18	17

As an example of how to read this chart, say you have a Chevy 350 engine and you want to obtain twelve pounds of boost. (This chart is for a BD 6-71 blower, Stage I only.) A blower underdrive of –5 will give you the 12 figure you need. However, this doesn't mean that you'll end up with a compression ratio of 12:1. To figure that out, you need to look at this chart.

This chart shows the final compression ratio combining the static compression and the amount of blower boost (for BDS 6-71 blower). The maximum final compression ratio for street driven vehicles, running today's unleaded gas with a blower, should not exceed 10.8:1. If higher ratios are desired you have to use higher octane fuel. Super-

Holley 650 carbs are installed over adapter plate above the blower.

high-performance engines use alcohol, which is another story.

If your engine has a compression ratio of 8:1, then if you add four pounds of boost you'll end up with a ratio of 10.2:1. The final compression ratio must be carefully calculated before installing other internal engine parts, since pistons, rings and other parts must be chosen based on the final compression ratio of the engine. An engine that carries too much boost for its parts will bend connecting rods, chew up main bearings, burn pistons and so on.

All the figures used in the chart were calculated by Blower Drive Service for sea level altitude only. To figure out what the compression ratio is at higher altitudes, use this formula:

$$FCR - \frac{(altitude) \times .2}{1000} =$$

Corrected Compression Ratio

Final compression ratio chart
Compression ratio

Blower boost	6.5	7.0	7.5	8.0	8.5	9.0	9.5	10.0
2	7.4	8.0	8.5	9.1	9.7	10.2	10.8	11.4
4	8.3	8.9	9.5	10.2	10.8	11.4	12.1	12.7
6	9.2	9.9	10.6	11.3	12.0	12.7	13.4	13.4
8	10.0	10.8	11.6	12.4	13.1	13.9	14.7	15.4
10	10.9	11.8	12.6	13.4	14.3	15.1	16.0	16.8
12	11.8	12.7	13.6	14.5	15.4	16.3	17.3	18.2
14	12.7	13.6	14.6	15.6	16.6	17.6	18.5	19.5
16	13.6	14.5	15.7	16.7	17.8	18.8	19.8	20.9
18	14.5	15.3	16.7	17.8	18.9	20.0	21.1	22.2
20	15.3	16.2	17.6	18.9	19.8	21.2	22.4	23.6
22	16.2	17.0	18.6	19.8	20.9	22.4	23.6	24.8
24	17.0	17.9	19.5	20.9	21.9	23.6	24.8	26.0

Then fuel fittings can be connected carefully. Be sure not to overtorque aluminum and brass fittings.

Higher altitudes will decrease the final compression ratio, since the sea level air pressure (14.7 psi) decreases with altitude, affecting the final amount of air pressure.

When using a fuel injection system, you will also have to change injector size at higher altitudes, such as when running in Colorado.

Finally, Blower Drive Service has a chart of recommended blower drive ratios depending on engine compression. This is for a 6-71 blower using ordinary pump gas. These figures are only approximate, since fuel octane, blower condition and engine performance requirements vary.

Recommended blower drive ratios
Engine compression ratio

Engine cid	6	6.5	7	7.5	8	8.5
289	-15	-18	-20	-23	-25	NR
330	-8	-10	-15	-18	-20	-23
350	DIR	-5	-10	-12	-15	-18
390	+5	DIR	-5	-8	-10	-15
430	+10	+5	DIR	-5	-8	-12
460	+15	+10	+5	DIR	-5	-8
500	+20	+15	+10	+5	DIR	-5

Sources of blowers

There are several manufacturers of top quality blowers. Since the blower case itself is often rebuilt from a truck blower, these are pretty much the same from all companies. The difference between blower makers is in the accessory parts and how these are designed. For example, the Dyer blower is a low-profile Chevy blower that will fit under the hood. Other blower makers might use the same blower case, but the mounting flange and other pieces won't be as compact.

The widest selection of blower kits is sold by Blower Drive Service. They have blower kits for fifty-eight different motors, covering virtually every American make. In addition, they can diagnose and repair blowers made by either themselves or other makers. They also sell carburetors, plumbing kits and other items, as well as complete blown engines.

Dyer, located in the Chicago area, also has a top line of blower kits. Many are used by truck pullers and racers in the Midwest. They also provide excellent service and work with many top

With air cleaners in place blower installation is finished and other standard engine accessories can be installed.

Photo shows finished Chevy 350 engine with Dyer blower, intake manifold, carburetor adapter and Holley carburetors. This engine will produce from 500 to 550 hp. Blowers are ideal for off-road competition because they develop low-end horsepower very quickly.

racing engine builders such as Quarter-Mile Competition Engines in Chicago Ridge, Illinois.

Weiand Automotive has a long-standing reputation for top-notch blower kits, blower manifolds and other accessories. They sell a complete small-block Chevy street blower kit for the 283, 302, 327, 350 and 400 engines. They sell a beautifully finished "A" kit that fits the Chevrolet 283, 302, 327, 350 and 400 ci engines using the smaller 4-71 blower. This kit is also available for the Chrysler 426 Hemi engine with 6–71 blower. The kit also comes for the same Chevy engines with a 6-71 blower. (With the expense and trouble of installing a blower, unless you have the smaller displacement engines the 6-71 is the recommended choice.) The big-block Chevy motors—396, 400, 427 and 454—also can use the A kits with 6-71 blowers. Blower manifolds are not included. The A kits feature the Weiand exclusive one-piece aluminum front case cover/ nose drive. These blower kits have a show-quality custom finish that would look great in any vehicle.

The Weiand B kits are less expensive and don't use the one-piece aluminum front case cover/nose drive assembly. Instead, the nose drive is mounted directly to the stock GMC 6-71 front cover. These B kits are for the Chrysler 391 Hemi, 426 Hemi, Chevrolet 283, 302, 327, 350, 396, 400, 427 and 454 engines. Although these engines are not all found on pickup trucks, with Advance Adapters' help you can bolt one into your pickup, whether it's from the '50s, '60s, '70s or '80s.

When installing a Weiand blower, they recommend that a capacitive discharge or multispark ignition unit be used. The distributor curve should be approximately thirty-two degrees total with street gas, and be all in by 3400 rpm with eight to ten degrees initial timing.

Edelbrock has a unique Edelbrock/KF Supercharger for the Chevrolet 2.6 liter V-6 engine. This supercharger is street legal in California, so it's street legal just about everywhere else. It produces thirty percent more low- to mid-range horsepower, quicker acceleration and a great improvement in pulling power, which is what you need for pulling a camper or trailer. If you have a Chevy 2.8 liter V-6 this is definitely the way to go.

5

Aerodynamic exterior changes for better handling and styling

For some years the "spoiler" has been used on sports cars and minipickups. On minis the spoilers have some positive aerodynamic effect, but not as great as they do on low-riding sports cars. A well-designed spoiler helps performance in two ways: by achieving an aerodynamic downforce, and by directing air around the tires to help reduce drag. This is why the spoiler often protrudes from the side and in front of the front tires.

In addition to the spoiler there are two more components of ground effects kits that help your pickup achieve full aerodynamic benefits: the side

This unusual 1978 Chevy Luv lowrider has a custom-made front spoiler.

The painted grille adds to the smooth styled look of the Luv.

This windshield is on a Nissan pickup. It keeps air, rain and dust from blowing in the windows when they're partially open.

dams and rear valance. The side dams act as sheet metal extensions to extend the vehicle's body down toward the ground. This helps keep air from swirling under the vehicle and in front of the tires. The air is directed along the sides of the vehicle, in much the same way as the sides of a speedboat force the water to flow along the sides.

The rear valance not only looks good but also improves performance by cutting down on the swirling air in the wake of the vehicle. Typically, when a pickup is moving, air flows over the front hood, cab, along the bed and then downward. A rear valance keeps the airflow smooth toward the ground, reducing aerodynamic turbulence that increases wind resistance and drag.

If this discussion seems to imply that a vehicle should move through the air smoothly the way an

Here's a Mazda with the full HoTTops conversion, including front spoiler, side dams and convertible top.

This is how the new Ranger GT looks with factory installed ground effects. Front spoiler and side dams as well as rear valance are included. Pinstriping was added by owner.

airplane does, it's because a vehicle *must* move through the air efficiently if it is to achieve better performance and gas mileage. At speeds over 55 mph the primary resistance to forward motion in a vehicle is not the inertia of the truck's weight or the friction of the tires on the ground, but wind.

Air at sea level exerts a constant pressure of fourteen pounds per square inch. This increases gradually as a vehicle moves, and greatly increases over 55 mph. At faster highway speeds, this makes air the greatest enemy of good handling and gas mileage.

The only way to effectively combat the aerodynamic resistance your pickup encounters is to both lower it and install a ground effects kit. In fact, these two items, the lower suspension and ground effects, are what make the lowrider or slammer pickup so unique, stylish and such an improvement over previous pickup designs.

There are currently many brands of ground effects kits for two-wheel-drive pickups. Before buying any kit, you should check out several aspects of the kit's quality and installation. These are extremely important and will make a great difference later on.

The first consideration is the quality of materials in the ground effects side dams, valance and front spoiler. Good kits are made of ABS plastic or good quality fiberglass. Fiberglass has the advantage that anyone with fiberglass experience can modify it. And with some trucks, such as full-size Chevys, the only kit available might be made of fiberglass. So you are forced to go with the kit that will fit your truck.

Generally, ground effects kits are very difficult to modify, unless you have a fiberglass kit that is a little bigger than your truck and you have experience working with fiberglass. So don't get just any mail-order generic ground effects kit and expect it to fit your truck like a glove. If it's not made for your particular truck's body, it won't fit.

Another important consideration is installation. The better kits do not require holes to be drilled directly into the truck's sheet metal sides. Usually, attachment is made on the inside flanges of the fender and the flanges under the side of the truck. This way, you will not drill into anything that's easily seen on the truck body. The edges are usually held by rivets or screws.

How are the sides held up? By the same two-sided tacky tape that auto body shops use to attach trim to a car or truck body. This tape has long been proven to stand up to weather and changes in temperature, so using it for side dams is no prob-

This customized Chevy S–10 pickup features Bushwacker ground effects painted the same color as the truck. Bushwacker

lem. And if the tape ever does work loose, it can be easily replaced without damage to the ground effects parts or the truck body.

There are three parts to ground effects kits: the front spoiler, side dams and rear valance. These can often be purchased separately, so some truck owners buy the front spoiler and side dams together, then add a rear roll pan made by the same or a different manufacturer. If you change manufacturers with the roll pan, there is a possibility that the side dam and roll pan edges will not meet. In that case some bodywork will have to be done to repair the gap.

Although the side dams are what really make the "California look," you can install only a front spoiler and rear valance or roll pan for a great looking truck. This is less expensive and involves less work. There are several manufacturers such as Bill's Custom Louvering that can make custom roll pans for virtually any vehicle.

You can also install only a rear roll pan, or front spoiler. The nice thing about lowrider pickups is that there are no rules. Every truck is unique. If you only have a roll pan it can be painted the same color as the truck body, and with some good body graphics you can end up with a great looking truck.

Bushwacker Road Hugger ground effects kit

The ground effects kit used for these photos is made by Bushwacker and is available for many different truck models (not for full-size pickups, however). A complete list is included in this chapter. The Bushwacker kit is actually three separate kits: one for side dams, one for the front spoiler and one for the rear valance. These are sold separately and can be purchased individually as needed. So you can combine a Bushwacker front spoiler with a steel roll pan, for example. Or if you damage a rear valance, you can easily replace it with a new one without buying an entire new kit.

Front spoiler

These front spoiler instructions apply to Bushwacker front spoilers that fit the Ford Ranger, 1982 and up, and Chevy S–10 pickup, 1982 and up. These tools will be used in the installation, as recommended by Bushwacker:

1. clean wiping rags
2. degreasing solvent such as Prep-Sol
3. electric drill, small portable one okay
4. $5/16$ inch drill bit
5. crescent wrench
6. pliers
7. screwdriver
8. pencil
9. utility knife with sharp blade
10. $9/32$ inch drill bit

Painting

It is recommended that the spoiler be painted prior to installation, which is much easier than painting it on the truck. However, you may want to do most of the fitting and drilling before you paint it. The Bushwacker ABS plastic is of such good quality, however, that if the color (such as black) is right for your truck, you don't need to paint it. It will look great without painting. However, be sure to handle it very carefully since it can be scratched. To prepare the spoiler for painting, wipe it with a degreaser such as Prep-Sol and wipe outer surface with a tack rag prior to priming. A polypropylene primer such as Ditzler DPX800 *must be used* to ensure color coat adhesion. The color coat should have a flex additive such as Ditzler DX369 to prevent paint cracking or checking. This is because the ABS is flexible and will constantly flex while under aerodynamic pressure when the vehicle is moving. Before using any paint, check to see if it is compatible with these two Ditzler products, or use the primer and flex additive for the particular brand of paint you intend to use. Check out all of these details before you paint the spoiler, side dam or valance.

Removal and installation

1. Remove stock front spoiler. Remove clip nuts from spoiler and save for reuse.

2. Fit Road Hugger spoiler up to bumper and mark hole locations onto spoiler. Remove spoiler and drill marked locations with $5/16$ inch bit. Apply clip nuts to drilled holes. Reapply spoiler onto bumper and loosely secure.

3. Position end of spoiler onto lower fender and mark location of fender fastener. Repeat with opposite side. Remove spoiler and drill marked locations with $9/32$ inch drill bit.

4. With a utility knife cut out bottom of light pocket using squared edges of pocket as a guide. Drill $9/32$ inch holes through indents in sides of the light pockets. Repeat for opposite side.

5. If light hole plug is used continue with step 5. If light kit (Bushwacker part no. 000091) is used proceed to step 6. Apply light decal to plug and push into light pocket from backside of spoiler. Using clip nuts supplied, fasten over both spoiler and light plug with nut side toward center of plug. Secure with screws provided. Repeat for opposite side.

6. When using light kit part no. 000091, light hole plugs and hardware may be discarded. Remove screws from light bezel and save. Holding light lens bezel and housing together, insert from backside of spoiler into light pocket. Locaters on bezel should snap into holes drilled in step 4. Secure spoiler to light with screw provided. Follow wiring instructions included in light package after step 7 is completed.

7. Apply spoiler to bumper and secure with original fasteners. Secure ends of spoiler to fenders using original fasteners.

Pickup valance
Painting

The valance is made of ABS plastic and it will show surface damage if it is cleaned with lacquer thinner or enamel reducer. You can use a general purpose degreaser such as Prep-Sol. If you prefer to paint it, use a lacquer, enamel or polyurethane automotive paint. As noted above, use Ditzler DPX-800 or similar polypropylene primer, and a flex additive such as Ditzler DX369 to promote adhesion and prevent paint cracking. If your brand of paint is other than Ditzler, check out the proper polypropylene primer and flex additive for that brand.

Installation on Ford Ranger and Chevy S-10 pickups

Here are the tools and materials you will use: electric drill (portable drill okay), pop-rivet gun, $1/2$ inch wrench, $3/16$ inch drill bit.

Install valance using the following procedure:
1. Remove rear bumper and mounting brackets, if so equipped.
2. Remove tailgate.
3. With valance off the vehicle, pre-drill all pop-rivet locating indents with $3/16$ inch drill bit. Do not drill sheet metal with the $3/16$ inch bit.
4. Clean inside edge of bed side dams and apply mounting tape even with edge. Leave release paper on tape for now.
5. Install valance into tailgate cavity and line up with bed side dams. Using $3/16$ inch pre-drilled holes as a guide, drill (with bit provided) and rivet center two holes. Pull bed side dam away from valance and remove release paper from tape. Realign panels and press firmly together. Repeat for opposite side.

6. Where side dam panels and valance overlap, drill and rivet on underside. Again using pre-drilled holes as a guide, drill and rivet top mounting flange in an alternating pattern from center until secured. Next, drill and rivet two end mounting flanges.

7. Install license plate into cavity. *Note:* It will be necessary to remove the license plate to gain access to spare tire crank release hole. No provision has been made for a license plate light but a light can be installed if required in your state.

8. Replace tailgate.

Side dams

Follow directions noted earlier for painting and priming the ABS plastic side dam parts. Be careful to use a cleaning solvent, primer and flexible paint compatible with the ABS plastic material. If the black pieces match your truck you may wish to leave them unpainted, since the factory ABS plastic finish looks good enough for immediate installation.

Tools and materials you will use:
1. clean wiping rags
2. degreaser such as Prep-Sol, do not use lacquer thinner or enamel reducer
3. tape measure
4. grease pencil
5. electric drill, portable drill okay
6. $7/32$ inch drill bit
7. screwdriver
8. $3/8$ inch wrench
9. masking or duct tape
10. pop-rivet tool

When installing the Bushwacker Road Hugger ground effects side dams, brackets like these are used to support the side dams from the bottom. They're first bolted to the lip under your truck's sheet metal, where the holes won't show, then bolted in place.

This view of the underside along the body shows how the side dams are held in place. The bottom of the brackets are then bolted to the plastic air dam sections. The brackets are flexible for a good fit.

Install side dams as follows:

1. Check fit of each part in proper location by holding up to vehicle side and making visual check. Adjustments may be made by sanding or scraping areas that have interference.

2. Remove all dirt and wax from side of vehicle in the areas where ground effects will be applied. Use clean rags and a degreaser such as Prep-Sol as the solvent. Dry thoroughly.

3. Using a tape measure and grease pencil, locate and mark holes for the mounting brackets on the bottom edge of the sheet metal about ½ inch

After the bottom brackets are bolted on, the ABS side dams are moved aside, as in this photo, and the double-sided high tack tape applied between the side dam and truck body. This tape will hold the side dam pieces securely in place and is virtually weatherproof.

in from the turned-under edge of the metal. See instructions for precise locations.

4. Using an electric drill and $^7/_{32}$ inch drill bit, drill through sheet metal at each mounting hole location. Duplicate this procedure on both sides of the bed.

5. Using a screwdriver and ⅜ inch wrench, attach appropriate mounting bracket to each location. Make sure the bottom flange of the bracket points in the direction indicated in the instructions. See photo for example of bracket installation.

6. Apply two pieces of masking or duct tape to the top edge of each part. Place part in its proper location, making sure the bottom edge of the part is tight against the bottom edge of the mounting bracket (as in photo). Secure in place by pushing tape against vehicle.

7. While parts are taped in place, mark the mounting bracket holes onto each part using the mounting bracket holes as locaters. The holes should be approximately ½ inch *in* from the edge of the lower flange of each part.

8. Remove part from vehicle and drill $^7/_{32}$ inch holes through each part at locations marked on lower flange.

9. Reapply parts to vehicle as outlined in step 6 and attach to mounting brackets with hardware included in kit. See instructions for correct hardware applications.

10. While the part is being held in place by the masking or duct tape, hold top edge of part with one hand, and pull out or push in the bottom edge of the part with the other hand. This will line up the bottom edge of each part with the other ground effects on the side of the vehicle. It may be necessary to overbend the mounting brackets so they will spring back to the proper position.

11. After all parts have been aligned, remove masking or duct tape from part. Pull part away from vehicle and remove protective strip from the adhesive tape. Push the part back in place making sure pressure is applied to the full length of the tape. Apply pressure several times to ensure good contact to the body panel.

12. Recheck the alignment of each part, then drill the first hole in the wheelwell opening using the ⅛ inch drill bit provided in the hardware packet. Insert pop-rivet and fasten in place with pop-rivet hand tool. Check alignment again, then drill and fasten pop-rivet in second hole. Consult instructions or photo for hole location.

The final installation will not require any holes to be drilled in sheet metal sides of the vehicle. The only holes drilled are hidden on the inside of the body metal flanges. You can see from the photos how this is done. The sides of the side dams are held to the body by automotive double-sided high tack tape, so there is no damage to body paint or sheet metal. This is also an excellent way to attach ABS

This photo shows how beautifully the side dams fit on the truck. The ground effects kit is relatively easy to install, *but the way it's designed it's easy to line up for a smooth aerodynamic look.*

plastic since there is excellent adhesion between the tape and plastic.

Applications for Bushwacker Road Hugger kit

Bushwacker Road Hugger ground effects kits are sold as separate components. These are the front spoiler, side dams and rear valance. The front spoiler is made of Bushwacker's Dura-Flex 2000 thermoplastic, which is flexible on impact but keeps its shape. It extends about seven inches below the bumper, and complements the Road Hugger side dams. All front spoilers are furnished in black, but can be painted with proper preparation. (See earlier instructions for installation.) Spoilers include openings for driving or foglights, or Road Hugger mock light inserts. Light kits can be purchased separately.

Light kits for spoilers have a maximum legal wattage of fifty-five watts using quartz halogen bulbs, and come with all necessary hardware.

Side dams are custom fitted and include eight pieces, two part numbers to a set. Order cab and bed pieces separately. They descend about three and one-half inches below stock rocker panels. They cannot be used with Bushwacker fender flares.

Rear valances are one-piece and mount beneath the tailgate. They include hidden fasteners and permanent adhesive tape. Kits come with mounting hardware and complete instructions.

The following applications are descriptive only. They tell you which trucks can use Bushwacker Road Hugger ground effects kits. Consult their catalog or a distributor for the most recent information and specific part numbers.

The front spoiler replaces your own and has optional turn signals. These connect to the vehicle's wiring. Simple instructions enable you to install the front spoiler easily.

The rear valance fits flush with the tailgate and the Bushwacker side dams for a clean aerodynamic fit. What you're seeing here has not been painted, this is how good the parts look out of the box. With a black truck, the parts do not need painting unless you wish to change the color.

- Chrysler trucks
    Front spoiler, side dams and rear valance are all available for these models and years:
    D-50, 1987-89 standard cab, standard bed
    D-50, 1987-89 standard cab, long bed
    D-50, 1987-89 extend-a-cab, standard bed
    D-50, 1987-89 extend-a-cab, long bed
- Ford
    Front spoiler, side dams and rear valance are all available for these models and years except where noted:
    Bronco II, 1983-88 front spoiler only
    Ranger pickup, 1982-88 standard cab, standard bed
    Ranger pickup, 1982-88 standard cab, long bed
    Ranger pickup, 1982-88 extend-a-cab, standard bed
    Ranger pickup, 1989 standard cab, standard bed
    Ranger pickup, 1989 standard cab, long bed
    Ranger pickup, 1989 extend-a-cab, standard bed
- General Motors
    Front spoiler, side dams and rear valance are all available for these models and years except where noted:
    S-10/S-15 pickup, 1982-89 standard bed
    S-10/S-15 pickup, 1982-89 standard cab, long bed
    S-10/S-15 pickup, 1982-89 extend-a-cab, standard bed
    S-10/S-15 Blazer/Jimmy, 1982-89 front spoiler only

- Mazda
    Front spoiler, side dams and rear valance are all available for these models and years except where noted:
    Pickup 2WD, 1986-89 standard cab, standard bed
    Pickup 2WD, 1986-89 standard cab, long bed
    Pickup 2WD, 1986-89 extend-a-cab, standard bed
- Mitsubishi
    Front spoiler, side dams and rear valance are all available for these models and years except where noted:
    Pickup, 1987-89 standard cab, standard bed
    Pickup, 1987-89 standard cab, long bed
    Pickup, 1987-89 extend-a-cab, standard bed
    Pickup, 1987-89 extend-a-cab, long bed
- Nissan
    Front spoiler, side dams and rear valance are all available for these models and years except where noted:
    Pickup 2WD, 1986 ½-89 standard cab, standard bed
    Pickup 2WD, 1986 ½-89 standard cab, long bed
    Pickup 2WD, 1986 ½-89 extend-a-cab, standard bed
    Pickup 4WD, 1986 ½-89 front spoiler only
    Pathfinder, 1987-89 front spoiler only
- Toyota
    Front spoiler, side dams and rear valance are all available for these models and years except where noted:
    Pickup 2WD, 1984-88 standard cab, standard bed, domestic
    Pickup 2WD, 1984-88 standard cab, standard bed, import
    Pickup 2WD, 1984-88 standard cab, long bed, domestic
    Pickup 2WD, 1984-88 standard cab, long bed, import
    Pickup 2WD, 1984-88 extend-a-cab, standard bed, domestic
    Pickup 2WD, 1984-88 extend-a-cab, long bed, domestic

John Baker Performance Street Dream ground effects kit

The John Baker Performance kit fits the 1987 and up Mitsubishi and Dodge minipickups. To give you some idea of what's involved in installing the kit, here's a list of parts, including hardware and tools:

- Front spoiler: Includes one full-width valance, five oval head self-tapping screws. The panel has openings for optional auxiliary lights. Leave as is if lights are not desired. Outboard of these are molded-in contour lines which may be cut out to allow a flow of air to the front brake areas. This will help keep them cool if you do a lot of city driving.
- Side skirts: One long side panel, one end cap, eleven oval head self-tapping screws, two special

flat-headed screws and two screw caps for these. (One set for each side of the vehicle.)
- Rear valance: One center panel, two end panels, nine self-tapping oval head screws, four nuts, bolts and washers.
- Required tools and equipment:
  hdraulic floor jack (optional)
  electric or portable drill
  $3/32$, $3/16$ and $1/2$ inch drill bits
  small-slot screwdriver
  two jack stands (optional)
  medium Phillips screwdriver
  10 mm box-end wrench
  pair of pliers
- *Note:* The hydraulic jack and jack stands are used when the vehicle will be raised off the ground for ground effects kit installation. The vehicle does not have to be raised for the kit to be installed; however, the kit installation will be much easier (you'll have a lot more elbowroom) if the vehicle is first jacked up, supported by jack stands and then worked on.

The following sections will cover installation of the ground effects parts separately:

Front spoiler

1. Remove stock valance (recommended but not required).

The John Baker Performance ground effects kits make a beautifully aerodynamic vehicle out of your Dodge or Mitsubishi mini.

2. Locate on lower bumper flange two oval bolt heads under parking lights. Spoiler must be clearanced at these points for flush fit. Hold spoiler in position, mark for bolt heads and drill panel with $1/2$ inch drill bit. An assistant is recommended since once the large $1/2$ inch hole is drilled, it's impossible to shift it a fraction of an inch or so.

Here's what you get with the John Baker Street Dream package: sun visor, tonneau cover, spoiler, fender flares and optional weathershield. For Mitsubishi and Dodge minipickups.

3. Refer to *front spoiler* installation page of installation instructions. Drill $3/16$ inch holes as indicated. Hold spoiler in position against bumper, mark for holes, drill bumper with $3/32$ inch bit.

4. Attach spoiler with oval head self-tapping screws provided. *Note:* The critical part of this installation is the first alignment needed for the ½ inch holes. Do this step carefully.

Side skirts

1. Do one side of truck at a time. Refer to *side skirts* illustration in instructions to locate attachment holes for long panel and end caps. Drill panels with $3/16$ inch bit. Temporarily fit long panel, mark body for drilling with $3/32$ inch bit, mark and cut in front panel flange to clear body bolt inside wheel opening.

2. Drill body holes, attach long panel with oval head self-tapping screws *and the one special flat-headed screw* as indicated in illustration. Install special cap over flat-headed screw.

3. Drill $3/16$ inch holes in end cap where indicated, mark for $3/32$ inch holes and drill out. *Note:* Fiberglass panel edges may need filing or sanding for flush fit. Install with oval head screws provided and the one special flat-headed screw where indicated. Install special cap over flat-head.

4. Repeat steps in this order for the opposite side of the truck.

Rear valance

1. Drill panels where indicated in *rear valance* instruction sheet with $3/16$ inch bit. Remove rear bumper if truck is equipped with one.

2. Start with either end panel and remove two 10 mm bolts from rear inner flange of wheel opening. Repeat on opposite side of truck.

3. Some, but not all, trucks' exhaust tail pipe may interfere with *right* end panel. If so, cut out half-circle around molded-in lines with snips or keyhole saw. You may want to make a rough cut with a saw first, then smooth the inner edges with a rasp file.

4. Mount both end panels *using wheelwell bolts only*, but do not tighten.

5. Position center panel and drill attachment holes in body panel with $3/32$ inch bit. Secure with oval head self-tapping screws provided. *Note:* If rear bumper is to be reinstalled, notch panel for brackets at this time.

6. Match trailing edges of end panels to outer ends of center panel. Drill attachment holes with $3/16$ inch bit. Secure with nuts, bolts and washers provided.

7. Tighten wheelwell bolts. Reinstall rear bumper if desired.

John Baker Performance Street Dream kit for Dodge and Mitsubishi

The John Baker Performance Street Dream kit consists of four items: fender flares, front spoiler, sun visor and tonneau cover. These are designed to

be installed together and blend together stylistically. If you buy the complete Street Dream package, you won't be stuck with a spoiler that doesn't fit with the front fender flares and so on. The parts are made to fit together.

These items are included in the kit:
• Fender flares: Four fiberglass fender-opening panels (packaged separately in pairs for the front and rear) with appropriate sheet metal screws.
• Front spoiler: Includes one full-width panel, five oval head self-tapping screws, two nuts and bolts for attaching spoiler ends to fender flares. Panel has openings for optional auxiliary lights. Leave as is if lights are not added.
• Sun visor: Optional one-piece roof panel, one dozen special flat-headed screws, twelve caps.
• Tonneau cover: One full-size bed cover, appropriate lengths of self-adhesive Velcro tape.
• *Note:* Vehicle does not have to be raised, but for practical purposes it is much easier if you raise the front end, support the truck on jack stands and remove front wheels. This will make installation of the spoiler and front fender flares much easier.
• Required tools and equipment:
  hydraulic floor jack
  two jack stands
  wheel wrench for removing wheels
  electric drill
  drill bits size ⅛, $3/32$ and ½ inch
  Phillips screwdriver
  file or coarse sandpaper
  tube of silicone sealer

Fender flares

1. Start with any flare and position it against fender and align with body contours. Have assistant push flare in and up at forward upper corner of wheel opening. Flare edges may need filing or sanding to fit flush against fender.

2. Use drill and ⅛ inch drill bit through flare and into rolled-under fender opening flange. When you drill the hole, be sure to center it in the flange.

3. Insert a sheet metal screw in hole, but do not tighten it right now.

4. Move to upper rear corner of fender opening, drill as before, start screw.

5. Drill holes and start remaining screws at even intervals around perimeter of fender opening. Tighten all screws while in on flare.

6. Repeat steps for remaining flares, taking care to align each one, and file if necessary for a smooth, tight fit.

Front spoiler

1. Remove stock valance. This step is recommended but not required for installation of new spoiler.

2. Locate on lower bumper flange, two oval head bolts below parking lights. Spoiler must be clearanced at these points for flush fit. Hold spoiler

in position, mark for bolt heads, drill panel with ½ inch drill bit.

3. Drill $3/16$ inch holes where indicated. Position spoiler under bumper, mark for holes, remove spoiler and drill bumper with $3/32$ inch drill bit.

4. Attach spoiler with screws provided. Drill through fiberglass and flanges of spoiler and front flares and install small nuts and bolts. This will ensure that spoiler and flares are held together tightly.

Sun visor

Visor may appear to be too narrow for truck, but you will find that it fits properly.

1. Scribed mark on visor indicates holes for twelve supplied flat-headed screws. Drill all with $3/32$ inch drill bit.

2. Position visor on roof making sure it is centered. Drill through holes in visor and through roof, again using $3/32$ inch drill bit.

3. Put a small bead of silicone sealer around holes in roof and on underside of visor to prevent moisture seepage.

4. Install visor with screws provided. Place supplied plastic caps over screws.

HoT Tops ground effects

HoT Tops of Tempe, Arizona, has done a great deal of creative work developing ground effects kits, rear window neons and convertible top conversions. These vehicles can use HoT Tops ground effects aerodynamic styling kits. The following models, years and sizes are available. Consult with HoT Tops for the most up-to-date information.

• Chevrolet/GMC
  S-10, 1982-88 GMC S-15, long bed
  S-10, 1982-88 GMC S-15, standard bed
  S-10, 1982-88 GMC S-15 king kab
  Blazer, 1982-88 GMC Jimmy
• Toyota
  Minipickup, 1984-88 long bed
  Minipickup, 1984-88 standard bed
  Minipickup, 1984-88 extra-cab
• Datsun
  Minipickup, 1980-83 standard bed
• Nissan
  Minipickup, 1984-86 long bed
  Minipickup, 1984-86 standard bed
  Minipickup, 1984-86 king kab
  Minipickup, 1986½-88 standard bed
  Minipickup, 1986½-88 king kab
  Minipickup, 1986½-88 long bed
• Mazda
  Minipickup, 1986-88 long bed
  Minipickup, 1986-88 standard bed
  Minipickup, 1986-88 cab plus
• Dodge/Mitsubishi
  Minipickup, 1987-88 long bed
  Minipickup, 1987-88 standard bed
  Minipickup, 1987-88 extra cab

• Dodge Dakota
  Minipickup, 1987-88 long bed
  Minipickup, 1987-88 standard
• Isuzu
  Minipickup, 1981-87 standard bed
  Minipickup, 1988 standard bed
  Minipickup, 1988 long bed
• Ford Ranger
  Minipickup, 1982-88 standard bed

East Coast Customs ground effects for full-size Chevy and minipickups

East Coast Customs of Maryville, Tennessee, makes some unique ground effects kits. They can fit truck applications that other ground effects kits cannot handle. Most ground effects kits on the market are made for smaller pickups. If you have a Chevy S-10 there are a great deal of choices you can make. But with a larger pickup, your choices are few.

Here's a list of applications for East Coast Customs ground effects kits, front spoilers, cab extenders and so forth. The full address of the manufacturer is listed in the Appendix. Be sure to write and ask if a kit is available for your truck, if you don't see it here, because they are always adding new applications.

• Chevrolet S-10 pickup
  Seven-piece ground effects kit available for 1982-88 short bed trucks. It's part no. T-C10. Includes four rocker panels, two rear quarter panel extensions and front spoiler. The front spoiler is sold separately as part no. T-C15. You can also get a rear valance panel (roll pan) tailgate insert part no. T-C20, and tailgate spoiler, part no. T-U25. One unique item for the S-10 is a hood scoop, part no. T-C12. It's 3 ½ inches high, twenty-five inches long and twenty-six inches wide. All of these S-10 items can be shipped via UPS.
• Chevrolet S-10 pickup
  Another ground effects kit, the G-100, consists of eight pieces, including a front spoiler, two rocker panels, four bed extensions and rear bumper replacement panel. These two items can also be purchased separately: a front spoiler (G-120) and an S-10 cab extender (G-110).
• Chevrolet S-10 Blazer
  East Coast Customs has a five-piece ground effects kit (T-C35) that consists of front spoiler, two rocker panels and two rear quarter panel extensions. Fits 1982-88 Chevy S-10 Blazers.
  Another S-10 Blazer kit, the G-200, fits 1982-88 S-10 Blazers and Jimmys and includes front spoiler, two rocker panels, two door panels and two rear quarter panel extensions. The G-210 front spoiler fits the S-10 Blazers and pickups. Another seven-piece ground effects kit fits 1982-88 Blazers and Jimmys and includes a front spoiler, two rocker panels, two door panels and two rear quarter panel extensions. Available separately is

This full-size Chevy uses a roll pan made by Bell Super Tech. It fits the stock vehicle by attaching five ¼ inch screws across the top and two on each side. It can be painted the same color as the truck. A license plate light has to be added.

an S-10 Blazer front spoiler. All items can be shipped UPS.

Ground effects for full-size Chevy trucks

• Reduce wind drag with a fiberglass cab extender. Fits 1988 Chevy fleetside trucks only, part no. G-450. A ground effects kit for the short bed fleetside and stepside is part no. G-400, for 1988 only.

• Front spoiler for 1988 trucks is the G-425 that can be fitted with foglamps or GM parking lamps #915220.

• Ground effects for 1973-87 Chevy short bed fleetside trucks is part no. G-500, and features simple bolt-on installation.

• Two-piece truck front spoilers fit 1973-80 and 1981-87 Chevy trucks, part no. G-510.

• Cab extender for 1973-87 Chevy short bed or long bed fleetside trucks, part no. G-525.

Ground effects and spoiler for Nissan pickups

• For the 1986½-88 pickup, you can get the front spoiler separately, part no. T-N15.

• Ground effects for the Nissan is available in a seven-piece kit, including four rocker panels, front spoiler, two rear quarter panel extensions and hardware, part no. T-N10.

• Rear valance for the 1986½-88 Nissan is part no. T-N20.

• Nissan tailgate spoiler is a universal item that fits most minitrucks, part no. T-U25.

Toyota ground effects

A seven-piece package includes four rocker panels, two rear quarter panel extensions, front spoiler and hardware, part no. T-T10. Fits 1984-88 short bed Toyota trucks.

• Toyota front spoiler can be purchased separately, part no. T-T15, fits 1984-88 Toyota minis.

• Toyota tailgate spoiler, part no. T-U25, fits all minitrucks.

• Toyota cab extender, part no. G-600, fits 1984-88.

• Toyota rear valance panel (roll pan) for 1984-88 Toyota trucks, part no. T-T20.

Pop Top Minis ground effects and aero wings

These vehicles can use the Pop Top Minis ground effects kits shown in the photos. Installa-

Here's two photos comparing the look of a stock bumper to a roll pan. This Nissan pickup has standard taillights and aftermarket chrome bumper.

But the second photo shows an older Datsun pickup with blue dot taillights and a roll pan. The roll pan and tonneau cover give it a much more aerodynamic look.

tion procedures are similar to those already mentioned. Be sure to thoroughly read installation instructions before installing any kit, and note manufacturer's specific requirements.

Ground effects applications:
- Toyota: 1984-89
- Nissan: 1984-86
- Nissan H.B.: 1987-88
- Nissan H.B. E/C: 1987-88
- Mazda: 1986-88
- Dodge: 1979-86
- Dodge: 1987-88
- Mitsubishi: 1979-86
- Mitsubishi: 1987-89
- Chevy S-10, S-15: 1982-89
- Chevy Blazer: 1984-88

Note: Kits are available for 1989 and later vehicles. Consult recent catalog for kits and availability.

Aero wing applications:
Bedwing: universal for most trucks
Shellwing: universal for most trucks
Bedwing with light: universal for most trucks
Shellwing with light: universal for most trucks

Tailgate covers and steel roll pan

Installing a roll pan on your truck will add styling and a smooth lowrider appearance to the rear. Roll pans are often custom made by small manufacturers, so there are a number of options that can be added to the roll pan. These include louvers, which can match the louvers on the tailgate cover, taillights and a recessed license plate holder. You can keep the stock taillights, but the truck will look much better with the taillights built into the roll pan. Many roll pan taillight sets, like the one shown here made by Bill's Custom Louvering, come with blue dots for that "hot pink" look.

This tailgate cover for a Chevy full-size pickup is made by Bill's Custom Louvering and comes with several options. More louvers and a Chevy bow-tie emblem can be included.

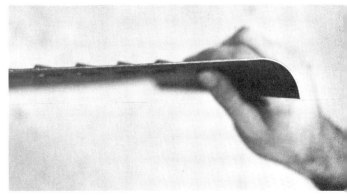

A close-up of the edge shows how it's curved to perfectly match with the curve of the tailgate. It fits perfectly at both the top and bottom for an easy installation. This one will he welded to the stock tailgate.

This custom-made roll pan was fabricated by Bill's Custom Louvering. It includes two options: the 1946 Ford   *oval taillights with blue dot inserts, and the recessed license plate holder.*

Close-up photo of the taillight shows how it is easily installed in the roll pan.

Tailgate covers offer another exciting way to dress up the rear end of a truck and smooth it out. These can be custom made by companies such as Bill's Custom Louvering, who can add such touches as louvers, the Chevy bow-tie logo, the Ford logo, Chevrolet lettering and so on. Tailgate covers give that finished, filled-in super-smooth look to the rear end of a truck. Any truck without a tailgate cover and roll pan is just not finished aerodynamically.

Installation

To install a steel roll pan like this one, follow these steps:

1. Jack up the truck (or raise it up on a lift) making the bumper and wiring accessible. If the truck is lifted up on the ground, use jack stands to support the frame while you're working on the truck.

2. Remove license plate.

3. Disconnect taillight wiring. This is found at the rear fender just behind the wheel. With the Chevy pickup, there are two plugs that should be disconnected.

4. Loosen and remove bumper mounting bolts on both sides. The bolts will not be used again. However, keep the bumper and hardware together in case you want to replace the bumper in the future.

5. Cut the two wires going to the taillight, and resolder them with stock connectors as in the photo.

6. Line up the roll pan on the rear, and drill the installation holes. The roll pan is held at the top by a bolt through the flange of the bed, and at the side of the back of the fender.

7. Do this for the opposite side of the truck.

8. Remove the roll pan, after fitting, and paint it.

9. The roll pan license plate recess does not allow enough room for a license plate light. You can buy a license plate frame with a built-in light and that will work fine, if a lighted license plate is required in your state.

10. After painting, install the taillight assemblies, secure each one with two screws and connect wiring. The roll pan does not allow for a white back-up light, so if you want back-up lights you will have to rig up your own. Simply install white lights on the rear, and splice into the wire that feeds the back-up light.

In all the roll pan takes about two hours to install. Painting and steel preparation work is additional. But for a professional finish the roll pan should be carefully sanded, primed and painted with the same type paint as the truck body.

The inside of the roll pan shows the recessed taillight holder and outside edge. Two bolts hold the roll pan to the vehicle on each side.

To install the new steel roll pan, remove the old bumper and taillight wiring sockets (these are plugged into the fender). At this point, only one bolt has been attached.

Close-up photo of the roll pan shows how it's mounted to the truck. The two holes above the roll pan are the sockets for the old wiring.

In this photo the two bolts are in place and tightened, and the wiring for the taillights has been connected. Simply press the connector into the old wiring spot and the lights are connected to the vehicle's wiring system.

Custom roll pans to fit most pickups are available from Bill's Custom Louvering and other manufacters (see Appendix).

Headlight covers

An easy and inexpensive way to improve the appearance of the front end is to install headlight covers. These make the headlights flush with the front body line of the truck, improving aerodynamics somewhat and appearance at the same time.

The headlight covers described here are the Euro Lens covers from Extang Corporation in Ann Arbor, Michigan, and can be applied to most new mini and full-size pickups. These are held to the headlight frame (bezel) on the inside edge using

Velcro strips. The strips are first attached to the headlight bezel, then the headlight cover is slipped over the Velcro for a tight fit.

Using Velcro strips is a much better way to attach the headlight covers than using screws. The thin, fragile headlight bezel was not made to take screws, and if you use a screw-mounted cover the bezel will eventually crack and need to be replaced. The job is rather simple but must be done carefully and precisely so the headlight cover will appear flush with the truck's front end when installed.

Before buying headlight covers there are several things to keep in mind. One is that in all states it is illegal to drive with the tinted or smoked (dark)

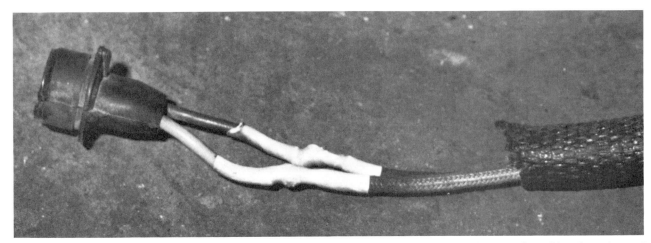

To connect new oval taillights to your wiring system, simply cut the old wires and solder the new ones on. The heat-shrink tubing will cover the soldered sections of wiring to prevent corrosion.

Place three Velcro strips on the bottom and three on the side for each headlight cover. This is for the double-beam Chevy pickup headlight.

headlight covers on at night. You can install the headlight covers for show only. And in California, all headlight covers are illegal. In most states it is legal to drive with them on during the day, and it may or may not be legal to drive with the clear covers on at night.

Also, trucks can vary a great deal in the design of the headlight frame around the light. This makes for a different type of installation as well as a different size and shape of headlight cover.

For example, with the truck shown here, a 1988 Chevy full-size pickup, there are two styles of headlight cover available. One size, a much wider one, fits the double or twin headlight system. With this system, there are four headlights up front.

Next, carefully slide the Velcro edge of the headlight cover over the Velcro until it's held by the Velcro tabs on the bezel. Use a credit card to disengage the Velcro if it needs repositioning.

When the brights are switched on, all four lights are turned on. With the more common dual light system there is only one headlight and it has a regular and bright beam combination. Keep this in mind, as well as the style of grille you might have, when you order headlight covers.

Extang's Euro Lens was chosen because it is made of acrylic plastic that is seven times stronger than glass, and it is also clearer than glass. The Euro Lens is also twice as thick as most other headlight covers, one-eighth inch versus one-sixteenth found on most others. This gives additional protection from gravel and other highway hazards. The Euro Lens also has a unique rubber frame that protects the edge of the lenses and gives a more finished look.

Extang Euro Lens will fit these vehicles:
• Chevrolet: 1982–88 El Camino, 1988 big pickup and Blazer with dual lights, 1988 big pickup and Blazer with quads, 1988 S-10, S-15 pickups and S-10 Blazer
• Dodge: 1981–85 full-size pickup, 1986–88 full-size pickup
• GMC: 1988 big GMC pickup with quad lights, 1988 big GMC pickup with dual lights
• Jeep: 1986–88 Jeep Commando and Wagoneer
• Mazda: 1986–88 Mazda pickup
• Toyota: 1987–88 US-style Toyota pickup, 1987–88 import-style pickup

Installation on a Chevy pickup

1. The first step in installing headlight covers is to thoroughly clean the headlights and bezels. Make sure they're clean, and then dry them completely. Wipe the area inside the bezel (where the Velcro will be attached, see photo) with alcohol to make sure there's no grease present.

2. Place four or five Velcro tabs on the bottom of each headlight bezel. Place the long side of the tabs one-quarter inch in from the outer edge of headlight bezel as in the photo.

3. Place four or five Velcro tabs on the top of each headlight bezel one-quarter inch from the edge, as in step 2. In some installations there may be Velcro tabs on the sides or there may not. To see if you need Velcro tabs installed on the sides also, see if there's the fuzzy Velcro on the rubber frame. Remember, Velcro has two parts, the fuzzy fabric and hooked, rougher side. The rougher side is what goes on the bezel and the fabric is built into the rubber frame of the headlight cover. If there's no fuzzy Velcro on the sides of your headlight covers, you don't need to install any Velcro tabs on the sides.

4. If you do need to install Velcro tabs on the sides, place three Velcro tabs on each side.

5. Insert the bottom of the headlight cover into the headlight opening.

6. Tilt the cover back into place and firmly place it in position. You can use a credit card to

prevent the Velcro from grabbing until it's in the proper position. With a little practice you'll have the covers fitting perfectly.

Installation on a Chevy S-10

The Chevy S-10 uses a different type of lens cover. This does not use a rubber gasket around the outside edge, as the pickup lens already described does. Instead, it is a solid acrylic one-piece wraparound design. This design only requires the use of three Velcro attaching points: one on the bottom, one on the side and one on the top horizontal edge, as in the photos. This makes for a tight, easy installation.

Maintenance

Do not wash the truck with the headlight covers installed. Remove them and wash the truck separately. Avoid wiping the headlight covers often. Although the acrylic plastic material is fairly scratch resistant, like a windshield it will eventually show scratches the more you wipe it. To clean the headlight covers, use a mild soap or plastic cleaner (be sure it's made for acrylic plastic) and wipe gently. Do not use abrasive cleaners, gasoline, solvents or other automotive cleaners. To remove

This photo shows the Chevy pickup with the Extang Euro Lens tinted headlight cover installed. It's a clean, snug fit that will stay put at highway speeds.

tar, use naptha or kerosene. You can protect them with automotive wax.

Remember, the tinted (dark) covers cannot be used with the headlights on. In many states you

This 1986 Datsun 720 pickup has custom-made mirrored Plexiglas headlight covers. They match the chrome bumper perfectly. Mirrored Plexiglas is expensive and *difficult to work with, but this job was beautifully done by Randy Fritz of Indianapolis, Indiana.*

may be able to leave the clear lenses on, but first check with state highway regulations.

Tonneau cover

Why include tonneau covers in a chapter about aerodynamics? Simple. Because tonneau covers, like most other accessories, do two things: 1) they provide a better appearance to a pickup and keep the inside of the bed cleaner, and 2) by covering up the box they reduce the air drag caused by the air being trapped in the pickup box. When you travel down the highway at even, slow speeds of 30 mph or so, the air blows over the front, over the cab, and then swirls down into the bed and gets trapped by the tailgate in the bed.

A tonneau cover reduces (but doesn't totally eliminate) the drag caused by the pickup box by smoothing out the surface of the box. Of course there are different ways of installing a tonneau cover, and some are more rigid than others. Many truck owners try to make their own cover and use a piece of plywood under a piece of vinyl.

When they're finished, they find out that there's more to a good tonneau cover than looks. It

has to be tightly anchored to the side rails and tailgate. This is because a very strong suction effect is created by the wind passing over the tonneau cover at highway speeds. One truck owner I know had the tonneau cover sucked off the back of his Chevy S-10 by the wind at 55 mph. This can be very dangerous to people driving behind you: imagine the damage a large piece of three-quarter-inch plywood can cause when it hits a car windshield!

What you need is a system of installing the tonneau cover that will hold it onto the box at highway speeds, but will allow it to be easily removed for access to the box. One of the best solutions to this system is the Extang Corp. Tuff Tonno sport rail system. This uses an aluminum rail screwed to the inside box flange to hold the tonneau down, plus it uses cross ribs to support it. This way you can snap the tonneau cover on in minutes, and remove it just as quickly.

Other tonneau installation systems use Velcro or snaps. Snaps are more difficult to install, require that you drill a large number of holes into the truck body and eventually rust. They are also rather ugly and become an eyesore if you ever decide to per-

This tonneau cover was custom made by HoTTops and installed on a 1988 Ford Ranger. Design was by the truck owner.

manently remove the tonneau. Velcro systems do not hold as well, and there is always some difficulty having it seal tightly at highway speeds. The Extang Corp. Tuff Tonno is available for most pickups, and has stayed on when used by off-road racers at speeds up to 110 mph!

Installation of a John Baker Performance tonneau cover

1. Supplied adhesive-backed Velcro will surround four sides of bed just below top edge. Thoroughly clean a two-inch strip with wax and grease remover to remove any wax, grease and other substances. This is very important for the Velcro to adhere properly.

2. Peel off two inches of Velcro backing to expose adhesive surface. Start at any bed corner by pressing Velcro to surface.

3. Peel backing off as you go, keeping Velcro reasonably tight, and press Velcro firmly in place. Trim off excess at corner, proceed around bed and across tailgate.

4. *Do not attach* tonneau cover for at least twenty-four hours to allow adhesive adequate time to cure. Also, be sure vehicle is left in garage or area where temperature is appropriate for adhesive cure. (See adhesive instructions.)

The Tough Tonneau cover on a Chevy uses the same aluminum rails. These are attached to the sides of the bed so you don't have to drill holes on the outside, exposed sheet metal.

Custom hard tonneau cover

Unless you have a well-made, tight tonneau cover, or have a nice custom-made vinyl tonneau cover that you only use for shows, you will want to eventually have a solid tonneau cover that can be kept permanently on the pickup box. There are

This 1969 Chevy has been dropped and features a custom-made tonneau cover with the Chevy bow-tie logo.

A piece of plywood under the tonneau material gives the entire cover rigidity.

This 1978 Chevy Luv has an unusual hinged and locked tonneau cover made out of a piece of sheet metal placed over plywood. The sheet metal has the same glossy surface as the rest of the truck's body.

some manufacturers that make rigid tonneau covers, but it may be easier (due to the difficulty of shipping something as big as a rigid tonneau cover) to make your own.

These photos give you some ideas. The best way to make your own rigid tonneau cover is to start with a foundation of plywood. This is available in standard four-by-eight-foot sheets. You can also buy plywood faced with oak, mahogany and other veneers. By itself this wood, when stained

The rear of the Luv features a roll pan, two chrome tail pipe tips and an aerodynamic wing.

and covered with a weatherproof urethane finish, will look nice on the truck if wood goes with your truck's interior. If you have a custom oak dashboard then an oak box cover would look great.

Starting with the plywood foundation, you can then use other materials on top of it to go with any style of truck. You can have an upholsterer do a custom-made vinyl top, with a design you specify, or you can have the cover painted to match the truck. The Chevy Luv in these photos has a rigid pickup box cover that's covered with sheet metal, then painted the same color as the truck. The wing on the back makes the whole truck look smooth and aerodynamic.

If you do choose to paint the rigid box cover, it must be covered with sheet metal first so it will look just as smooth and glossy as the rest of the truck. Only sheet metal (or fiberglass) will allow you to use regular automotive paints. Fiberglass is not rigid enough over a large area (unless it's very thick) to remain stiff on the highway. If you use a piece of sheet metal to cover the plywood, you can then stylize the truck with paint graphics or pinstriping, and match the entire truck to the designs on the hood and sides.

The advantage of a rigid top is that you can hinge it to the box rail behind the cab and lock it. This way no one can steal your spare tire, tools and so on. In order for it to be aerodynamic at highway speeds it must be firmly locked down anyway.

6

Exterior changes and modifications: convertible tops and tilt beds

One of the most exciting and radical changes you can make to your compact pickup is to make it into a convertible. When combined with ground effects and body graphics, a nicely done compact pickup is as stylish and sporty as any vehicle on the road, with much less cost.

With a kit from HoTTops of Tempe, Arizona, you can change almost any minipickup into a convertible. The old roof becomes the removable top. HoTTops

Initially, convertible top conversions were popular in California and Arizona, where they were first developed. As the idea became popular, it spread across the country very quickly through exposure in such magazines as *Truckin'*. And as usual, the convertible top conversion is far ahead of what Detroit auto makers are doing with minipickups.

Only one came out with a pickup truck with a convertible top in 1989—Dodge, with its Sport Convertible. The other sport truck makers have yet to make convertible tops available, even though they are very popular.

After their initial wave of popularity, the conversions lost some popularity when it was discovered that some of the tops leaked badly. The conversions worked fine in southern California and Arizona, where it does not rain that often. But in the more northern, midwestern and eastern states, truck owners had many complaints that the tops leaked like sieves.

But most of these leakage problems have been corrected. There is now one reputable conversion kit that can be said to be virtually leakproof. The most weatherproof soft top conversion is made by HoTTops of Arizona. An applications list and description of the kit can be found in this chapter, and the address can be found in the Appendix. Vehicles with this conversion kit have gone through car washes and garden hose soaking tests without leaking scarcely a drop of water.

This is not to say that other conversion kits will not be perfected. There may well be others that are not as popular but are still leakproof. If you want to know how well a conversion keeps out the rain, talk to a person who's installed one. They range from very happy with the conversion to very unhappy because of leaking problems. One truck owner told me that every time it rains, no matter how little, his front seat becomes soaking wet. He's so disgusted that he plans to silicone up the front hardtop seal, cover it with waterproof vinyl and bolt it down!

A lot depends on the quality of the installation. Conversion kits are not easy to install, especially for the beginner. It's something best left to the experienced auto bodyman. Close tolerances have to be followed for the parts to fit, since (with the hardtop and targa top conversion) you reuse your roof and back window frame. Cutting off too much material in the wrong spot (or not making a

The Dodge Sport Convertible, new for 1989, is the only current pickup with a convertible soft top. It folds nicely in the back. The Dodge Sport Convertible is a mid-size pickup.

straight cut) will cause great problems that can only be corrected by purchasing a new roof section, and this is very expensive.

For now, the safest route to go is to stick with these recommended manufacturers and have it installed by an experienced bodyman. It would be even better to have it installed by someone who has done a convertible conversion before, but this is not always possible. Feel free to go with a different manufacturer than those mentioned here, if you know of someone with a weatherproof conversion.

If you want to do a convertible conversion on your truck, you should also be aware of the fact that some trucks are easier to work with than others. Generally, the Japanese trucks have a more solid, reinforced type of rear window frame and roof support. This makes it easier to cut them, since they're more rigid for targa top conversions. Of course, when installing a soft top conversion the quality of the kit is of first consideration. But with hardtops and targas the quality of the vehicle's sheet metal and construction are critical.

Targa tops, soft tops and hardtops

There are three ways to open up your cab to the sun and wind: 1) targa tops, 2) soft tops and 3) hardtops. These conversions are available as kits through several manufacturers. Not all vehicles can be converted. Most minipickups, particularly those manufactured in the last five years or so, can be transformed into convertibles of some sort. Popular minis, such as Nissans and the Chevy S-10, have a number of kits available for them.

Three of the top manufacturers of conversion kits include HoTTops, Pop Top Minis and RATICAL. You will find a list of trucks that can use their convertible top kits later in the chapter.

Targa top conversion

The targa top conversion is a partial hardtop convertible. Instead of cutting out and removing the entire roof and rear window as with the hardtop, the targa top replaces the roof section. Sort of like making the entire roof into a sunroof. The advantage of the targa top is that it keeps more structural strength in the rear window and frame area, and if you own an extended cab mini (which can't use a hardtop conversion) the targa top is the only way to go.

Installation of the targa top involves cutting the roof at the front and rear with a saber saw or reciprocal saw such as a Sawzall. Rubber gaskets are installed on the front and rear joints to make the roof waterproof. It locks down, but can be removed at any time by unlatching the roof section from the inside.

Here's a general description of how to install a HoTTops targa top:

1. Carefully position the templates (cutting guides) on the roof of your vehicle. These will guide you through the cutting operation.

2. Before cutting, do two things: a) loosen the headliner inside the cab and let it hang down in front of the rear window, b) put two equal lengths of duct tape on the roof to protect the painted surface from the Sawzall's guide shoe.

3. Have an assistant watch where the blade is going from below, and also have him hold the roof to keep it from vibrating. Cut the roof with a Saw-

This Chevy S-10 has been made into a convertible using the HoTTops hardtop conversion kit. Note the plastic molding behind the seat.

Above the windshield, the rubber seal extends across the top to keep moisture out of the cab.

123

zall (with fine hacksaw blade) following the lines on the templates.

4. Be careful to cut the cab precisely, particularly at the door frames. The old roof will become the new targa top.

5. Carefully remove the section of sheet metal that has been cut out of the roof. Use an assistant to hold the other side so the paint on the roof won't be scratched.

6. Install the cab support brace over the rear window area to stiffen the sheet metal.

7. Install the rear ABS plastic molding. This will hold the targa top in place in the rear section.

8. Install the female bow and hold-on strip on the front windshield headliner. Screw down with hardware provided.

9. With Sawzall, carefully cut away window frame sections.

10. With tin snips, carefully cut away one-quarter inch of the back of the roof insert. This allows the roof section to fit firmly into the new ABS molding for a tight seal.

11. A stiffener bar is installed inside the targa top roof section to keep it from bending. Now reinstall the headliner on the targa top section, and also trim it to finish it on the rear section of the roof. This can be done by an upholstery shop. Window seals and urethane components are sealed to prevent leaks, and mounting latches are added to finish the conversion.

Applications for HoT Tops targa tops

HoT Tops targa tops are available for the following vehicle models and years. Consult HoT Tops for latest application list.

- Toyota: 1984 to present
- Nissan: 1984 to 1986 (king and standard cab)
- Mazda: 1986 to present
- Mazda/Ford: 1977 to 1985

After the roof is removed, a high-quality molded plastic cap is installed across the back and over to the window. The top fits into the hole that can be seen in the photo for stability.

- Dodge/Mitsubishi: 1987 to present
- Dodge/Plymouth: 1979 to 1986

Applications for HoT Tops hardtops and soft tops

HoT Tops hardtops and soft tops are available for the following models and years. These are complete kits that allow the entire roof and rear window section to be removed, as in the S-10 photos.

- Toyota: 1973 to present (three different kits depending on year of vehicle)
- Nissan: 1984 to present
- Datsun: 1973 to 1983
- Mazda: 1986 to present
- Mazda/Ford: 1977 to 1985
- Dodge/Plymouth: 1979 to 1986
- Dodge/Mitsubishi: 1987 to present
- Dakota: 1986 to present
- Isuzu: 1981 to present (two different kits, depending on year)
- Chevy S-10: 1982 to present
- Chevy Luv: 1981
- Chevy: 1972 to 1980
- Chevy C-10: 1973 to 1987
- Ford Ranger: 1982 to 1988

Hardtop convertible kits by Pop Top Minis, Inc.

Pop Top Minis, Inc. also makes a hardtop convertible kit for many pickups and minipickups.

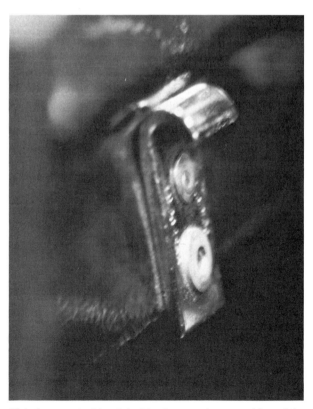

This heavy steel hook holds the rear bottom sides of the hardtop down, while there are also latches above the windshield.

A close-up photo shows how the S-10's engine has been installed in the center of the vehicle. This photo also shows the four-way hydraulic controls. This truck has manual controls: pull the lever to raise and lower the bed. However, electric controls or remote cable controls are also possible.

These kits also keep your vehicle's sheet metal top for use as a convertible top. The kits range from $325 to $375 and include complete instructions, templates and measurements, all sealing parts and hardware, and sealants such as silicone, contact cement and weather-stripping.

The following tools and equipment are needed:

1. reciprocating saw such as Milwaukee Sawzall for cutting the sheet metal accurately
2. drill
3. screwdriver
4. hammer
5. file, utility knife and masking tape
6. socket set
7. tape measure, pencil and scribe
8. cutting pliers and 6-foot straightedge
9. safety glasses

Normal first-time installation time is about ten hours.

Applications for Pop Top Minis convertible conversions

• Toyota: 1974 to 1988, three different kits depending on year
• Mazda: 1986 to 1988
• Dodge: 1979 to 1988, two different kits depending on year
• Mitsubishi: 1979 to 1988, two different kits depending on year
• Nissan: 1984 to 1988

The hydraulic cylinder pulls on the long angled bracket, causing the bed to tilt up. Hydraulic cylinders can be used to push or pull under power.

- Chevy S-10, S-15: 1982 to 1988
- Chevy Luv: 1972 to 1980
- Isuzu: 1981 to 1988

Tilt or lift beds

When you purchase a tilt bed kit, you purchase several expensive items. Chief among these are the hydraulic pump and hydraulic cylinder. The pump supplies the hydraulic pressure needed to actuate the ram, while the ram does the actual lifting of the pickup bed.

There is a way to power your hydraulic ram using your power steering pump. This will be described here in some detail. There are many advantages to doing this. One is that you won't have to buy an expensive hydraulic pump. This is usually a starter motor connected to a hydraulic pump unit. The starter pump runs off of your vehicle's electrical system and powers the pump. Installing this pump involves a lot of extra work: mounting the starter motor and pump to the pickup's frame, then running the electrical connections to your engine compartment. These parts are also expensive.

A cheaper way to achieve the same result is to install a valve on your power steering unit's hydraulic line that will divert the hydraulic fluid under pressure to the rear tilt bed ram. This uses your car engine as the source of power, instead of a starter motor, and runs lines directly to the rear tilt bed ram. The only limitations to this system are that you won't have a great deal of hydraulic pressure, just enough to lift the pickup bed when it's empty. You won't be able to dump a bed full of gravel, if that's your goal. However, if you wish to lift the bed just at custom shows or when on display at the local drive-in, it will work just fine. The other limitation is that since you are using the pressure from the power steering system, you can't drive while tilting the bed. Since virtually all tilt beds are done for custom show trucks anyway, this is not a real concern for anyone building a truck for shows. After all, with the conventional electric hydraulic pump, you won't be tilting the bed while you're driving anyway. The safest way to install this system is to install it on a show truck that is never driven on the highway. For safety reasons, you should not drive any vehicle with a power-steering fed tilt bed on the highway.

Reinard Helder of Helder Manufacturing (see Appendix) has worked out the details of this tilt bed system. You can also purchase tilt bed kits from mail-order supply houses. An excellent source of hydraulic kits and parts for these applications is Low Rider Hydraulics and Custom Accessories in San Jose, California. They have a great deal of experience in designing and installing lift bed kits, and can sell you either an entire kit or any parts you will need. (See Appendix.)

Installation

No matter how you power your lift bed, there are several basic design ideas you must use for a good installation. A lift bed installation involves several key components. One is the actual hydraulic unit, consisting of a source of pressure, a valve and a cylinder. The source of pressure must be a high-quality pump. It can either be electric and be a self-contained system, or it can be your power steering unit (for display trucks only). An average power steering pump produces about 1,500-1,800 psi, enough to lift an empty pickup bed.

The valve is another critical component. There are different types of valves, but the type that's best for a tilt bed is the "four-way" valve. This type, shown in the photo, is used with a "double-acting" cylinder.

The best way to understand a double-acting cylinder is to compare it with a hydraulic floor jack. With a floor jack, you pump the handle to create pressure in the cylinder, raising the jack arm. When you want to lower the jack, you turn a release valve, which releases the pressure and lowers the jack arm.

A double-acting cylinder, the kind you will need with your tilt bed, is different. This cylinder uses pressure *both* ways. It uses pressure to push the rod out of the cylinder, but then it also uses pressure to pull the rod back. (The rod is actually pushed both ways, but the "push-pull" idea is easier to visualize.) So for your tilt bed, you will need pressure to raise it, and pressure to lower it.

With double-acting cylinders there's more power on the push motion, although the rod is strongest on the pulling motion, since the distance traveled by the rod is shorter. To get the maximum strength out of the rod, have the rod pull to lift the bed up (such as the one in the photo) and push to lower the bed.

Once you have all the parts you need, for example, after you have bought the bed lift kit, you need to do several other modifications to your truck for the tilt bed installation. Aside from the hose and electrical connections that will have to be made, you will also have to fabricate a new subframe for the bed, and a hinging system for the bed. The best and strongest way to build a subframe is to make it out of box tubing. This can be done at any good welding-fabricating shop.

To make the measurements, first loosen the bolts that hold the pickup bed to the frame. With two men on each side, lift the bed and carefully remove it from the vehicle. You can remove the tailgate first to make it lighter. Then, measure the distance to the bed mounts, and make these the centers of the two sides of your box frame. Fabricate the box frame first, then add the hinges and mounts. Hinges can be as simple as two tabs of flat iron, with a hole drilled for a pin (or bolt). One tab is bolted to the frame, the other to the box sub-frame of the bed.

It's a good idea to make another set of tabs on the opposite side of the bed. This way, you can bolt or pin down the bed on both sides, making it as secure as the original bed mounts. When the pickup bed is lowered, it will rest on the truck's original frame. If you want to make it nest into the frame securely, build a V-shaped register, such as you see on dump trucks. This involves fabricating two V-shaped sections out of plate steel, one on the box frame, the other on the truck frame. When the bed is lowered, the two V-sections will nest together, mating for a secure fit. You should also include some tabs so the bed can also be bolted down for highway travel.

A V-shaped register is a good idea since it will also keep the bed from rattling on the highway when it's empty. To make your show truck totally rattleproof, design some bed bolt-down mounts that use big rubber washers, the same as those used on body mounts. Keep these under pressure by tightening the bolt going through them, and you'll have a tight, quiet bed for city and highway driving.

Another way to dampen noise is to cut a big mudflap, such as those used on semi-trailers, into strips. Place these under the box frame before it's bolted tight. The rubber gasket will keep everything solid and silent.

The other fabricating work you'll have to do will be to build a bracket for the hydraulic cylinder, and also a mounting spot for the pump, if the power steering pump is not used. The trucks in the photos can give you some ideas about how to do this. Always bolt brackets to the frame, do not weld them if it can be avoided. New frames are heat treated, and the heat given off by welding can weaken them.

Using a power steering pump

Your power steering pump can be used to power a lift bed. This is because most steering

A close-up photo shows how the bed lift was installed. The cylinder is located on a cross-member made of steel tubing mounted inside the frame rails. It has a bolt mount so it can rotate upward as the bed lifts. The bed's sub-frame is made of channel iron and angle iron.

pumps use 1,500-1,800 psi, enough to lift an *empty* bed. To install a bed lift using your power steering pump, you will need the following parts:

1. Four-way valve. This is fed by the high-pressure line coming from the power steering pump, with a line going to the power steering box. Two lines from it will go to the cylinder that lifts the bed, since the cylinder is double acting.

2. Hydraulic cylinder, with suitable lift (in inches) to raise the bed, using whatever bracket or

The hydraulic pump, electrically operated, is securely mounted to the frame, part of it going just under the cab. Electric switches can also be used to raise and lower the bed.

This Toyota pickup has a bed that tilts in dump-truck style to the rear.

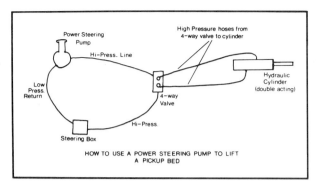

*Use a four-way valve and double-acting hydraulic
cylinder to operate a tilt bed from a power steering
pump. If you have manual steering, just add a power
steering pump for the hydraulics. Or, you can add a
second power steering pump to your vehicle.*

"arm" you have designed to lift the bed. See the
photos for some examples.

3. Brackets for mounting the four-way valve,
lifting arm and so forth, and hoses for all connections. Hoses must be rated at about 4,000 psi for
safety.

The basic idea behind this power-steering
powered design is that the hydraulic pressure from
the power steering pump is diverted, with the four-
way valve, to the hydraulic cylinder. Two high-
pressure lines must go to the cylinder for the
power-up, power-down action. You will need to
add about three to four quarts of hydraulic fluid to
the system, but you will not need a bigger hydraulic
fluid reservoir. This is because the four-way valve
and double-acting cylinder always work under
pressure. There is no "drain" mode or pressure
release valve that will release fluid for storage.

When the four-way valve is not open, it is
solidly shut, and fluid under pressure is automatically diverted to the power steering box. However,
for safety reasons, you should not install this type
of system on a vehicle driven on the highway. It's
best when used on a vehicle for show.

If you have a show truck, you can also use this
type of setup (with a kit from Low Rider Hydraulics) to build a hydraulic system that will lower
your show truck to the ground at custom truck
shows. This will give you an extra-low lowrider, one
that will definitely be lower than other trucks.
When the show is over, start the engine and use the
cylinders to raise the truck up so you can drive it
onto a trailer for the trip home. It is not legal to
drive a vehicle suspended by hydraulic cylinders.

There is one safe way to use this system and
still drive your truck around on the street. This is
possible if your truck has manual steering. You can

then add a power steering pump and use the
engine to power the hydraulic bed lift only when
needed.

If you have an older pickup, or a truck where
power steering was optional, then it would be
inexpensive to simply go to a wrecking yard, get the
power steering pump bracket and hub off of an
engine like yours, and then add it to your engine.

You need to drive the pump with a belt. This
can be run off the crankshaft, or you can add a
double pulley to your alternator, since you'll only be
using the power steering pump occasionally.

If you have enough room on your engine, you
can install a second power steering pump (rebuilt
steering pumps are not that expensive) on your
engine. This one can be used only for the tilt bed,
while the other one can remain as it is for running
the power steering.

The main rule to remember is that the power
steering pump can only run one thing at a time;
either the bed lift cylinder or the steering box, not
both. And you should *never* (with the power steering setup) lift the bed while the truck is moving.

To summarize, there are several different ways
to power a bed lift system. These are:

1. With a bed lift kit with independent hydraulic pump and lines.

2. With a system that runs off the high-pressure side of your power steering pump.

3. If you have manual steering, you can install
a power steering pump on your engine and use that
exclusively to lift the bed.

4. You can add a second power steering pump
to lift just the bed. This has to be completely independent of the steering pump and box, with its own
belt and hoses.

5. You can lift the bed by hand with a manually operated hydraulic pump. These are available
war surplus for about $15 to $50, depending on
how big the pump is. This type of setup will use a
one-way cylinder rather than the double acting.
The double acting can be used, with a valve
installed on the lines going from the hand pump to
divert the pressure from one hose to the other. All
of these systems (except the hand pump) require
the same type of hydraulic lines, four-way valve
and double-acting cylinder.

Helder Mfg. is an excellent source for all the
parts you'll need to complete this project. You can
also get custom-made steel parts, such as hinges,
lifting arms and so forth, from Helder Mfg. Low
Rider Hydraulics is the best source for hydraulic
parts, kit and hinges. Of course, a great way to build
a tilt bed would be to consult a welding-fabricating
shop that also works with hydraulics. Their experience and expertise will make the job much easier.

7

Body graphics

Since the 1950s, American car owners have customized, stylized and individualized their vehicles with paint work. And for good reason. All cars come from the factory looking the same. Sure there are some "custom options" such as the type of upholstery fabric, color of the vehicle and so on.

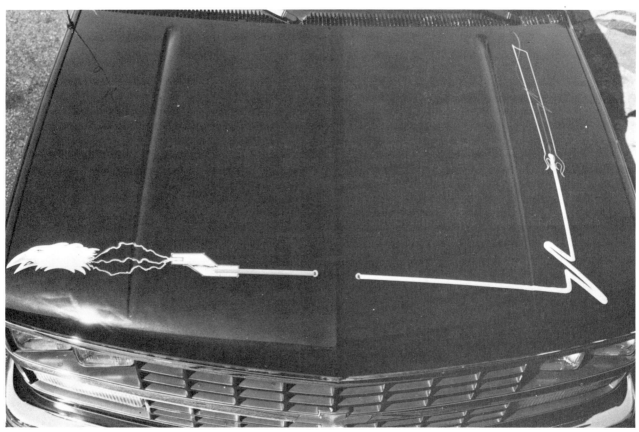

This Chevy hood displays what "Billy the Kid" calls the "history of truck graphics." On the top right are the beginning of pinstriping: fine lines and varied colors. Next are the neon tubes, and finally, an elaborately painted design of an eagle's head. Note that the design fills only two sides of the hood; this makes it asymmetrical. Also, it uses a variety of colors (Billy once pinstriped a truck using 42 different colors!).

This Nissan features some beautiful body graphics work as well as ground effects kit by HoTTops.

But these are still installed by the factory and have that factory look.

With sport trucks there is a whole new revolution and interest in vehicle artwork. Not since the "van art" of the 1970s has there been such an explosion in body paint and graphic art as you now see in lowriders. But the type of graphic art design and style used for lowriders is not the same as was used in vans. There are several important differences. You have to understand what these differences are to know why vans and lowriders require different painting techniques.

The biggest difference is in the size of the vehicles. Vans had large, flat surfaces that were seen at eye level. These were then used as "canvases" by airbrush artists to make large colorful murals. These murals often included mountain lakes, city skylines and other large and detailed subjects.

But lowriders are much smaller, lower and have long narrow sides. You can't paint large murals and have the truck look good. Consequently, good lowrider art is more subtle and sophisticated. There's nothing wrong with using murals, airbrushing and the other techniques that

This 1985 C-10 Silverado is painted using both pinstripes and a neon tube "zapped" down the side.

A close-up of the Silverado shows how the neon tube design was used as a "focal point" to bring the eye to the door, where there are fine pinstripes and the word Silverado.

have been around for a long time. But the design ideas you'll find in this chapter are considered to be the best, and have been created by the most respected truck painters and graphic artists in the country.

Everyone wants the California look on their lowrider truck. What is the California look, and how do you get your truck to look this way? These questions will be answered in this chapter. In reality, the California look is the look found in the trucks featured by magazines published in California, like *Truckin'* magazine. But the California look was partially created in Arizona, Texas, Kentucky, Oregon and Indiana, as well as other areas.

This is because places like Arizona have pioneered items such as the convertible top conversion (through the company HoTTops). The Quickor (distributed by Warn Industries) ground effects kits were developed in Oregon, and they were one of the first. Bell Super Tech in California did a lot of early work on lowering kits.

Another major reason for the great variety of paint styles found in sport trucks is the great vari-ety of trucks themselves. There are stock trucks, stock custom, lowriders, customs and minis. For many people the design and style melt together into the California or New Wave look.

The body lowering, aerodynamics and body graphics all contribute to the California lowrider look, but in this chapter we'll talk about only one aspect—the body graphics.

This chapter will also cover in detail the body paint, paint graphics, graphic decals, pinstriping, window tinting and neon lighting accents that you can put on your truck.

Body paint work

There are two kinds of body paint work that can be done to beautify and individualize your truck. These are 1) pinstriping and 2) paint graph-

This louvered tailgate, installed on a 1967 GMC pickup, was painted to go with the truck's overall color scheme and design.

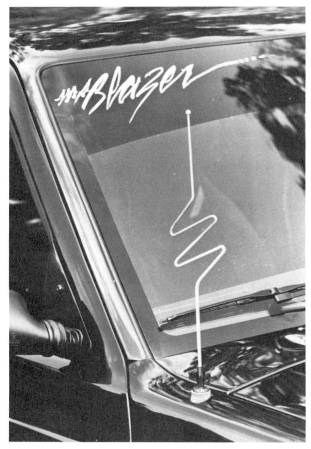

This 1987 S-10 Blazer has an antenna bent by Main Street Graphics in Indianapolis, and the word Blazer stylishly painted on the window. It also has some window tinting.

The striped paint scheme is followed up and over the pickup bed.

Next, the paint scheme follows the rear window, breaking for the louvered rear window cover.

ics. Pinstriping is the use of fine handpainted lines and designs applied by brush. The most common form this work takes is scrolls, flourishes and body accents. It is also possible to enlarge pinstriping to include some abstract art and geometric designs, as you'll see later.

Paint graphics is similar in that it uses color to beautify a truck's appearance, but is different in that paint graphics are applied with a spray gun and cover larger areas. Also, paint graphics involve the extensive use of masking and color overlays to achieve different paint schemes, designs and creative effects.

Using an airbrush is a way to obtain fine shading, contrast and lines in paint graphics, but the

Finally, the painted stripes follow over the roof to the hood, where they end in a winged silhouette graphic design.

huge van-type murals are generally considered inappropriate for minipickups and are not accepted as part of the California look of current lowrider art.

Of course you can do whatever you like with your truck, and there's no one who can tell you what to like or dislike.

Here's a short list comparing pinstriping and paint graphics:

Pinstriping
- less expensive
- larger areas covered
- more intricate designs
- use names for focal points
- gaudy if too big

Paint graphics
- more materials, higher price
- brighter colors used (candies)
- more confined areas to work

Design concepts for lowriders

Because minipickups have a long, low profile there are certain designs that will look better on them than others. Keep in mind that when you look at a lowrider you are looking *down* at the vehicle's hood and sides. You are able to see the whole hood at once, something you can't do with full-size pickups with 40 in. tires and a lift kit.

So the paint graphics and pinstriping have to be more subtle and more sophisticated. You have to learn a different set of design ideas for minis than for big pickups and vans. One custom painter whose designs are widely recognized as being creative and original is Billy Christine, or "Billy the Kid," of Main Street Graphics in Indianapolis, Indiana. Eight years ago, for example, he first painted neon tubes down the sides of the trucks. Three years ago he was doing pinstriped graphic designs on trucks, before most magazines even thought of featuring minis with that type of graphics. And his work has been widely imitated by painters in California and other parts of the country. Billy the Kid is also able to articulate and share his creativity with others, and doesn't mind teaching other people how to create their own designs.

He has given these guidelines for painting lowriders. They give a good idea of how to lay out a graphic design, but the best way is to actually see his work in the photos of this book. From them you can get an excellent idea of what he means by "focal point," "composition" and other ideas.

Billy says, "Graphics should start and stop. There's a beginning and an end. Between these is a 'focal point,' a point where the eye catches a logo, abstract design, or dry brushed area. It can also be a small picture if it's done properly. The focal point should stand out from the rest of the graphic and catch the eye.

"The focal point can be used to achieve different effects. For example, if you have a short truck and you want to make it look longer, move the focal

This 1987 black Blazer uses a neon tube on the side and fine pinstriping in its subtle body graphics.

point toward the rear of the truck. This will give a longer line for the eye to follow from the front. Also, a long truck can be made shorter by moving the focal point forward. This will give it a shorter length before it's broken up by the focal point.

"Composition, or lack of composition, is where people make the biggest mistakes. They think, 'hey, this looks great, let's do more!' They don't know when to stop. Usually, less is better than more. A truck is not a signboard, so don't paint it like a sign. Pinstriping and paint graphics should enhance the truck's appearance, not distract you from it by being too busy. New Wave art is great, but many people who like it carry it too far. A 'wave' should not be just a big splash down the side of a truck. It should be part of the truck.

"Another mistake is to follow a body line with a paint graphic or pinstriping. The problem is you're then tied into the body line so you can't leave it. I once painted a hood on the body line, but then was forced to follow it.

"Hoods look best when painted *asymmetrically.* The best way to understand what asymmetrical means is to understand what symmetry is. Symmetry is the likeness of two sides to each other. The right side is *exactly* like the left. Sides that are symmetrical are mirror images of each other. That's not what you want. Here's how to paint asymmetrically: paint only one corner and have it come down a side, or paint only one corner and part of one side. This will look better than trying to decorate the truck like a signboard. Truck hoods don't need to be filled up, neither do the sides. A subtle graphic is always more powerful than a big

one that fills up the side. You don't have to balance out a composition on a hood or side. It's okay just to paint one corner of the hood, or part of the side, it's all in how it's done.

"When I paint a truck I try to get to know the truck owner, if he or she is into cruising or off-road driving, or is more conservative. I won't paint a woman's truck the same as a man's if she doesn't want me to. She might want to enhance her femininity with the truck, and that's fine. In fact, the key to success is to make a lady's truck look like a lady's

Close-up photo of the focal point of the truck's body graphics. The neon tube is pink and the pinstripes medium blue, with the Blazer in light green.

This 1983 S–10 Pro Street is owned by Main Street Graphics and has a 1969 Chevy V–8 engine as well as graphics by Billy the Kid.

truck. If you can do that, you're in on all the others. I do what I feel will both please the customer and enhance the appearance of the truck.

"But don't get the idea that I categorize people into male or female, or use any other categories. Every time I paint a truck it's different, and I really don't know what will work on the truck until I actually do it. I've done good work on trucks and wiped it off because I didn't feel it suited the truck."

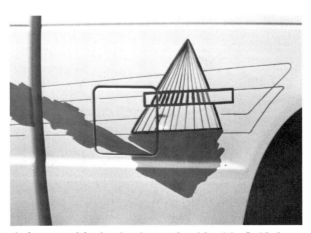

A close-up of the focal point on the side of the S–10 shows the design, which was done in shades of pink and purplish green.

The fine stripes come from behind the front wheel, as they're wrapped by rough pink brush strokes which end in the abstract design.

Every custom painter is different and does things in a slightly different way. But these general design ideas are what is considered to be the best for minipickups, and if you look at trucks that are painted well you'll find that these concepts are in the truck even if the painter or truck owner wasn't aware of them.

Here's some general guidelines for how to do pinstriping and paint graphics. These techniques won't make you a master without years of practice, but they'll give you a good idea of how to do your own paint graphics if you're already familiar with a paint gun and have painted some cars, or you want to try simple pinstriping.

Pinstriping

In some ways pinstriping is easier than paint graphics, because it requires less equipment and masking work, and the paint is less expensive. But pinstriping requires a steady hand and can get as difficult as you want to make it. If you want to try out some ideas, though, this section will help you get some good results. The good thing about pin-

This painted "Pro Street Mini Truck" logo has an abstract design behind it and window tinting. It's another creative way to individualize a truck with paint graphics.

striping is you can always get some paint thinner and wipe off your mistakes! So you can try different ideas without doing any harm to your truck's factory paint job.

Another creative way to paint a name on your truck. This is Billy the Kid's Main Street Graphics truck. There's pinstriping and fine airbrushing (as well as a minutely drawn skyline inside the letters) with "graphics" airbrushed on.

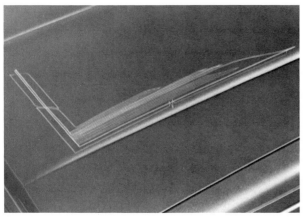

Here's an example of an asymmetric hood. It's only painted in the bottom right corner, using an amazingly fine set of extremely fine lines. These lines draw the attention of the viewer to the design. The hood becomes a painted object, not just a billboard for a mural or symmetrical design.

The basic enamel paint for pinstriping is the 1 Shot brand. It comes in half-pint sizes in a great variety of colors. The Eastwood Co.

Equipment

The basic equipment you'll need to do pinstriping includes the paint, solvents and brushes. You'll also need layout tools which include a wooden yardstick, grease pencil, one-foot ruler and different kinds of masking tape. The layout tools are essential for laying out the design and keeping the paint within your design boundaries. The layout tape is not essential when you're good. In fact, old-time painters thought that using tape to make straight lines was a cop-out, only done by amateur painters. If you're a pro, you should be able to paint a straight line all the way down a truck's side by hand. If you're an amateur, then use tape to make a straight line. It's the only way you can do it!

Billy the Kid uses basic 1 Shot commercial sign painter's paint. There are various brands of commercial sign painter's paint and a pure acrylic enamel is best. This comes in a small number of basic colors. If you want a variety of different shades of purple or blue, for example, you have to mix your own using the base 1 Shot paint colors. The best way to mix your own paint colors is to mix

them in small baby food bottles. These small bottles are big enough to contain a workable amount of paint but small enough to handle and mix easily.

The paint is rather thick when it comes out of the can, so you have to mix it with a little Penetrol, a small amount of Smoothie (a leveling additive) and paint thinner. A little experience will show how thin the paint should be for various effects. For extremely fine lines, thin the paint more. Keep in mind that light colors such as white, yellow and pink require two coats. The paint is rather transparent and with only one coat you won't get a solid color.

For fine line work, the brushes Billy the Kid uses are Dominican reds, which are extremely fine and sharply pointed brushes. The paint bristles are actually longer than the handle. Using these brushes requires a smooth stroke and steady hand,

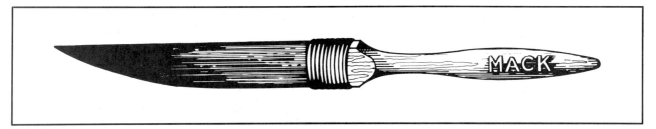

Another basic popular tool is the long "sword" brush. It's extremely useful for painting thin, even lines. The Eastwood Co.

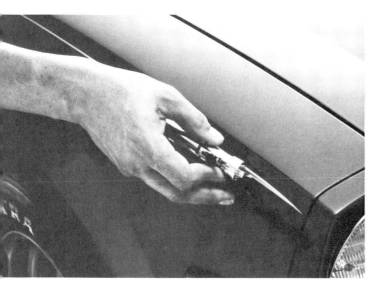

An accurate way to paint fine lines is with the Beugler tool available from The Eastwood Co. It uses a variety of different-size wheels to transfer paint to the vehicle. Wheel head sizes range from ⅟₆₄ to ⅛ inch. The Eastwood Co.

but remember, you can always erase your mistakes with a rag damp with paint thinner.

Good pinstriping work requires a mastery of masking tape skills. Tape is available in different widths, with different widths and numbers of masked lines. Basically, there are two kinds of tape, depending on whether you're going to lay guide-

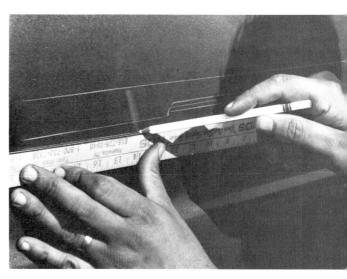

The grease pencil is then used to make fine lines for the curved sections and fine pinstriping.

lines, or paint up against the tape. The tape that you use for painting is tackier.

Another way to lay down stripes is with the Beugler tool, featured here in a photo. It's available from the Eastwood Company, and is an excellent way to lay out fine lines. It may or may not be easier to use than a brush and tape, depending on your skill. However, it does offer another technique for painting pinstripes.

Laying out a design

To begin pinstriping design work, first wash the vehicle thoroughly and make sure it's dry. You can start laying out a design idea directly on the

To begin laying out a design on a truck's sides, don't hesitate to draw directly on the paint. Use a grease pencil, since any mistakes can be easily wiped off with a dry cotton cloth. Here Billy the Kid uses a wooden yardstick (wood is best because it doesn't scratch) and a grease pencil to rough-in horizontal lines.

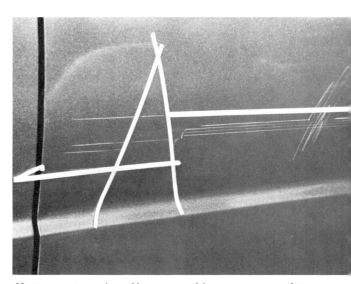

Next, narrow strips of layout masking tape are used to mark out the edges that will be painted by hand brush. The triangle shape is the basic outline for a geometric design.

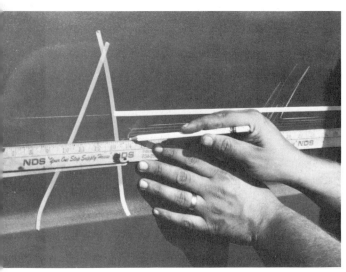

Next to the geometric design, more fine lines are marked out with the grease pencil. At this point, Billy is just experimenting and seeing how things will look.

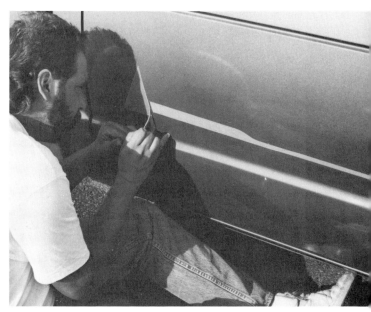

After painting some of the horizontal lines, he begins to paint the triangle-shaped geometric design.

vehicle's paint with a grease pencil available at art stores such as the Schwan Stabilo. This pencil is available in different colors, depending on the color of the truck's paint, and will help you draw out squares, triangles, swirls, flames, waves and so on without putting any paint on the truck.

The grease pencil can be painted over, and after the paint is dry, the other guidelines can be wiped off with a soft cloth. If you don't like the design you've made, you can wipe it all off and start over again. A wooden yardstick is good for tracing out straight lines with the grease pencil, since the

soft wood won't scratch the truck's paint or the metal.

When laying out a design, you may first want to try something on paper, but don't hesitate to go right out to the truck with a grease pencil and start marking it out. Working on the truck itself will also give you a better idea of how the graphics will

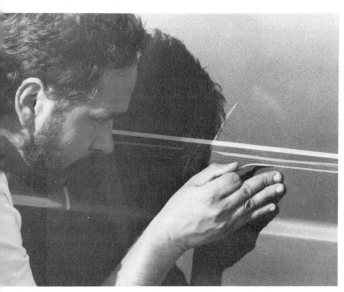

With a fine pinstriping brush, Billy begins to paint in the horizontal lines of the design.

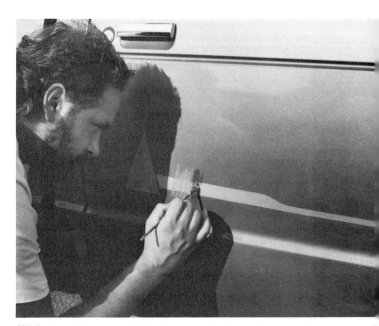

With the "dry brush" technique (using thick paint) Billy accents the geometric design with brush strokes. This will be the focal point of the design.

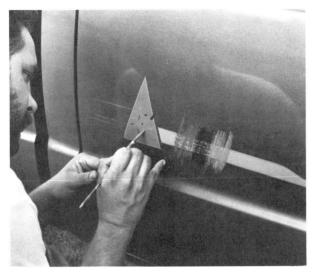

Billy adds dabs of different colors inside the triangle.

Finally, Billy paints along the other side of the triangle, and will follow this line down to the rear of the truck. Putting the focal point on the door makes the truck seem longer.

actually appear on the vehicle, and gives a better sense of scale and perspective.

Pinstriping traditionally uses the striping tape, which is actually two layers of tape. First the tape is applied to the vehicle, then the outer cover is lifted out, revealing two stripes that can be filled in by brush. Other kinds of masking tape are available that can lay out four or six extremely fine lines, but these are better suited for spray painting.

One commonly used pinstripe style is the Fresno quarter line. This is a stripe one-quarter inch wide with fine borders on each side, the borders are a different color than the stripe. The advantage of the Fresno quarter line is that it is wide enough to cut across the body lines and dis-

This 1985 C–10 Silverado features a neon tube and pinstriping.

Here's a beautifully painted 1988 S-10 Chevy painted in neons with some abstract designs.

tract the eye from the factory shape of the body. You can use it to break up or accent body lines. You can also paint zig-zag or rough lines and then border them with fine pinstripes.

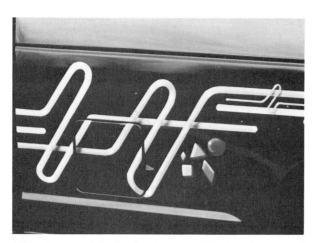

This close-up of the focal point shows the use of neons and abstract designs. The artist kept to the rules of neon tube painting: don't make sharp turns, and airbrush to achieve a 3-D effect.

Another way to break up a body line is with a painted neon tube. This is just a neon tube painted on the side of the truck. When you paint neon tubes, you have to remember that the neon tube you are trying to portray has certain characteristics. One is that most neon used in commercial neon signs is seven millimeters wide. Neon comes in millimeter sizes, and seven is the standard. Another thing is that there are only two real colors in neon lights, red and blue. These two colors can be combined to make pink. Every other color you see is obtained by using colored glass.

Another limitation to neon, besides the colors and width, is the shape. Since neon lights are bent glass tubing, the bends are usually gentle and have a somewhat large radius. So don't make sharp pointed zig-zags out of neon tubing on a vehicle's side. It just won't look like neon, since everyone knows neon has gentle curves and bends.

Neon should look like it flows down the side of a truck, and flows around the corners. Don't make extremely straight lines or sharp bends, they just won't look right. After the neon tube is painted, highlight the edges with a slightly darker color; a darker blue, for example, if the neon is light blue. This will make it look like a blue tube. Also, when

Here's another design for a focal point. In this one a stripe is zapped into a neon tube, then zapped back to a stripe that follows the length of the truck.

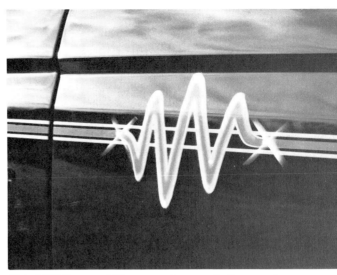

This 1988 Ranger GT has a stock ground effects package, but paint graphics have been added on the hood and sides.

you're finished with the paint work you can use an airbrush and spray a fine white line on the top one third of the tube. This is one way to use airbrushing to accent the work, and will make the tube look three dimensional. The best airbrush for the job is made by Paasche. Two of their airbrushes are shown in the photos.

A careful look at the trucks in these photos will give you some idea of how creative (and difficult) pinstriping can become. It's one form of painting that's definitely limited only by the creativity of the painter.

Paint graphics

Pinstripes are one technique of applying paint to a truck body, but paint graphics are another widely used technique that can be used to achieve different effects. Paint graphics are very popular, and are used extensively by owners of 4X4s and vans, probably because the spray painting involved is familiar to many painters, who use spray guns everyday in body shops. The real artistic touch comes in when the design, layout and overlaying of colors is used to create beautiful effects.

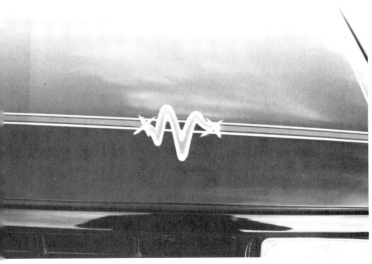

A close-up of the hood shows how it's been done in three stripes (the center stripe is the largest) with a graphic neon "zap" in the lower right corner. This asymmetric location breaks up the monotony of the stripes and gives more excitement to the graphics. A similar, larger graphic design is on the door.

To do your own airbrush work you can get started with this H set featuring the single-action external mix H airbrush. Paasche

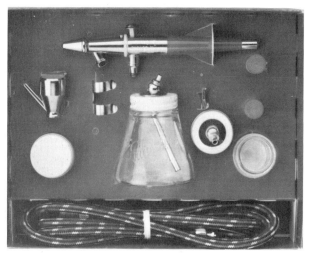

The VL model Paasche airbrush is available in this kit which contains everything but paint and a compressor. Great for doing neons and abstract art on trucks. Paasche

Begin laying out the areas to be spray painted by using masking tape. First, thin strips of masking tape are laid out horizontally. Note the curve over the rear wheelwell. This will later prove to be an important part of the paint graphic design.

When using paint graphics, you have to keep the limitations of the technique in mind. Remember that with pinstriping you are mainly using fine lines, but paint graphics use large panels or wide stripes of paint. Whereas with pinstriping you are enhancing the lines with color, with paint graphics you are enhancing the colors by giving them *shape*.

Although you can make extremely fine stripes and points with pinstriping, with paint graphics you have to end a section of paint with a width of at

least two inches. This is because the paint will peel off if tapered to a point. This one fact will limit some of your design ideas. You also have to cover the paint with clear when you're finished, and this requires additional masking.

Paint graphics share some basic design concepts with pinstriping, but these are also a little different. For example, with paint graphics there is also a focal point, but it is where the line of paint

Here's the "before" shot of the Chevy pickup painted in this sequence of photos. The plain black sides look boring. But they'll soon look much different.

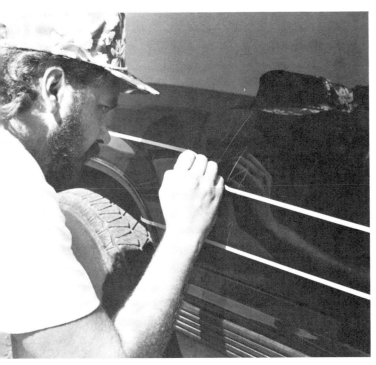

Now Billy is marking out a "torn" effect using a grease pencil. Using a grease pencil helps him try out new ideas without laying down any paint.

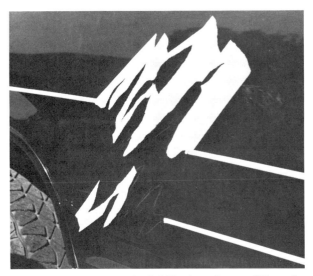

Next, to achieve a torn look Billy ripped some 3M masking tape into pieces and stuck them to the side of the truck.

curves up in front of the rear wheelwell. If it's a long bed, you can shorten the visual length of the truck by moving the paint curve forward, closer to the door. If you have a short bed and you wish to make it look as long as possible, move it back toward the wheelwell. This idea is easier to understand by looking at the photos in this section.

Basic steps

You must remember that although with pinstriping you are laying down specific lines and designs, with paint graphics you are doing a different type of painting work: you are laying down areas of color whose shape is defined only by the tape masking you do. Since you're using a spray gun rather than a fine brush, the paint is covering broad areas at one time. This is the basic concept behind paint graphics and becomes very important when working with candy paints where you are applying layer after layer of paint and the layers combine with each other to create different colors and effects.

There are seven basic steps that must be followed when creating paint graphics. Some of these steps involve a lot more time and work than others:

1. Wash the truck thoroughly and dry with a chamois to prevent any water spots.

2. Clean the area you plan to paint by wiping it with Prep-Sol, Pre-Clean or some other automotive cleaning solvent. This will remove any wax, grease or oil from the existing body paint.

3. Carefully lay out the outline of the design scheme you have in mind. At this point, you're only interested in the outside boundaries of the design. Allow one-quarter inch on all sides for the clear (which will be applied last) to cover all the paint work.

4. Scuff sand the existing paint with #1200-1500 ultrafine sandpaper. This will break the surface of the factory paint job and allow the new paint layers to adhere better. After sanding, clean with a tack rag. This should be automotive quality to keep the surface clean.

5. Spray the entire area to be painted (including the area that will be covered with clear) with an adhesion promoter such as DuPont's 222. This will

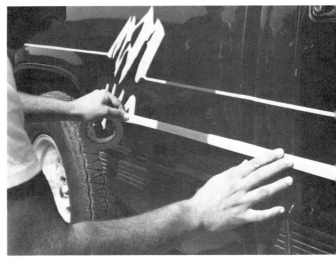

After the torn focal point is masked out, Billy lays wider masking tape down for the spray painting.

The wider masking tape is applied around the torn area as well. This will make it easier for the painter at the bodyshop to paper and tape the truck later.

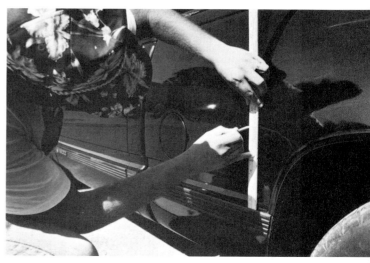

To transfer the design to the other side of the truck, Billy marks the measurements on a wooden yardstick, then marks where they should be located on the blank side of the truck. Mark both sides of the door, and the wheel-wells.

ensure that the subsequent layers of paint will stick better to the original body paint and will last longer. If you are using some other brand of paint, use an equivalent to the DuPont 222 adhesion promoter. After the adhesion promoter is dry, apply masking tape one-quarter inch *over* the area that has been sprayed with adhesion promoter. This is to make sure that the adhesion promoter is under the layer of clear which will be put on last.

6. Mask off the rest of the truck body and apply the layer of basecoat. For light colors, apply white basecoat. If your paint work will be black or

dark blue, use a black basecoat. The basecoat, particularly the white basecoat with candy colors, is essential since it allows the true rich color of the candies to come through.

7. At this point the preparation has been completed and you are now ready to paint the design you have laid out.

Creating designs

There are two basic kinds of paint you can spray to create designs. These are the spray enamels and "candy" paints. The candies, particularly

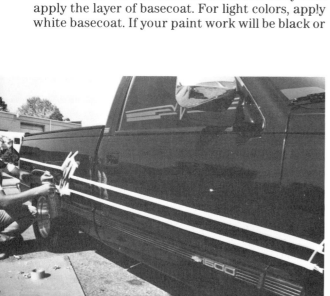

This is how the paint graphic is laid out with all the masking work completed. It takes years of experience to be able to lay out masking tape like this in a perfectly horizontal line by hand.

Using the ruler measurements as guidelines, Billy tapes the first fine lines of masking tape to copy the design to the other side.

The completed tape job (on the other side of the truck) looks like this. Later, the spray painter will add more tape and paper.

the new neon colors, are very popular with low-rider painters. In fact, it is the use of candy neons that sets lowrider paint art apart from that used on vans and 4X4s.

The difference between candies and enamels is that candy paints are tinted clears, where enamels are solid colors. What this means is that the more you layer the candies, the darker and richer the colors get. With enamels, subsequent coats don't change the color. Also, with candies you can lay one color over another and mix them on the truck to

After spray painting on the white basecoat, fine 3M pinstriping tape, with eight lines, is used to mask the side of the truck where a finely lined design will be.

Wide masking tape and paper are laid out on both sides to protect the rest of the truck from overspray.

create a third color. Spray blue on yellow and the color you get is green.

Most candies are either urethane enamels (clear) or lacquers. Either one is good for paint graphics, although the House of Color brand has a good selection of neons, which are now available in six colors. These six colors can be combined to form many others. You can obtain a color chart from House of Color that shows how the colors change when one candy color is applied over another.

Painting with candies becomes a project that must be carefully organized. If you want green to be in the graphic, for example, you must plan how it will be created, since it is the result of painting yellow over blue or blue over yellow. You may have a large section of blue that you want to end in green. Apply the blue first, then cover it with yellow to make the green. You can fade-in the colors by overspraying a little into the blue. But if you want the color to end abruptly you must wait for the blue to dry (so it's dry enough to take masking tape), then tape over the blue and apply the yellow to the section you want to be green.

Applying paint graphics is a difficult process of masking over any part of the truck you *don't* want to be painted, then removing the tape and doing this again. Complicated paint jobs require a dozen or more tape setups and removals. Each time any new color is applied, you have to decide what you want to do with the other colors: should you paint over them and create new hues and colors? Or tape them and make a solid border between colors?

What you do is determined by the design you have created, but you can see that if you don't have a design in mind you can find yourself in trouble when the spray gun is loaded with paint and you're not sure where it will go. This is why spraying candies and creating paint graphics is such difficult work.

It becomes even more difficult since you usually want to match both sides of the truck. You have to apply the same number of coats to each side or the colors won't look right. Candy paints are best applied in thin, even coats. Apply the spray gun in a quick, even motion, and don't hesitate over any point, even for an instant. If you do, the paint will come out darker. Keep a written record of how many coats (or passes) you made over each area, so you can duplicate it on the other side.

If you've created a large graphic, you can match one side of the truck to the other by carefully measuring up from the bottom of the sheet metal with a wooden ruler. Mark the ruler with a grease pencil to help you lay out each side. For example, your graphic might start four inches up from the bottom of the rocker, and stop five inches up the door. While you're doing this, keep in mind the one-quarter inch border you need for clear when it's finished.

If you're just beginning to do your own graphic designs but you have experience using a paint gun, you may want to tape and paper the sides all the way down, then draw out your design with a grease pencil. This will give you some idea of how it will

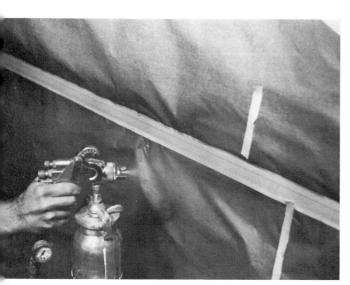

The "candy" paint is applied over the pinstripe tape to achieve the fine lines. Note that the rest of the truck (and the rest of the painted areas) have been covered with tape and paper. Paint graphics require that the unpainted portions be taped and papered for each coat. This is what makes paint graphics such tedious work.

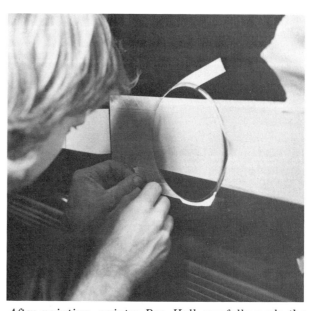

After painting, painter Ron Hall carefully peels the masking tape off the truck. Be careful not to lift off the paint film. Use a razor blade to cut the paint film when necessary. Usually, you won't have to wait more than an hour before removing the masking tape.

Unfortunately, this black and white photo doesn't do justice to the design by Billy the Kid and skillful paint *work of Ron Hall. But you can see how the plain black truck was transformed using paint graphics.*

This full-size Chevy has body graphics on the sides that are made up of nothing but tape. There are six different colors, creating an explosion of color and design down *the side of the truck. It's much easier and quicker to do a truck in tape than in pinstripe paint.*

look. The more time and effort you spend planning out your design, the less trouble you'll have down the road. This is particularly important if you're painting candies, which are much tougher to apply.

When the painting is done, remember that the clear has to be applied within twelve hours. After the clear is properly cured (consult the manufacturer of the clear for drying time) it can be buffed. The clear will bring out the colors, brighten them up and also protect them from weathering. Be sure

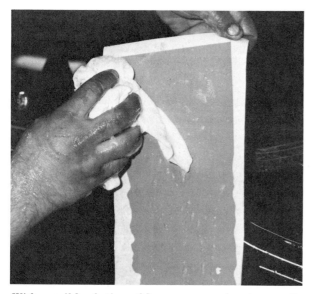

With a mild solution of Ivory soap and water, gently wipe the decal (after it's been separated from the backing). Also make the surface of the truck wet.

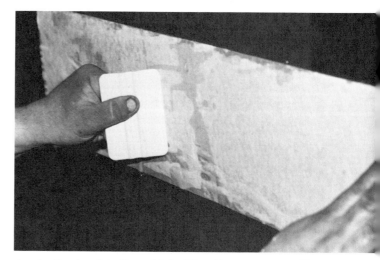

Apply the decal to the vehicle. The slippery soap will enable you to move it around a bit. Then use the plastic squeegee to firmly squeeze out the soap and water from under the decal.

that the clear is the same type of paint as the candy you're using (urethane or lacquer).

Equipment

Body graphics must be applied with a spray gun, but since you're not painting the entire body of a truck, you can use a smaller and less expensive spray gun than is generally used for automotive paint work. A widely used spray gun for general work is the Binks #7. Paasche also makes a gun that's good for small spray work, called the Model 62.

Whatever gun you use, you should make sure it has proper air pressure, a compressor that can keep a steady supply of air and a filter to filter water out of the air before it enters the gun. The slightest amount of water will spit out the gun and ruin an otherwise beautiful paint job.

When mixing paints, particularly candies, be sure to carefully follow the manufacturer's directions for preparation, thinning and mixing. This is because all paints are not the same, and the manufacturer knows how their paint can be applied most effectively.

Decal graphics

The most recent development in body graphics has been in the area of vinyl decals. These are rather large decals (up to three feet long) that can be used either by themselves or in combination with pinstripes (either paint stripes or tape) to create complete body graphic designs on vehicles. The great advantage to decals is that you can select a specific design (such as a palm tree, splash or sunburst) and place it anywhere you like. You can then use the design to enhance pinstripes or just add them to the factory pinstripes.

Another advantage is cost. To do your truck yourself with decals and pinstripes will cost from $100 to $150, whereas hiring an expert painter will cost $400 to $500 or more.

The major disadvantages are that you are limited by the selection of designs available (making your truck look like everyone else's with the same decal). However, right now not that many trucks have decals, and there's a wide variety of colors and sizes available with the same design. Combinations of designs and pinstriping layouts can always create a unique vehicle.

One way to use decals creatively is to hire an expert taper to do the tape lines. You can have him incorporate the decals you like, placing them where you want on the truck, then enhancing them with tape. If you put the decals on the truck yourself, remember to use the design concepts outlined at the beginning of this chapter. That is, use a focal point for the eye to catch, and keep the design on the hood asymmetric. Place a decal in just one corner, or in the center with different lines running into each corner.

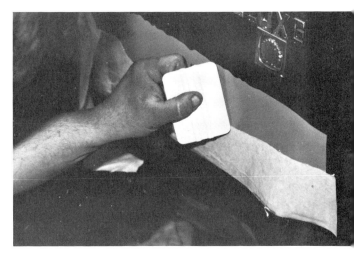

With the decal attached to the vehicle, carefully peel back the paper, while using the plastic squeegee to remove air and smooth out the decal.

You can also enhance taped lines and decals with vinyl lettering. You may want to place a truck name or phrase on the truck. Vinyl lettering is available from several companies.

With decals, you can always remove them after a year or so and change the design. This option is always much cheaper than hiring a professional to do the job over again. Most truck owners can only afford to have the truck painted once.

How long do decals last? When properly cared for and applied with an adhesion promoter such as Rapid Tac, decals will last seven years or so, depending upon the amount of hot sun and other elements they're exposed to.

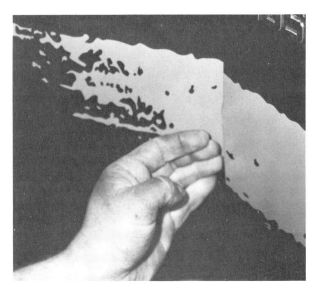

If the decal goes over the door crack, carefully cut it with a razor blade and tuck the decal on the surface inside the door and door post.

Vinyl decals

Most large decals are made of vinyl. The actual decal is sold to you sandwiched between two layers of paper. One layer, called the backing paper, carries the vinyl pieces. The other layer, the application paper, holds the vinyl in place while it's being installed. To install vinyl decals, you will need the decals, a plastic squeegee, a liquid called Rapid Tac which promotes adhesion (if you want a permanent decal) and a clean surface. To apply a decal to your truck's body, the first step is to clean the surface before applying the decal. If the truck has wax on the exterior paint, the wax must be removed if you want a permanent decal application. This is because the wax will prevent the adhesive on the vinyl decal from bonding as tightly as it would to paint. If the vehicle has been recently painted, wait at least a week after the paint is thoroughly dry. Decals can be applied in winter, but this should be done in a warm garage. Conversely, don't apply vinyl decals when it's ninety-nine degrees outside and the surface you're decaling has been standing in the sun for four hours. If you apply a decal on a hot day, let the vehicle stand in the shade first and make sure the side to receive the decal has cooled off.

There are different ways to prepare paint and glass for decaling. Clean glass with a window cleaner, and wipe until completely dry with a lint-free cloth. Make sure the glass is free of dust, dirt, grime and other adhesives.

Paint surfaces

Paint surfaces such as the body sides and doors will need thorough cleaning and de-waxing where the decals will be applied. First clean the truck with a solution of laundry or dishwashing detergent and water, or some commercial car cleaning solution. Thoroughly dry, then wipe with Prep-Sol or some other paint-preparation solvent to remove wax and any oil or grease. Lacquer thinner, Xylol and VM&P naphtha may also be used. Dry surface with a lint-free cloth before the solvent evaporates, since the solvent may evaporate quickly, leaving the grime on the paint.

Applying vinyl decals

After the surface has been prepared and you've determined where the decal is going to be located on the truck body, you are ready to apply the decal. Do this carefully, since the decal cannot be removed and replaced once it has been applied to the truck. It can be removed but you'll need to

This is how the finished decal will look. Adhesion can be strengthened by using Rapid Tac.

buy a new one if you want to replace it in a slightly different position.

Get the decal ready to be applied by laying it down flat on a hard, very smooth surface, such as a smooth formica kitchen counter top. Lay it down with the vinyl (color side) against the table. Use the small hard plastic squeegee (available at automotive trim shops) to press the vinyl onto the application paper. The application paper holds the decal in shape while you're installing it. Rub the small dots and edges into the application paper so they'll stay in place after the backing is removed.

Next remove the backing paper. Carefully peel it back at a forty-five-degree angle. If any vinyl sticks to it, roll the vinyl back flat on the table and rub with the squeegee. The vinyl must adhere to the application paper. Pay special attention to the edges and small pieces to make sure they stick to the application paper.

Once the backing paper is removed, the adhesive is then exposed and ready to adhere to the surface. A wetting agent such as Rapid Tac can be used at this time. The Rapid Tac will make the paint more slippery, so it's easier to move the decal around and position it, but it will also promote the chemical bonding of the decal to the paint so it will stay on the truck longer. Rapid Tac also minimizes problems such as bubbling up of the vinyl.

Place the decal where you want it, and when you're sure it's in position, squeegee the vinyl (which at this point is under the application paper) against the body of the truck. Start at the center and work outward, to avoid creating any bubbles.

Once the vinyl has been completely squeegeed to the body, the application paper must be removed. Start at one corner and slowly peel the application paper off. If the vinyl starts lifting, squeegee it flat.

These directions are somewhat different if Rapid Tac was used (and for virtually all applications it should be). A drying period will then be needed. If so, first apply the decal to the truck body as mentioned above, but instead of removing the application backing, first squeegee out the excess moisture, working from the center outward in all directions. Allow enough time for the decal to bond, then remove the application backing. Use of Rapid Tac will make the decal installation much easier.

It is best not to wash the newly applied decal, but the surrounding area may be cleaned of any pencil marks, water spots and so forth. A warm environment (during winter months) will greatly help in making a strong bond between the vinyl and body surface.

Some auto bodymen use a heat gun to rush the decal application. This is not recommended. If this is the first time you're applying a decal, you will probably ruin it by applying heat. A blow dryer produces much less heat than a heat gun, but it should not be used to install the decal. Use it instead to remove decals if that becomes necessary.

How to combine single color decals into multicolored decals

For our purposes, the color that appears most in the decal will be called the "primary" color, while all the other colors that are added will be called "secondary" colors.

First, determine which areas are to be in the primary color. With an Exacto or other sharp, pointed knife cut around each of the sections that will *not* appear in the primary color, cutting *only* through the application tape and only *around* each of the unwanted sections.

After determining the placement of the primary color, remove the backing paper on only those sections of the primary color that are to be used in this application. The application tape should have remained as one piece, with holes in it, and should still retain proper placement between the sections. Application should then proceed as it would for a normal decal to put the primary color in place.

Simply cut around the sections of the secondary colors, remove each and apply to the area that they belong in relation to the primary color, resulting in a graphic with multiple colors.

This explanation is more complicated than the actual installation, and you should try cutting out sections before applying the decal. Practice with colored construction paper (the kind you buy in art stores) since this is much cheaper than experimenting with expensive vinyl decals. This will also help you decide upon your design and perfect your cutting skills.

Cutting out sections of decals is very tedious, difficult and exact work and should only be done with some practice, and then only after you're sure of your skill.

There are three kinds of decals featured in these photos, the "brush strokes," "grid" and "splash." Generally, the brush strokes decals are usually put side by side, at an angle to the bottom panel, starting at the bottom. The grid is used along a body contour, usually the bottom panel. Then you can take the top row or two and start running it upward at an angle. Then use the larger boxes off one of the lines, preferably placing them at different angles than just horizontal. The splash can be used anywhere.

The decals used in these photos were made by a company called Freelance Lettering in Indianapolis, Indiana. They can be purchased through Accent Distributing in Indiana.

Letraset vinyl letters are available in fine art stores. Alternatively, you must use vinyl lettering found in trim shops. When using lettering, use them

This "ART FX" rear window neon is on a Mazda, built by HoTTops of Tempe, Arizona. HoTTops

sparingly and don't make them too big or have them cover too large an area.

Rear window neons

If you really want to attract a lot of attention at a drive-in or custom truck show, come equipped with a full-size rear window neon, like the one shown in these photos. These are all from the HoT-Tops company. They are specially designed by Craig Smith, and there are fifteen generic styles to choose. Cost is about $200.

How does a neon light work with a truck? The light comes with special 5,000 volt transformers powered by the truck's twelve-volt system. These transformers are what make it possible to use neons in a truck and they're also rather expensive.

Another rear window neon by HoTTops is this Coors sign. There are 15 different rear window neons available from HoTTops. HoTTops

Mounting a neon light inside your truck is rather easy. The neon tubes are spring-mounted inside a clear acrylic box. This box is shaped like the rear window of your truck. It's installed on the inside of your truck. Then, the two transformers are mounted inside the vehicle, connected to your truck's twelve-volt wiring system, and they can be turned on by the flip of a switch. There is a dark inside cover for the neon light so the neon won't light up the inside of your vehicle. You can rig it up to beat to music or just turn it on with the flip of a switch.

The spring-mounted neon tubes can be left in the truck. Most normal driving will not break the neon tubes. After all, most outdoor neon signs last for years through winter weather, storms, high winds and other vibrational hazards without damage.

Neon license plate frames

Another company called Street Neon of Houston, Texas, makes neon light frames. They come in red, green, blue, yellow, pink, purple and white. Since most states require that the license plate be lighted at night, the neon frame is legal in most states. Also, the neon license plate frame doesn't twinkle or blink on and off like the license plate frame using the small electric bulbs. License plate frames with blinking lights are illegal in many areas.

The neon tube is permanently mounted inside a plastic frame, which fits over the mounted license plate. The license plate is clearly visible with the neon license plate frame on. A small transformer for the neon, five inches high, three and one-half inches wide and one and three-quarter inches deep, is mounted inside the rear of the vehicle with two mounting screws. It's sealed in a weatherproof box.

Glass tinting

In addition to being an important part of the Euro Look, glass tinting has several other positive advantages to offer your minipickup. For example, by reducing the amount of sunlight entering your vehicle, you will make the cab of your truck cooler on summer days (increasing your comfort and lessening the need for air conditioning). You also make it more difficult for potential burglars to see what you have inside the truck, you reduce the amount of shattered glass that will enter the vehicle in an accident (using the film application) and you reduce the amount of damage done by sunlight to interior seat fabrics and upholstery materials.

There are two ways to tint windows. The most common way is to use a plastic laminate, which is applied, while wet, to the inside of the window. When properly applied, a good quality laminate will provide many advantages for a long time. As you may know, there are many different colors and degrees of darkness to be found in glass tint laminates. You can get a rose color, smoke gray, blue, green, amber and a top tint for eye-level protection, as well as the common dark tint colors.

Window tinting comes in a range of "darknesses" or the degree to which they block out light. Many states now have laws limiting how dark the tint can be. Usually, these laws are rather vague. For example, one state says that the tinting cannot be so dark as to make the driver unidentifiable at dusk! Of course, some persons may be able to identify drivers under different lighting conditions. But keep in mind that a police officer usually cannot stop you merely because of your window tinting. Window tinting can usually be checked only after you have been stopped for some other traffic violation, such as speeding or making an improper turn.

But enforcement of state laws varies from community to community. Usually, even those states with tinting laws don't bother law-abiding citizens driving minis with tinted windows. Before having any glass on your vehicle tinted, however, it's a good idea to check with local authorities and those who may know (such as a tinting shop) how stringently these laws are enforced. You can always remove tinting from the window if it is found to be illegal.

Everyone knows that tints vary in darkness. In reality, laminates are rated by percentages. You can buy laminates varying from a rating of five percent to eighty percent. What this percentage rating refers to is the "vision factor" associated with that particular shade. For example, a rating of five percent means that the vision factor into the vehicle is five percent. In other words, ninety-five percent of ultraviolet light is blocked out. This is just about the darkest shade you can get. Windows covered with five percent laminate are virtually black.

At the other extreme are the very light tints, which would be eighty percent. These are very light and serve to block out small amounts of glare. They are hardly noticeable, but would serve to keep the interior a little cooler on hot days in areas where the laws are very strict. Most of the trucks you see have a thirty-five percent laminate. These allow you to see thirty-five percent into the vehicle. The thirty-five percent laminate is a good general laminate for side windows, where you want to keep out most of the sun but want to be able to see traffic clearly. The darker five percent would be used for a back window on a pickup, or the hatchback of a sports car—situations where you don't need to see out, but you want to block out most of the light.

There is one other process used to tint automotive glass, and this is chemical coating. In the Chicago area there are only two shops that do chemical coating, the Mr. 50s shops in Harvey and Berwyn, Illinois. Chemical coating uses a dye, similar to printer's ink, that is drawn by gravity over the

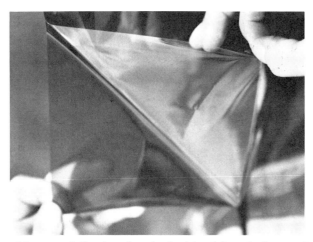

After carefully cleaning the inside of the window and cutting the film, slowly separate the film backing from the window tinting laminate.

portion of glass to be tinted. It actually coats the glass, so there's no film to bubble up or come off. Chemical tinting is much more difficult to do (although doing a good laminate tinting job isn't easy, either). There are also shops in California and Florida that do chemical tinting.

Chemical coating also has other advantages. It can darken curved windows, and windows with heater lines, perfectly.

The following section will give a general outline of how to install window tinting, but keep in mind that an excellent tinting job is difficult to do. It requires good, professional laminates as well as experience and expertise. The advantage to having a professional do the job is that you get a warranty. Some shops offer a lifetime warranty, so if the laminate ever bubbles up, it will be replaced for free.

If you plan to do your own window tinting, purchase a good quality of laminate. Generally, the

Then spray the laminate and glass surface thoroughly with a soap and water solution.

The laminate is applied to the glass, and then sprayed again. At this point it is thoroughly wet on both sides.

The laminate on the right is totally free of air bubbles and excess moisture. At this point, the installation is nearly complete and the adhesive on the laminate will begin adhering to the glass.

laminates sold in discount auto parts stores are not good enough for a good job. They're made of inferior materials and contain inferior adhesives. You should be able to purchase good quality laminates from a window tinting business. The cost runs from $3.50 to $6.50 a running foot. This is the best window tinting laminate you can buy. You may also be able to buy some tools from the tinting shop, such as a squeegee and spray bottle. Some shops don't want you to do the job yourself, and may be unwilling to sell you professional quality materials.

Installation

To apply a laminate to your windows, follow these steps. Although the steps seem simple, they require a high degree of skill and careful work.

1. First, cut the laminate to the width you need for the window. Remember, you'll have to leave about one-quarter inch around the glass without laminate, so the laminate won't rub against the window moldings when the window is raised and lowered.

2. To apply the laminate, you need a spray bottle with a solution of soap and water. This is to keep the laminate wet while it's being applied. You'll also need a small automotive squeegee to smooth out the laminate after it's applied.

3. Clean and thoroughly dry the window you're going to laminate.

Carefully squeegee the moisture out from under the film, using an automotive squeegee like the one shown which is made of solid rubber.

Another way to dress up a window is with window etching. This pattern has been carefully sandblasted into the glass and is permanent.

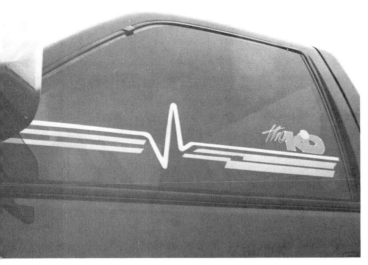

Here's a beautiful example of window tinting graphics. Different shades of plastic laminate, rose and blue, were placed between the tint laminate and the window glass. Where the laminates overlap, light is reflected and a silver strip is created. This was done by Billy the Kid of Indianapolis, Indiana.

4. The laminate comes with a film backing. Carefully pull the backing off the laminate, while an assistant sprays it to keep it wet.

5. Wet the inside surface of the window thoroughly.

6. Apply the film to the window, being careful to align it before it begins to adhere. Be gentle so you don't crease the film. If you do crease it at this point, you'll have to go back to step 1 and cut another piece of film.

The rear window of this pickup has been removed for tinting.

7. Carefully squeegee the film onto the window, starting from the bottom middle and working out to the sides and top. Squeeze out any air or excess water.

The plastic film contains an adhesive that helps it stick after it's applied. The film can be removed if it's installed improperly, but this has to be done immediately, otherwise a new piece of film has to be cut and applied.

If you notice a great number of bubbles, there may be several reasons for them. One is that the grade of laminate you're using is inferior. It could be stretching while it's being applied. Another is that you didn't apply a film of soap and water to the entire inside surface of the window and the laminate. Third, you didn't do a good job with the squeegee or squeezing out all the air and soap film, or there may be fine pieces of dust or dirt on the

Another vehicle with window tint graphics by Billy the Kid. Each part of the design was cut out of plastic laminate—an extremely tedious and difficult process.

To replace the window, position a piece of string inside the rubber molding, as shown here. One person pulls on the string from the inside, seating the window molding.

As the string is pulled, the glass seats in the molding. Have an assistant push the glass from the outside to solidly fit the window molding in place.

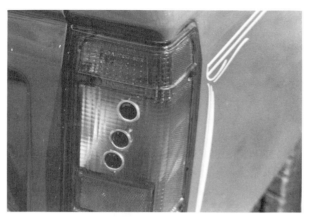

This 1988 Ford Ranger has three blue dots in each taillight. To drill holes for blue dots, be careful to drill slowly or the plastic lens will crack.

glass. Remember, it takes a great deal of skill to do windows perfectly.

While you can do the laminates yourself, chemical tinting can also be done at professional shops. If you want a perfectly smooth job on sharply curved glass, such as a windshield, then chemical tinting is the only way to go.

One style of Billy the Kid's "Hot Tennas," stylized radio antennas for pickups. These are made of stainless steel and replace stock radio antennas. Surprisingly, their diagonal bends improve radio reception! For a pleasing look, the top of the antenna should be kept in a vertical position.

Here's a Nissan pickup with just one blue dot in the taillight. Blue dots can be installed in virtually any taillight.

8

Interior upgrading: upholstery and electronics

The body graphics and ground effects discussed in previous chapters will greatly enhance the style of your truck's exterior. But there's more. The interior can be stylized to suit your personal taste with everything ranging from new upholstery and carpeting to electronics such as stereo systems, radar

This 1983 Chevy S–10 dashboard and door panels have been painted in 1957 Chevrolet turquoise, a beautiful, classic shade of blue. Vinyl can be painted if it is done carefully, and a paint such as DuPont Lucite acrylic lacquer is used.

This Nissan door panel has had several custom modifications made to it by the owner. The entire door panel (all vinyl parts) has been painted the same bronze color as the truck; the Nissan emblem, windjammer, window tinting and Alpine speaker have been added.

detectors and security systems. This chapter will cover some of these areas and give you ideas as to how to customize your truck's interior.

Dashboard and door panel modifications

One of the most difficult parts of the interior to modify is the dashboard. Along with the door panels, it's one of those "built-in" parts of the truck that seem to defy changes. But there are some things you can do to customize and individualize your dashboard so it can go with your exterior body graphic design and stand out at custom shows.

Painting

One of the easiest ways to customize the interior vinyl, including both dashboard and door panels, is to paint them. They can be painted and will turn out very professionally if done properly. Any interior vinyl part to be painted should be spray painted with a spray gun after it is removed from the vehicle. If it is impossible or too difficult to remove it, remove the door handles and other parts, and carefully tape and paper over the other exposed parts such as the windows, seats and so on.

A good paint to use for painting vinyl is DuPont Lucite acrylic lacquer. This adheres well and is available in almost any automotive color, since it is a standard automotive paint. The white S-10 Pro Street in the photo had the dashboard painted a beautiful 1957 Chevrolet turquoise blue color, one of the nicest colors used in the 1950s. Some people don't like to use color with an interior, but remember you can also paint the interior black, gray, red or any other color. When spraying, use

This dashboard has been custom made out of aluminum, then polished to a mirror finish. The neon graphics are formed using a bead roller, a very difficult job. The result is a beautiful and unique dashboard.

The instrument panel molding of this Ford Ranger has been replaced with a piece of custom-made walnut. The wood was carefully cut, sanded and urethaned for a high-gloss wood finish.

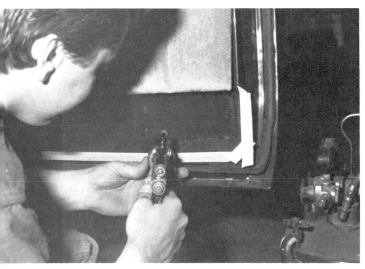

Then place contact cement on back of carpet and press into place. Contact cement is all that is necessary to hold carpet to door.

To glue carpeting to a door panel, first install the upper door panel section (it's attached with clips or screws), then glue the carpet to the lower section. Here contact cement is sprayed onto the bottom section of the door. Contact cement can be brushed on. Use masking tape to cover areas not to be cemented.

light, thin coats because the paint is absorbed into the vinyl to some extent.

Replacing a door panel

To remove your door panel, open the door wide and locate the screws that attach the door panel to the door's sheet metal. If the door panel doesn't have screws, it's held in by clips. These are the button-type clips that expand after they're pushed into a hole. Gently pry the poor panel off at the edges (starting at the bottom corners) to remove it.

A replacement door panel can be custom made out of vinyl upholstery material and carpeting. The usual method is for an upholstery shop to first measure out a piece of panel board, cut it to fit your door, then cut and sew vinyl and carpeting to fit the door panel. This usually requires specialized upholstery equipment and materials. The custom door panel is then attached to the door using the same clips or screw holes as the original.

The bottom section of carpeting can be attached with glue. Use a professional quality contact cement, applied to both the door and the carpet. Press the carpet in place for a permanent installation. The carpeting can be removed later. The advantage to using glue is that new holes do not have to be drilled. The accompanying photos show some custom door panels.

Seat covers

Several manufacturers make seat covers that are intended to be installed *over* your existing seat covers. These are particularly easy to install on minipickups with bench seats, since the top and

bottom come in one piece. They are an excellent way to protect your original seats from wear and tear. Performance Covers makes a good selection of replacement seat covers that are available through mail order. These come in six colors, can be removed and washed, are made of the same quality fabrics as original equipment, have a half-inch foam backing, feature shock cords for a tight fit, have an optional inflatable lumbar support and are Teflon treated and fire retardant.

The following installation instructions will give you an idea of how to install replacement seat covers.

These Pro Car seats are installed in an S–10. The easiest way to change seats and upholstery is to buy the entire seat and simply bolt it to the floor. Adapters can be used if bolt holes don't line up perfectly.

1. In order to install a bench seat cover, first see if the underside of the seat has enough space for you to reach under and install the shock cords. If it doesn't, loosen the two bolts on each end and remove the seat. This will later be reinstalled in its exact stock location.

2. For the back of the seat, if you have headrests, remove them by pressing button at base of support. Pull up slide cover over back, making sure welt cord in original seat matches cord in cover, so cover will fit exactly. Push vinyl flap with Velcro through slot to back of seat and attach to Velcro on inside of back.

3. Fit seatbelts through hole in cover.

4. For the bottom of the seat, fit cover so the front fits and pass vinyl flap between seat. Connect cords to grommet holes in front of cover. Side panels should be fitted between sliding track and the rest of the seat. You may have to loosen the bolts at each end of the track in order to have enough room to work with. You will have to make the track go as far as it will go. Be careful, as it's spring loaded.

5. Captain's chairs: With GMC models you have to remove some hog rings to be able to slide the back flaps through the back of the seat. With Ford models, if the cover has cut-outs for the armrests, do not remove them. If they do not, undo armrest cover at back Velcro and unbolt. Fit cover, cut slot and rebolt armrest. The new armrest cover fits over the existing cover. With Ford bench seats that have a center armrest, some have a drinks tray. Remove it, and cut slots as in the original cover.

Carpeting

You can replace the carpeting yourself, but there are several spots where the job will not look

To replace carpeting, first remove trim from doorsills and remove old carpeting and pad. Glue a pad to the floor, using contact cement, then the carpet can be glued to the pad.

These replacement seats are from Conversion Components, Inc., of Indiana. They also sell carpets, door panels, wood dash kits, ceilings, oak floor consoles and so on.

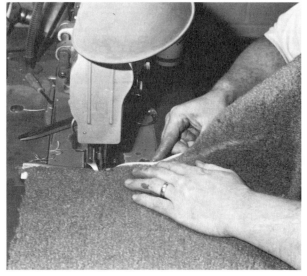

Finish edges by sewing up the edges. This will keep them from coming apart.

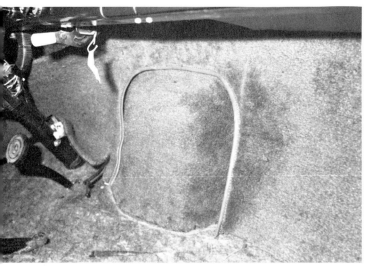

Cover contours on the floor with two pieces. First glue one piece of carpet to the pad, then cover it with a piece trimmed to fit around the contour.

To dampen noise, cover the rear of the cab with thick carpeting. This can be any color, since it won't be seen. Glue it to the pad or sheet metal with contact cement.

as professional without special tools, such as a sewing machine that can sew a hem on the carpeting for a finished look.

Installation steps are as follows:

1. To replace the carpeting, first remove the seat(s) from the vehicle completely. If the vehicle had carpeting in back of the seats, remove it from the rear firewall. Clean old carpeting scraps, glue and other remnants from the surfaces as thoroughly as possible. Try to get down to bare painted metal on the floor and firewall, if possible. Use of an adhesive thinner will make it easier to remove old, hardened contact cement.

2. Choose a carpet color that will blend with or accent both the dashboard and door panels (interior molded plastic parts) and the exterior color of the vehicle. If the vehicle is maroon, you may want to use gray for the carpeting. Or, you may just want to use a different shade of the same color that's on the vehicle.

3. Choose a synthetic carpeting that's been treated for resistance to soil and staining. Indoor carpeting will not work as well as carpeting intended for automotive use. The greater amount of dirt and dampness in a vehicle will quickly wear out the carpeting.

4. Before gluing anything to the floor, make sure it's clean and free of rust. If any rust exists, clean it and coat with a Rust-oleum paint for rust protection. If there are any holes, have these repaired by a body shop. Any holes left unrepaired will just let in more moisture that will wet the carpeting and create more rust in the future.

5. Before installing any carpeting, first put down a pad. This will make the carpet softer and will also dampen sound to make the interior

quieter. A pad about three-eighths inch thick or so will work well. Cut the pad into sections as large as possible. Avoid using small strips or squares to "make up" for mistakes in measuring. If you install large pieces they will adhere to the floor better and last longer.

6. Glue the pad to the bare sheet metal using a good quality contact cement made for carpeting. First coat the floor, then the pad. The pad can be pressed down to the floor for a lasting bond.

7. Cut the carpeting carefully, making sure to avoid putting seams under the driver's and passenger's feet. A vinyl heel pad can be sewn to the

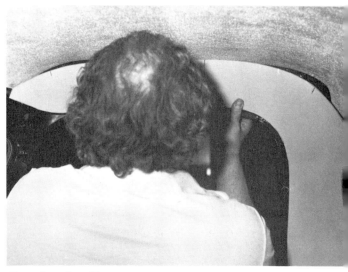

To make a headliner, first install the ceiling piece (it's velour glued to panel board), then take a piece of panel board and measure the fit inside the cab.

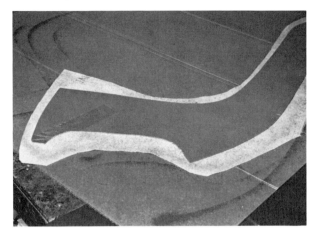

Carefully cut the panel board and piece of velour, then glue the two pieces together.

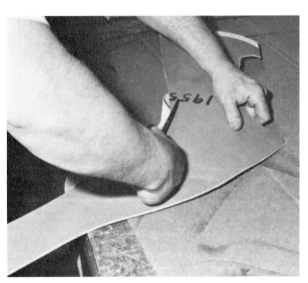

Cut off excess velour material from edges.

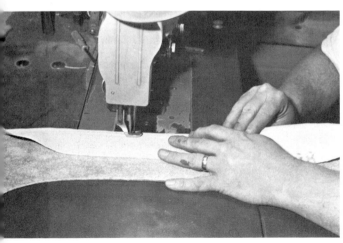

Sew a flap of velour material to the panel board.

driver's side if a suitable sewing machine is available.

8. Install the carpeting by gluing it to the pad. It will be held in at the sills by the chrome molding removed earlier.

9. If you wish to dampen noise behind the seat, first install a piece of thick carpeting on the rear firewall, glued into place. This does not need to match the color of the truck since it will be out of view.

Electronics

The modifications you can do to your mini-pickup don't end with the upholstery, carpeting and dashboard changes. You can also add all of the electronics that can fit into a car. These include a custom stereo system, radar detector and remote

Then sew the corner edge piece to the ceiling piece.

With ceiling piece and corners in cab, fit and trim off excess.

Finished headliner is held in place by rubber molding over rear window and over doors.

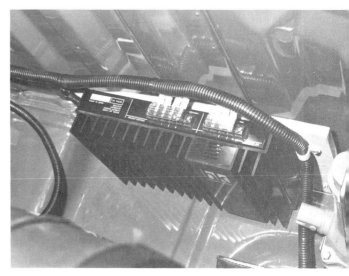

This Harman/Kardon amplifier is shown installed in a Nissan minipickup. Note the mounting board and careful, clean wiring work. These are important when installing electronics in any vehicle.

start system. In the following sections each of these modifications will be described separately.

Stereo systems

In recent years there's been a great improvement in the quality of stereo systems for vehicle installation. Because of the room inside a minipickup's cab, there's enough space to install large bass speakers behind the seat, tweeters up in the corners and mid-range speakers in the doors for a great-sounding stereo system.

There are several components to any stereo system. The heart of the system is the receiver/tape player/CD player. This can be as simple as a good AM/FM radio or as elaborate as the Sony CD player, which can stack ten compact discs and play them in any programmed order! Some of the better AM/FM stereo cassette players are made by Harman/Kardon, Sony, JVC, Craig and Alpine, among others.

The speakers are the next important component, and here as well there is a great amount of selection on the market. The important things to consider with speakers are the quality of the speakers, their location in the vehicle and finally their power.

The amount of watts needed to power the speakers will have to be accounted for by the amplifier(s) in the system. For example, say you are running two forty-watt and two twenty-watt speakers, for a total of 120 watts. Then the system will need, to run the speakers at their maximum, 120 watts. The amplifier you will use must be able to handle forty watts per channel for the two forty-watt speakers you intend to use. You can add additional amplifiers, which are very compact and virtually weather- and shock-proof, to boost the power of your system, in order to run your speakers at the maximum power output per channel.

In selecting a stereo system there are several guidelines to keep in mind. Speaker selection and power requirements can be taken care of by buying a complete system, but any good stereo shop will tell you that a component system, where the individual speakers are chosen separately, will deliver the best sound. However, if you're looking for a good-sounding system, any of the brand-name sys-

One way to mount speakers is in your own custom-made speaker box. Cut out holes in a piece of Medite, glue velour to the surface and install flush-mount speakers. This speaker box fits behind the seat in a 1987 Dodge Ram 50 mini.

Door mounted mid-range speakers in a Nissan mini. Use stock speaker holes, and make sure wiring doesn't interfere with window crank hardware. Keep speakers high up on door to avoid moisture and improve sound.

tems on the market will deliver good sound, and the installation will be rather easy.

Door panel speakers

Since new vehicles come with optional stereo systems, most door panels (the stamped sheet metal door section behind the vinyl) will already have holes in them for factory installed speakers.

Before going out to buy a set of speakers you plan to put in the doors, you may want to first remove the door panel and check the size of the factory holes. It's easiest to plan to install the speaker that will just fit in the door panel.

Most speakers (such as tweeters) have a built-in frame around them, which is designed to be installed on the door panel with only a small hole cut in the panel. To install these, locate the factory hole in the inner door panel, then cut out a small round hole for the speaker. Most of the speaker will be mounted outside of the door panel. Then, run the wires from the stereo behind the floor covering next to the door, through the door post section, into the door panel.

Try to keep the wiring (and the speakers) up as high on the door as possible. To determine the highest possible point, remove the door panel, and with the speaker in hand, see where it will fit before bumping into any window brackets, door reinforcements and so on. You can usually get one speaker next to the window crank, as in the photo, and one below it. If the speakers you have purchased are too deep for the door panel space, you can install some spacers, such as plastic washers, between the door panel and the speaker frame to bring the speaker out more away from the door panel. The rear of the speakers should not be bumping into anything, or be installed to where they are forced up against a section of the door's sheet metal.

Even though automotive speakers are made to tolerate temperature extremes and dampness, you should keep the speakers as high as possible to avoid moisture. The higher the speakers, the better the sound.

These two bass tubes are mounted behind the seat of a Nissan mini. They are held by plastic straps, but are acoustically self-contained for great sound.

This Boston Acoustics automotive tweeter is small enough to mount in the corner of a Nissan mini, yet delivers great sound.

Run the wires from the speakers through a flexible plastic tubing type of wiring protector, such as that black coil plastic used on new cars. This will keep the wires from being chafed. Keep some slack on the wires, so the door can be opened wide without pulling on the wiring. Keep the wire routing clean and simple, and where the wires are exposed, keep them covered. Make sure the wires don't snag or hang up on anything inside the door panel, such as a window crank. They may catch and break, or the plastic insulation might be gradually rubbed off.

Bass speaker

The advantage of a pickup truck is that you can install big bass speakers behind the seat for a great sound. The whole truck will vibrate to the hum of deep bass tones. You can purchase bass speaker tubes from several manufacturers. The ones in the photos here are from Southern Audio Services in Baton Rouge, Louisiana. The bass tubes are easy to install. Run the speaker wires from the stereo in the dashboard or (more likely) the amplifier, to the speaker tubes. Keep the wires covered and protected and allow some slack.

The speaker tubes will hang from plastic straps attached to the back of the bench seat. This will give the best sound as well as allow you to use the largest speakers you can fit behind the seat. You can make your own bass box or speaker box incorporating box mid-range and bass speakers out of Medite. This is a very dense, solid type of particle board, but it's much heavier and harder than particle board.

Cut the holes for the speakers with a saber saw. When you fit the box together, screw the sides and also glue them with construction glue, attaching the speakers with screws so they can be removed if necessary. This way you can have an inexpensive, removable speaker box that will give you great sound.

The advantage of the speaker box is that you'll be able to remove it from the truck and place it outside at a picnic, keep it in your garage while you're working on the truck, in the driveway while you're washing it or put it in your house as an extra set of speakers for your home stereo system.

Tweeters

Tweeters can be installed in either the doors or in the rear upper corners of the cab. Run the speaker wires under the floor carpet, near the door molding, then up under the panel of the cab to the speaker. There are many different makers of speakers. The ones featured here in the photos are made by Boston Acoustics and installed in a Nissan pickup.

To install tweeters on the cab's wall, first remove the headliner material from the cab. This is done by carefully prying the rubber molding away from the headliner, then loosening the headliner to pull it away just enough to fit some wires in. The wires then run from the tuner/cassette player, under the dashboard, under the carpeting, up the rear corner of the cab to the desired position. It should be placed up near the corner since you don't want the speaker to be right next to your ear. Obviously, small, high-quality speakers work best in these tight quarters.

Radar detectors

Radar detectors are like any other electronic products: they vary greatly in quality. While you can buy a relatively inexpensive radar detector that will do the job, the most effective radar detectors will detect radar under difficult conditions and can filter out the "noise" caused by microwave intrusive alarms and polluter signals.

Look for a radar detector that can tune to both the X and K frequency bands, the two bands used by radar. Also look for one that has electronic circuitry to filter out city microwave noise and polluter signals. The conditions under which it is most difficult for a radar detector to pick up radar signals are when the radar is coming from over a hill, around a corner or dead ahead on uneven (hilly) terrain. These signals are less direct but are still good enough to catch you speeding. The brand of radar detector that has been shown to be the most effective under these circumstances is the Whistler Spectrum 2 and Spectrum 3.

With pickup trucks it is also a good idea to have a remote type of radar detector. Most radar detectors have the pickup built into a box, like a stereo cassette player, and the entire unit is mounted under the dashboard. A remote unit uses a separate radar pickup, shaped like a car alarm siren, that is mounted behind the grille where it can pick up radar more efficiently.

These are particularly good for pickups since there's a lot of room up around the grille area, more than can be found with compact cars. A separate receiver is then kept inside the truck. It warns you of the presence of any radar, and includes the controls for the radar detector.

In addition to the Whistler Spectrum 2 and 3 brands, other brands include those made by Cobra, B.E.L.-Tronics Limited, Fox, Uniden, Sparkomatic, Gul and Micronta.

Remote starting systems

There are several good reasons why you may want to start your truck by remote control. On a hot day, you may want to remote start the truck so you can cool it off before you get into the vehicle. This will keep you from sitting on the hot upholstery, which is not only uncomfortable but may damage the upholstery if it's hot and soft.

In the winter months you may want to remote start your truck to warm it up before you get into it. Engines should also be warmed up to operating temperature on very cold days before they are driven. Or, you may want to start the engine several times at night so it doesn't freeze up by morning.

One good choice for a remote start system is called LA-Z-START made by C&A Control Systems, Inc. of Knoxville, Tennessee. This system can be used on any gasoline engine (carbureted or fuel injected) with an automatic transmission. It cannot be used on vehicles with manually shifted transmissions or diesel engines. They also make the Startguard remote starting system which also features a passive alarm system.

This remote starting system has many programmed features that will keep the vehicle from being stolen while it's running. After the vehicle is started by remote control (from up to 300 feet away) it will automatically shut the engine off if the engine begins to overheat, the transmission is removed from park, the brake pedal is depressed, the engine overrevs, the vehicle's hood is raised or the engine runs for more than fourteen minutes. After fourteen minutes the system automatically shuts off the engine. The vehicle cannot be driven until the key is inserted in the ignition, unlocking the steering column.

The system also monitors the engine. For example, if the engine stalls after starting, it will be automatically restarted. A carburetor linkage kit will manipulate the accelerator to release fast idle as the engine warms up.

When used in conjunction with a security system such as MaxiGuard, the doors of the vehicle (if the vehicle has power locks) can be kept locked while it is started. And with the MaxiGuard all of these operations can be done by remote control.

Installation can be done in about two to three hours, longer if the carburetor linkage kit is added. A digital clock can also start the vehicle at a preselected time during the day, such as when you are about to go to work in the morning.

Vehicle security systems

There are many brands of security systems, and most of them offer the same type of basic protection. When shopping for a vehicle security system, you should be aware of the tremendous number of security devices available. Here's a list of the most important ones. They'll give you a good understanding of what the vehicle security possibilities are and you can better decide which system you would like to get.

• Remote control vehicle security. In the early days of car alarms you had to arm/disarm the system using a key. This required that you drill a hole in the body of the car, and also made it necessary to go out and turn the key on and off every time you got in and out of the car. This was rather inconvenient when it rained, was extremely cold or hot. The current systems use a remote control actuator, similar to a garage door opener, but much smaller. The one made by MaxiGuard actually fits on a key chain and is the smallest currently available.

• Motion detector. When the vehicle is physically moved, such as when it is jacked up to remove the

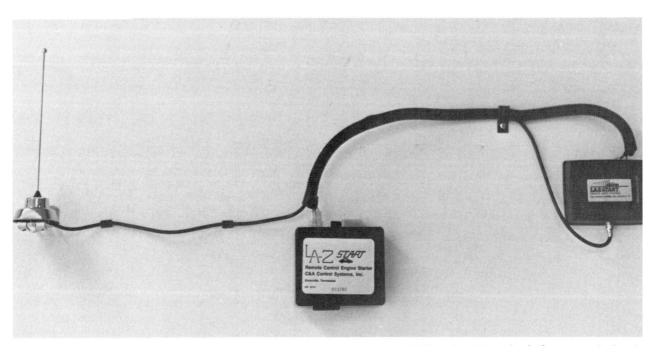

This display shows how the LA-Z-START remote starting system is hooked up to your car. An antenna, receiver and control module not only start the car, but will shut

the engine off if the hood is raised, the transmission is taken out of park or the brake pedal is depressed.

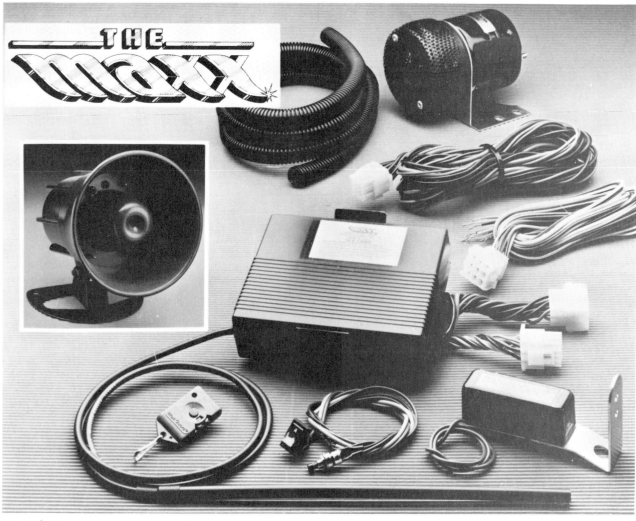

The MAXX security system by MaxiGuard supplies complete vehicle security, actuated by a small key-ring size remote button. MaxiGuard

tires or to be towed away, the motion detector will trigger a siren and flashing lights.

• Starter disrupt. Electronic modules are available that will make it impossible to start the engine without the ignition key.

• Hoodlock. Virtually all new vehicles have cable-actuated hoodlocks. A hoodlock is available that "locks" the cable in its closed position and prevents the hood from being opened. This can be installed where it can't be reached by anyone reaching under the vehicle.

• Glass Guard. This is a sound detector that uses an audio discriminator to listen for the sound of broken glass or sharp metal or wood contact on glass surfaces. It cannot be fooled by the sounds of rain, hail, keys jingling and so on. Available from MaxiGuard.

Look for these features when shopping for a vehicle alarm system. You may elect to only use

One component of any good system is a hoodlock. If the hood can't be opened, thieves can't work on the engine wiring to start the truck.

With a minipickup you have lots of room for burglar sirens. Here are two installed in a 1989 Nissan pickup. Note the plastic armored protection around the wiring. This keeps the wiring clean and secure for a reliable security system.

These two relays (one for each door) are wired to the individual doors and connected to your truck's electrical system.

certain optional features, such as the hoodlock and motion detector. These will be less expensive and will keep anyone from opening the hood, and will make it more difficult for anyone to steal your expensive tires and wheels.

Electric door releases

The installation of electric door releases has two benefits: 1) it gives your truck a sleak smooth look along the doors by allowing you to remove the exterior door handles, and 2) it provides the convenience of "push button" door releases. Just push a button on the outside and the door pops open!

This Mr. Gasket kit contains all the parts you need, including wire, relays and steel cable, for installing electric push-button doors in a GMC truck. Many other truck models and years can use the kit.

This is the door solenoid which, when activated, will pull a short steel cable and open the door.

The pickup used in these installation photos was a 1980 GMC. Most of the procedures will be the same for other truck models. There are some slight differences, though , which I will mention.

To begin the installation, first remove the inside door panel. This will give you access to both the inside door parts and the hardware for the outside door handle. Loosen and remove the outside door handle. There will be screw holes left in the door and these will have to be filled in, sanded and painted.

The parts for the electric door release are available in a kit from Mr. Gasket. The one used for this installation was part no. 6288. The kit includes all the essential hardware. It included everything necessary but the electrical crimp-type connectors used to connect the wires. It also included some pulleys used to change the direction of the cable inside the door (needed for some installations) but these were not needed for this particular truck and year.

Once you have the outside door handle removed, there are two parts to the installation: 1) installing the door solenoids, and 2) connecting the

Begin installation by removing door panel, handle rod and pull rod which hooks to door latch. Use screws to attach solenoid to door.

wiring. The door solenoids replace the handle and rod that open the door. A cable takes the place of the stiff rod, and a solenoid takes the place of the handle's lever action.

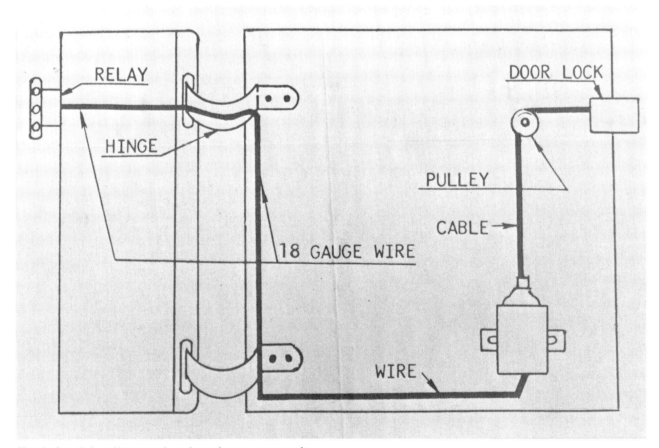

Here's the wiring diagram that shows how to connect the solenoid to the door lock. The pulley is not needed for all truck models.

In this photo the old door handle was positioned back in place to show where the handle is located in relation to the door solenoid.

Remove the inside door handle by removing screws that hold it in place. Then, screw the door solenoid to the sheet metal as in the photo. You will have to drill new holes for this. Try to line up the solenoid so it has a straight-line-of-pull on the cable. Also, place the solenoid near the old door

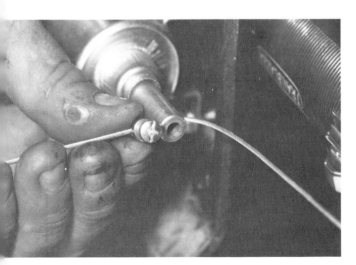

Hook one end of cable to door lock, and run other end to solenoid. A screw detent holds cable tight. It will have to be retightened after several weeks, since the cable will stretch a little.

Photo of door solenoid shows final installation, complete with activating wire. Solenoid is grounded to door, and wire from push-button gives it a positive connection.

Some bodywork will need to be done to make the door look smooth on the outside. This involves removing the han-dle, filling in the holes and painting to match original color of truck.

handle so there is enough room behind the door panel for the solenoid.

Installation of the cable is simple, but tricky. Place the cable through the hole where the rod used to connect to the door latch, and then run the other side through the solenoid, as in the photo. A small screw connector keeps the cable tight. Make the cable connection tight at first, but remember that it will have to be retightened later after it stretches from use.

Check the solenoid by touching a hot wire to the wire on the solenoid. If the solenoid plunger doesn't move, you have the cable too tight. Adjust until the solenoid plunger will open the door. Keep in mind that the plunger moves about ¾ inch but only has to move ½ inch to open the door, so you have ¼ inch leeway to work with.

There are two relays, and they are installed on the firewall in a convenient location. Each relay has three terminals, and these are labeled H, B and S. To install the wiring, run a wire from the solenoid to the H terminal on the relay. The S terminals are used for the switches, and the B terminals provide the positive connection. Connect one B terminal to the battery, and use an additional piece of wire as a jumper to jump to the other B terminal.

Four buttons are provided for opening the doors: two for the inside and two for the outside. The outside buttons can be placed under the rear window or in any other location. Inside buttons can be located by the driver's side under the dashboard, or at any other convenient location. This way the driver can open both doors.

Be sure to make clean, sure connections on the wiring, and make sure the solenoids and cables are tight. Don't leave any frayed wires where they can make a short.

9

Restoring old iron and building a pro street pickup

In recent years old pickup trucks have greatly increased in popularity and are now being restored to like-new condition by pickup owners all over the country. In some areas old pickups are as prized as high-horsepower 1960s muscle cars.

There are three ways to approach the restoration of a pickup: 1) restore it to original condition, 2) restore the body but modify the engine, drivetrain and electrical components with new replacements and 3) build a pro street pickup. Most

This 1967 GMC has been lowered and restored with bodywork and complete customizing, including a supercharged small-block Chevy engine.

This 1940 Chevy pickup was purchased as is with the cab in excellent condition. Running boards and other sheet metal are original. It has been drastically altered in the frame and suspension areas for quarter-mile racing. It has a small-block Chevy with Dyer supercharger.

pickup owners elect the second alternative, using new parts such as a Chevy small-block engine so they can keep the engine work to a minimum. It's also usually easier to use modern parts such as gauges, axles and so on, since the parts are much easier to obtain and repair parts will be easier to find in the future.

If you are contemplating a pickup restoration, read over the first parts of this chapter first. You may be surprised to find that some aspects of pickup rebuilding, such as the bodywork, are actually easier with pickups than they are with old cars. This is because there are several outstanding manufacturers and rebuilders of old pickup parts, such as Golden State Pickup Parts of California, that sell a great number of hard-to-find replacement parts. In fact, there are so many parts available for pickups that it is now much easier to restore a late 1940s, 1950s or early 1960s pickup than a car built in the same period.

Choosing a truck

The following section was put together by Seth Doulton, co-owner with wife Meridith of Golden State Pickup Parts, the original and oldest source for 1947–72 Chevrolet pickup parts. Over his many years of experience Doulton has compiled these guidelines for buying a used pickup intended for restoration. Carefully consider these points since they'll save you a lot of work and point you in the right direction.

This 1957 Cameo Carrier (the Cameos are the most valued Chevy pickups) came with new bed trim and a different fender emblem. Parts for these and other Chevy pickups are available from Golden State Pickup Parts.

The most difficult and crucial step you'll make in any restoration project is choosing a pickup that's "restoration-worthy." This means finding one that is solid where it's difficult to repair the sheet metal. But keep in mind that a truck can look like a total wreck and still be restoration-worthy if it's solid and substantial in the right places.

Doulton points out that you will have one of two goals in mind when you choose a truck: either the truck is for resale, or you plan to keep it for a long time and enjoy it. This decision has to be early on, since it will have an impact on virtually every part you choose for the restoration project.

If you plan to keep the truck, pay attention to the truck's body style and customized features. If you plan to sell it, stick to the most popular body styles and keep the modifications limited. Don't make any changes to the original body style or options. The potential customer may not like these, and it's usually difficult to find someone with the same taste you have in pickup customizing.

As for body style popularity, the hottest Chevy or GMC truck built between 1947 and 1966 is the 1955-57 short bed stepside with wraparound or

big back window. Because this truck is more desirable it makes it harder to find at a good price. Big back windows are worth anywhere from $500 to $1,000 or more.

If you plan to build or restore a stock truck, it's a lot easier and less expensive to start with a truck that hasn't been cut up or customized. You will have to pay more out front, but you'll save money and headaches in the long run.

If you plan to customize your truck it's not as critical that you find a cherry one to start out with.

In 1955 to 1966 trucks the hardest place to repair is the roof above the windshield. Rust in the lower body areas like the fenders, doors and rear cab can be repaired by using replacement sheet metal sections bought from numerous suppliers such as Golden State Pickup Parts. They can be purchased for about $20 and can be installed by anyone with sheet metal experience.

Rusted body panels and cut-out dashes are the biggest problems to watch out for. These are difficult and more expensive to repair. In the case of dashboards, it may be virtually impossible to find a

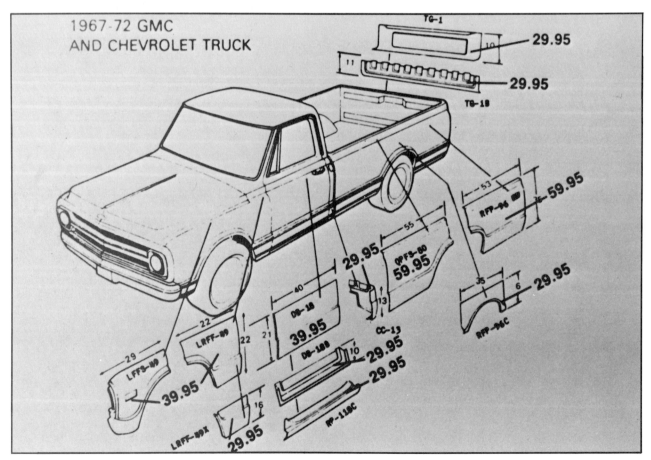

Here's some of the body panel sections that can be purchased for your 1967-72 GMC or Chevy truck. Panels *can be purchased individually, then painted and welded into place.*

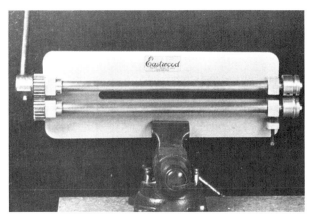

This bead roller creates beadwork on steel and aluminum panels. It's excellent for creating customized dashboard panels, or restoring sheet metal to original condition. It has an 18 inch throat, allowing you to create a bead 18 inches into a piece of metal.

A close-up of the bead roller shows how it presses a one-quarter inch half-rouch bead into a die. The bead made by this tool is not only decorative, it reinforces the sheet metal.

replacement original metal dashboard, depending on the part of the country where you live.

Another problem area on older Chevy/GMC trucks is the door hinge area. The metal post that supports the door hinges can be rotted out, making it impossible to hang a heavy metal door until the post is completely rebuilt with new metal. It will require a lot of custom welding work to rebuild the door post, but it can be done. If the door itself is rusted out, you can either have the door repaired by welding in new sheet metal (a difficult process that requires someone experienced in restoration work) or you can go to a junkyard and find a new door with solid hinge mounts.

The short wheelbase truck is definitely the most popular body style. Again, you must keep in mind both your personal taste and the type of restoration plans you have in mind for the truck. The short wheelbase is worth more than the long wheelbase in the same condition.

The limited edition Cameo Carrier pickups that were in production from 1955 to 1958 are a story in themselves. They were a stepside truck, standard with big back window, deluxe options and fiberglass fender skins that gave the truck the fleetside look that is still popular today. In fact, the Cameo was the forerunner of the fleetside pickup.

A Cameo today is worth about $1,000 more than a stepside in the same condition. But with added trim and hard-to-find parts a Cameo can cost as much as $2,000 more to restore.

Chevrolet pickup interchangeable parts

In any restoration project you will inevitably have to find some replacement parts. You may need a new door, or a bumper bracket, or a grille. The local junkyard might have a truck with a perfect grille, but will it fit your truck exactly? This following section will help answer many of these questions on interchangeability. These comments are based on the experience of Seth Doulton, who writes a "Chevy Corner" column for *Truckin'* magazine. Keep in mind that there may be crossover possibilities other than those mentioned here, and that some parts, such as brackets and so forth, may fit if slightly modified. A wire welder and torch will do wonders with any restoration project.

For sheet metal welding, this stitch welder from Eastwood provides an expensive and effective way to weld thin sheet metal. Stitch weld the sheets together, then fill in with weld for a tight fit. For welding sheet metal as thin as 20 gauge without burning.

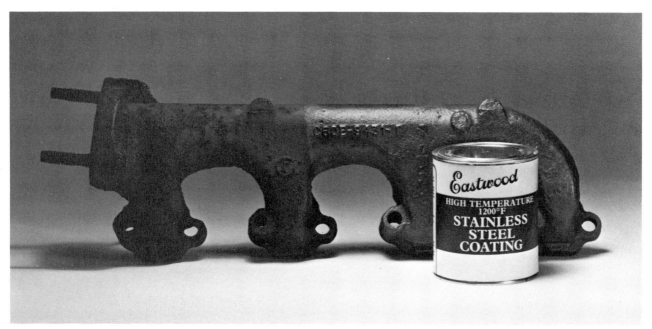

For great looking exhaust system parts on your restored engine, try this stainless steel paint from Eastwood. Just wire brush or sandblast your exhaust manifold and paint. Can be brushed on, and air dries in one hour. Will withstand up to 1,200 degree F. temperatures.

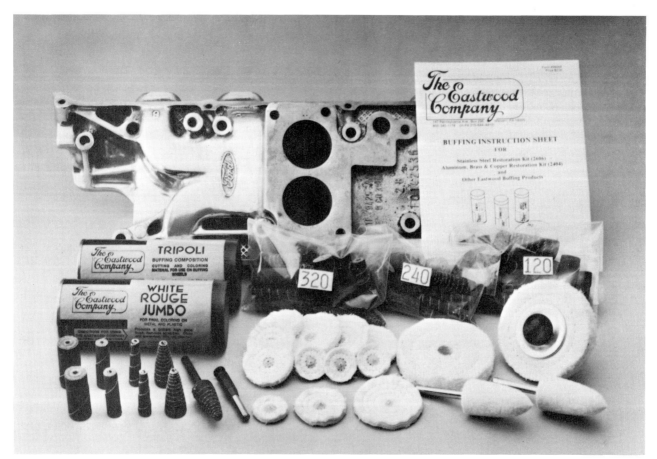

This aluminum manifold buffing kit from Eastwood has everything you need (except grinder/drill) for buffing an aluminum manifold to look like chrome. Good for all rough cast manifolds.

Bumpers from 1947 Second Series to 1955 First Series interchange. Also, 1955 through 1959 are the same with the exception of license plate bracket mounting holes in the center of the 1958 and 1959 model years.

Bumper brackets for 1947 through 1955 First Series interchange, as do the 1955 Second Series through 1957. The frame horn or middle bracket is the same on the 1958 and 1959, but the outer brace is longer because the 1958 and 1959 frame is longer from the center of the front axle to the front tie of the frame horn.

In dealing with fenders this factor also plays a part. The 1955 Second Series through 1957 fenders can be mounted on a 1958 and 1959 frame, but the front frame horns have to be shortened for proper front bumper fit (approximately two to three inches).

There is a slight difference in the 1957 fender where the grille mounts to the front. Level with the parking light there is an indentation and mounting hole. This can be reshaped easily to make a 1957 into a 1956 or 1955, or make a 1956 or 1955 into a 1957.

The 1947 through 1953 front fenders are the same. The 1954 and 1955 First Series have a reshaped front end to mate with the 1954–55 grille, that is also unique.

The 1947 through 1953 grilles are the same even though they were slightly different in certain

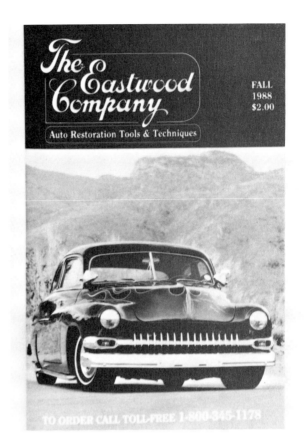

The Eastwood catalog is an excellent source for restoration tools, techniques and ideas.

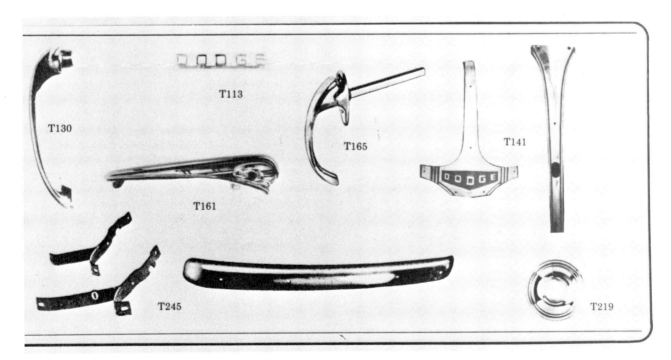

An illustration from the Roberts Auto Parts *catalog shows the variety of old door handles and Dodge insignia available from Roberts Auto Parts.*

years. Some were painted and some were stainless steel. It is possible to make changes to the 1947-53 front fenders to fit the 1954 and 1955 grilles. This will require custom fabricating work, however.

The doors on 1947 through 1955 First Series trucks will interchange. The 1951 through 1955 First have the vent window and the 1952-55 First have push-button door handles instead of the turn-down handles that the 1947-51 models have. Because of this, these doors also have different door latches and strikers.

Some people like the solid door window of the 1947 through 1950 trucks, so they exchange their 1951-55 First vent window doors.

The 1955 through 1959 doors are all interchangeable. Some of the 1955 Second Series doors have smaller, fine-threaded door panel screws and the 1956-59 models have larger, coarse-threaded door panel screws.

The 1947-53 cabs were alike, excluding the addition of a gas tank in the cab on 1948-55 First and the side cowl vent for 1947-50. The Early Hauler trucks were available all years with or without corner glass.

The 1955-59 cabs were identical and were available with small and large rear windows, all years.

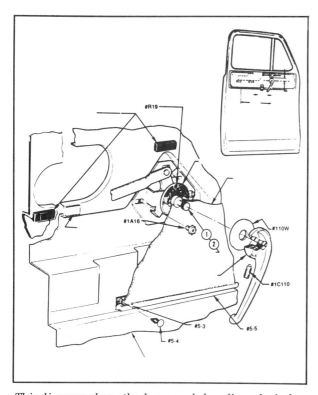

This diagram shows the door crank, handle and window hardware available from Golden State Pickup Parts. Use this diagram to order parts based on model and year.

The beds were alike from 1947 to 1953. The 1954 and 1955 models had bed sides that were only used in those two years. They were flat on the top rails like those from 1955-88, but they had rounded fender indentions for the round carryover 1947-53 rear fenders. Bed sides for the 1955-59 models were all the same. The 1947 through 1955 First Series used the same rear fenders.

When using a side mounted spare with a short wheelbase bed, the fender indention was deeper to accept the spare tire. In the long wheelbase the indention was smaller. The tailgate and front bed panel on the 1954 through 1959 stepsides were all the same. The fleetside bed was introduced in March 1958 and was also used in 1959.

Rear bumpers have always been an accessory and were the same from 1947 through 1953. The 1954 and 1955 First Series dipped down for the license plate in the center (this is very rare). The 1955-59 rear bumpers had the same dip in the center.

Early GMC and Chevrolet pickups

In the early years from 1947 to 1959 there was a noticeable difference between GMC and Chevrolet pickups. For example, the grilles were completely different and some of the dashes looked like they weren't even made in the same country. Some sheet metal was also different.

Front sheet metal and fenders from 1947 to 1959 were almost the same, with a few more holes punched in them to mount the massive grilles. The hoods were different all the way up to 1966. The grille was definitely the largest and the most apparent difference between the Chevy and GMC pickups. From 1947 up until 1972, the GMC grille dominated the truck field, and it was just a little more massive, with a lot more chrome added to the front end. Because of the size of the grille, more of the GMC trucks than Chevrolet trucks had chrome grilles.

With this large chrome grille gracing the front of the truck, it was natural to dress the rest of the truck with the complete deluxe trim package. The GMC's huge chrome grille and large number of chrome accessories was a reflection of the heavy use of chrome in the middle 1950s.

Another area of difference between the Chevy and GMC trucks is the dashboard. The GMC dashes from 1955 to 1959 were totally different; the only similarity in the two were the knobs and the metal dash strip between the windshield and the dash. Even the plastic knobs were different colors. The Chevy was black, the GMC gray. The glovebox cardboard in the GMC pickup was also two inches narrower than the Chevy's. The radio had a different outside appearance, but the electrical parts were the same.

The gauge cluster is the most noticeable difference in the interior. The gauges in the GMC are big and easy to read. The GMC came with a built-in spot in the dash for a tachometer or clock.

The cab and doors were the same, along with the mechanical parts that went with them, such as window hardware and door handles. The seat was the same, the only difference being the type of fabric that covered it.

The bed was identical, except for the different logos on the tailgates, being either GMC or Chevrolet. Back in the 1940s and 1950s the GMC and Chevy trucks were built on different assembly lines, whereas they are now made on the same assembly line. Right now there are about seven Chevys made to every three GMCs. The only changes are cosmetic; a decal here or there, the glovebox emblem, horn cap and body markings.

How to identify trucks

If you're strolling through a wrecking yard looking for an old truck, it may be very difficult to tell the truck years apart, particularly the early years. The easiest way is with an accurate photo book. This provides you with a number of photographs that can be used to identify specific models and years.

Another way is to use this list of characteristics compiled by Seth Doulton. You can take this book with you to the junkyard to see if a truck is the year you're looking for. If you have a 1950 Chevy pickup and need a particular item such as a door, then either look for the same year or a year that had the same door, as listed earlier. Either way, you must be certain of the truck's year if you expect the part to fit. And in many junkyards parts are not returnable, particularly if they have to be torch-cut or unbolted from the vehicle in the yard.

The Early Hauler Chevy pickups (1947-55 First Series) are the hardest to tell apart, year by year. Trucks made in these years had only very minor changes made to them.

The 1947 trucks brought new styling changes along with a stationary windshield and deluxe full-view rear corner cab windows. All the 1947s had floor-shift levers, three and four speeds alike. They also had an emergency brake handle on the right-hand side of the floor shifter. The running gear was a carry-over from the pre-1947 trucks, with unsynchromeshed transmissions.

In 1948 Chevy introduced the synchromesh three-speed transmission and moved the lever to the steering column. The emergency brake handle in the 1948 was moved to the far left side of the cab and was changed to a foot-operated mechanism. So if you're looking for a 1948, look for the shift lever on the steering column and a foot-operated emergency brake.

The 1947s and 1948s had the gas tanks under the front of the bed. In 1949 the gas tanks were moved into the cab behind the seat. The 1947 and 1948 had red needles in the gauges and the 1947-49 models had a large fuse block on the firewall.

From 1947 through 1950 the pickups had standard chrome bumpers front and rear. In 1951 the front bumper was standard and the rear was an option. The year 1952 was the only year when there was not a rear bumper available. In 1953 rear bumpers were reintroduced.

The 1947-49 pickups used lever shocks and GM introduced the modern tube shocks in 1950. The 1947 to 1949 trucks used a black cab opening windlace seal that was attached to the cab with a metal retainer. Midyear 1949, GM installed a track with a new style windlace that slid in the track.

The 1947-50 truck also had a left-hand cowl vent. The pickups built from 1951 to 1955 had only the top vent.

The most noticeable difference between the 1952 and 1953 were the side hood emblems. The 1952 emblems said "Chevrolet" and the 1953s said only "3100." Another interesting fact about the 1953 model was that it was the first year Chevrolet offered a side mount spare on pickups.

The year 1951 was the first year with vent glass in the doors. This change really updated the door of the truck along with adding extra ventilation to the cab. Some 1947-50 Chevy or GMC truck owners have traded in their non-vented doors for 1951-55 doors for just this reason.

The most predominant change would have to be the massive grille and one-piece windshield. The year 1954 was also the first year for major changes, including new dash gauges and steering wheel, just to name a few. Hundreds of small changes went along with the major changes, like dash knobs, parking lights, radios and other accessories.

Another change that showed up big in 1954 was the totally new bed. The design change in 1954 is still in use in the 1984 Chevy and GMC pickups. The new bed has taller sides and the top rails are flat, not sloped down as they are with the 1947-53 beds.

The rear bumpers from the 1954-55 First Series trucks have become one of the hardest to find and most sought after bumper of any pickup. It is flat like the front bumper and dips down in the center to reveal the license plate. The year 1954 also marked the change for taillights. Up until 1954 the trucks carried square taillights, but in 1954 they changed to the round design.

There are many more details involved than these, since GM regularly made small changes in many different items on the vehicles, not the least of which is styling. But this short list will give you an idea of what to look for when finding parts for your older Chevy pickup.

These two air-powered sanders are critical tools for any body restoration work. The larger one is for general, *rough sanding, and the small one for fine, smooth finishing.*

Basic restoration techniques

Restoring an older vehicle, whether it be a car or a pickup, is a difficult, frustrating, time-consuming project. However, with an older pickup you are virtually guaranteed a solid return on the money you have invested in parts (and to some extent your labor, too) if you use quality parts, keep to the truck's original design and do quality work.

Here are some small projects that will give you an idea of what kind of work is involved in any restoration project. The list given here is small, but will provide a good feel for the labor and techniques involved. For more detailed information, consult specific books such as body repair books. For engine work, see the chapter on engine rebuilding. Virtually all of the information is as true for older engines as for new ones. The only difference you'll have with older engines is obtaining parts. If the engine needs to be rebuilt, you can always find the gaskets by Fel-Pro. Fel-Pro makes complete gasket sets for every vehicle ever made in the United States, and virtually all foreign makes as well.

Bodywork

Bodywork on older pickups is usually easier to do than on cars, since the pickups used thick sheet metal (by today's standards) and had relatively simple construction. But some of the work you will need to do will be in difficult places. For example, you may have a rust problem with the sheet metal around the windshield, or the door post may be weak and rusted. These are tedious and difficult areas to repair, but the work must be done properly, using a wire-feed welder (preferred method) and new steel to achieve solid, long-lasting results.

Also, bodywork that has been done properly, using new sheet metal and welding, enhances the value of a pickup truck for later resale. The use of fiberglass or plastic body fillers should be kept to an absolute minimum. Whenever possible, use new sheet metal, welded into place, and carefully weld it to something solid on the body.

To give you an idea of the kind of work involved in pickup body restoration, read this section on rusty cowl repair. It's from the 1947-54 *Early Hauler Builder's Guide* published by Golden State Pickup Parts.

When it comes to rust on the 1948-55 pickups, it seems the most common spot is the lower corner of the cowl. If you have a truck built in this period with a rusty cowl, or you only seem to be able to find truck bodies at wrecking yards with rusty cowls, here's the solution to the problem. Golden State

Pickup Parts makes a repair panel that can solve the problem. If you don't know how to work with sheet metal, take the truck to a body shop that has demonstrated competence in sheet metal welding. Here's the step-by-step procedure:

1. Remove the fender and door for easy access.

2. If the rust is extensive you will need to cut a small panel out of sheet metal to strengthen the hidden pocket. Make it with a folded lip similar to the stock sheet metal. One way to make the sheet metal the proper size is to first cut it out of cardboard. Use another piece of cardboard for a mockup of the lip.

3. Hold the new piece of sheet metal to the cab with vise-grips. Then mark the cab. This is the spot where you will need to secure the sheet metal, so make sure it's a piece of solid sheet metal, not a section that has been weakened by rust.

4. Use an air chisel to cut most of the old cowl away. The air chisel cuts faster and will make the work easier. Later on you can cut more accurately.

5. Use tin snips or a sharp air chisel to make the final cut of metal out of the old cowl. The straighter and cleaner the cut, the easier it will be to weld the new metal in place.

6. Use the vise-grips to clamp the new panel to the truck cab. Now tack weld it every two inches or so to mount it to the cab. Start at the section nearest the door, and work outward. This will ensure a close fit to the cab. Use the Eastwood stitch welder for clean, careful welds. A good wire-feed welder is the best way. Make sure the temperature isn't too hot, or you'll overheat and warp the sheet metal. This is the critical part of the whole project, since bent or warped sheet metal will ruin the looks of the truck.

7. After the welding has been completed grind off the rough edges of the welds as smoothly as possible. Then use a metal conditioner to treat the bare metal, and cover with a metal-based filler to make it smoother yet. An all-metal body filler is best, since it will not absorb water and promote rust as plastic fillers do.

8. Sand the all-metal filler as smooth as possible, then paint with primer and body paint.

Windshield installation

One of the best ways to improve the looks of your old pickup is to install a new windshield. Windshields are widely available, but it's often expensive to have it installed. Follow these simple steps and you will be able to install your own windshield. The best way to do your own windshield is with new glass and new rubber. The old rubber will be very stiff, cracked and difficult to work with. Materials:

Nine feet of nylon cord, rounded off screwdriver, padded workbench and masking tape are needed. Of course, you must also have an original replacement windshield and new rubber molding. If your old windshield is in superb condition, you can reuse it if you can get it off the truck without breaking it. But new rubber must always be used.

Installation procedure is as follows:

1. Carefully remove the old windshield moldings and windshield, and then clean the "pinchweld" (the double section of sheet metal) into which the rubber fits. If there's any rust on the pinchweld, sand it and paint it with Rust-oleum rust preventative paint. A thin coat of primer will be sufficient.

2. Fit glass into the rubber. Start with center, top and bottom corners and push glass into place. Then pull rubber around rest of glass. Do one side at a time.

3. If you have stainless steel molding, lay glass with outside up. Start with corners. Hang one corner off the edge of the table for easy access. Pull rubber back and slide molding in. Make sure molding is in all the way before installing glass into truck.

4. If you do not have molding or if you are finished installing the molding, lay glass and rubber with inside up and bottom edge closest to you. If rubber comes off the glass, use masking tape to hold rubber on.

5. Rope the windshield. Start with the top of the windshield. Place the center of the string or cord at this point. Place string in opening of rubber that will fold over pinchweld. Make sure string is in as far as it can go and that it is pulled tight. Lubricate the rubber of the inside edge with liquid soap.

6. Place the windshield in the opening while you make sure it is centered. The string should be on the inside of the cab and at about bottom center. Pull the string with one person holding one side of the glass from the outside, while the person who pulls the string holds other half of shield by reaching around to the outside of the cab. Do not attempt to install the windshield without the help of another person.

7. Pull one side at a time. Pull string *not* out toward the back of the cab, but in toward the middle of the shield.

8. If rubber does not cover the pinchweld, take the screwdriver and gently lift rubber to the inside. If glass still does not pull in, tape glass from outside with an open hand. Don't hit it hard with your fist or the heel of your hand. Make sure to distribute the tap or pressure evenly. A hard rap or too much pressure in one spot will break the glass.

9. Do not install the trim yet. The windshield edge first has to be sealed with butyl rubber at a glass shop.

10. To install center outside molding use an awl from the inside while someone pushes the molding from the outside.

Cracked steering wheel repair

Many of the parts you need for the interior are readily available. These include gauge clusters, upholstery, carpeting, gauges and so forth. You may also want to replace the steering wheel, but the original wheel adds a good historical touch to the truck rebuilding project. To keep a cracked steering wheel in good repair, the cracks must be filed and filled in with epoxy. You'll need a set of small needle files, a larger triangular file, epoxy such as Evercoat flex patch and sandpaper.

These steps explain how to repair a cracked steering wheel:

1. Carefully remove the steering wheel. This usually requires removing a center nut and then using a bolt-type gear puller to pull the wheel off the stud. The steering wheel is force-fit on the stud and held down by a large nut and washer.

2. Clean the steering wheel using first soap, then a mild solvent to get any grime off the wheel.

3. Inspect the steering wheel to find the cracks. Be aware of the small finer cracks as well as the large wider ones. It's important to repair all the cracks.

4. Use a good, clean triangular file to file each crack out. Do this by filing a "V" groove down the center. What you are doing is removing the sharp edges and providing a good adhesion surface for the epoxy. Smooth out the edges so no sharp edges exist.

5. Clean all the dust off the wheel that was created by the filing. Use a blow gun to blow the dust out of the cracks. Mix the epoxy according to instructions (usually a 50-50 mix of resin and hardener) and fill in the cracks with a solid filling of epoxy. It's okay to leave a little bulge on the sides. These can be sanded down later.

6. Clean the epoxy off your finger with lacquer thinner or the recommended solvent.

7. After the epoxy dries (follow the instructions for *thoroughly* cured) carefully file off the excess. Use a small file to get as much off as possible. This will cut down on tedious hand-sanding time.

8. Use 80-grit sandpaper to sand down the whole wheel. The filled-in areas will take more effort. At this time, inspect the wheel again. If you find any new cracks you didn't see before, file them down with the V groove and fill them in with epoxy. Also, check the large cracks to see if any bubbles arose in the epoxy. If so, file these down again and refill with epoxy. Take your time since any small cracks you miss will almost certainly develop into larger ones later.

9. The nicest way to paint the steering wheel is with an automotive lacquer with a flex additive. Use lacquer primer first, then topcoat with the lacquer paint. Have an automotive shop do it if you don't have the painting equipment. At the end of this restoration the steering wheel will look and feel like new.

Painting

Painting an older truck cab and bed requires more preparation than actual painting work. Older bodies have both good and bad points. The good point is that they are made of much thicker sheet metal, which can be welded, ground, sanded and worked with more easily than the thin sheet metal found on new cars. The bad points are that they may be rusted out in places (such as in the cowl as already described), may require a lot of cleaning, sanding and grinding, and will need a thorough going-over to remove the years of dirt, grime and corrosion.

So in some ways there is more preparation work involved, in some ways less. Here's a basic how-to description of how to paint your older pickup's body. Of course, the actual preparation details, primers needed, and so on will vary depending on the manufacturer of the paint you intend to use. You can use an enamel similar to the original, or go to a high-gloss new paint such as the Sherwin Williams urethane enamel or some of the other new paints. These are available in colors that match original vehicle paint colors. Whatever paint you choose, be sure to buy the paint, carefully read the instructions and use only the preparation solvent and primer recommended. Nowadays many paints and primers are not compatible. So the type of paint you intend to use is really the first decision, and most important one, you have to make.

Steps for painting a pickup cab and bed:

1. Wash car with soap and water using high-pressure hose. A household detergent such as Tide is good for general cleaning. Rinse thoroughly.

2. Steel wool all chrome and moldings using #00 steel wool.

3. Remove all chrome, lights, bumpers and lenses.

4. If replacing windshield rubbers, cut back rubber approximately ½ inch away from painted surface with a razor blade or Exacto knife.

5. If not replacing windshield rubber, leave it in place until after the old paint is removed. Do not remove any of the glass at this time.

6. Tape up all cracks, doorjambs and cowl vent with two-inch masking or duct tape.

7. Place newspapers or cardboard sheets on floor around vehicle to catch the mess while you are stripping the paint.

8. Apply stripper per manufacturer's instructions. Brush only in one direction. Spraying will provide a more even coat. Be sure to use proper spray equipment with proper tip for stripper.

9. Apply stripper over a small, manageable area at one time. Do not apply in direct sunlight or when surface is hot.

10. After all paint, putty and plastic filler are removed, wash car thoroughly with soap and water and dry immediately.

11. Use a wire-feed welder to fill in cracks in sheet metal, breaks between joints, and weld in patch panels where required. Now is the time to repair the body as needed.

12. Grind and then sandblast welds to remove slag. Grind off any other rough spots from previous bodywork. At this time you should also sandblast any rough rusted areas. Get down to bare metal if possible. This will provide the best possible surface for future paint and will prevent rust formation.

13. Apply a metal conditioner to entire sheet metal surface per manufacturer's instructions. Work one section, such as a door, hood or fender, at a time. Scrub on metal conditioner and remove before dry. If the instructions for your conditioner are different be sure to follow them.

14. After you have gone over entire surface, do it again with a dry scuff pad.

15. Before painting, mask all rubber, glass and vehicle openings with masking tape and paper. At this time, you should apply a zinc chromate primer to help the paint bond. Use a zinc chromate primer that's compatible with the paint you've chosen to use.

16. Apply primer per instructions. This may involve using another metal conditioner or metal preparation solution. It will be the second primer you're using, after the zinc chromate.

17. Be sure to sand all areas that have been filled with metal body filler. Sand smooth in preparation for paint.

18. If you are removing the windshield, do it at this time. Sand exposed pinchweld areas with sandpaper and paint with suitable primer.

19. Coat with primer, following instructions as to drying time. Wait and sand as required.

20. Use second coat of primer as required by the paint you're using. Follow instructions for drying time.

21. Apply color paint, let dry and buff after appropriate waiting period. You must buff if using a lacquer. If you use an enamel, you'll have to wait longer between coats, for each coat to dry, before the final coat is applied and buffing can be done.

Note: Always follow manufacturer's recommendations as to primer and preparation, and allow adequate drying time. Preparation is the most important thing when painting any vehicle. Be sure to work in an area that's as dust-free as possible when painting. Preferably, do the bodywork, stripping and priming yourself and have it painted in a booth. A baking oven is an ideal way to achieve a good coat of paint.

Also, you do not need to strip the old paint off the truck in order to paint it. Of course, it's better to strip the paint, but stripping involves a great deal of additional tedious work. If you want a perfect truck that's restored as perfectly as possible, then strip the paint. Otherwise, there's nothing wrong with painting over the old paint, provided that it's been scuff-sanded first.

Rewiring

One of the greatest causes for problems in any restoration or rebuilding project is the wiring. Whenever you buy an older pickup (or need to rewire a newer one after a fire) the wiring is the most difficult area to lay out and restore.

Fortunately for pickup restorers and rebuilders, there is a company called Ron Francis' Wire Works in Chester, Pennsylvania, that has a great solution for this problem. They sell a replacement Component Panel that provides for all the electrical functions of a vehicle. This panel (with wiring and accessories such as switches and fuses) is all you need to completely rewire any pickup truck. It's a great blessing to anyone who purchased an old truck that has persistent wiring problems due to broken wires, corrosion and other problems.

It is also the best choice for anyone building a special project truck such as a Pro Street pickup from the frame up and needs a complete, reliable wiring system. When you order a wiring system, you'll be asked to fill out an order form which asks what year vehicle you have; the engine size; what type of alternator you have; whether it's a GM integral, GM external, Ford, Mopar, Motorola or Honda; what kind of ignition system you have; and what type of steering column you have. The Wire Works can supply original GM connectors, so it's best to use GM steering columns (available in wrecking yards) and integral alternators. These can be easily

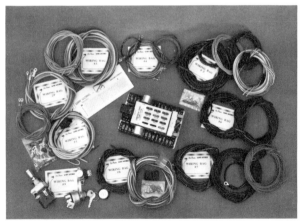

This complete wiring kit will enable you to wire virtually any 12 volt electrical system, on any American-made pickup truck. It's the best way to completely rewire your restoration or rebuilding project truck. The catalog is an education in how to solve wiring problems, from alternators to steering columns. Before redoing your wiring, consult with Ron Francis for the best and most effective way. Ron Francis' Wire Works

wired up, as well as the distributor, starter and so on.

The terminals on the component system circuit board are labeled and color coded, as well as the wires. So in the future you'll be able to quickly trace down a problem or change wiring without spending hours studying a wiring diagram with a bunch of hastily written notes that you no longer understand!

The Ron Francis' Wire Works also sells individual hard-to-find parts, such as electric gearshift indicators, dash indicators, voltage reducers, dash gauges and others. Anyone with any kind of wiring system problems, or just someone in need of spare parts, will find Ron Francis' Wire Works to be a project saver.

Frame modifications

The older trucks are great in the body, bed and accessory departments, but had very poor ride and handling characteristics with their I-beam axles and front leaf springs. The best way to build up your pickup to change the ride, handling and ground clearance is to change the front end. These photos feature a 1976 Mustang II front end on a 1940 Chevy pickup. The designers of this truck could never imagine that it would someday use a Mustang II independent front end!

If you plan to rebuild the entire front end, it's best to remove the cab (it's held on by just four bolts) and expose the entire frame for measuring, fitting and welding. Adding just the front end while leaving the cab on is not a good idea. The major result will be more headaches, mistakes and possibly a vehicle that is not level from front to rear without some additional changes. If you're going to do this kind of work, do it right and work with just the frame on the ground.

With this Mustang II replacement front end, the original frame rails were kept. The upper and lower control arm brackets were welded to the 1940 frame rails, and from there on it was a matter of installing the stock Mustang II parts. One additional part was the strut rod. This is a custom-made item purchased from Heidt's Hot Rod in Illi-

The front end shows the original radiator shield and frame. The engine is a Chevy 350 and was placed in the engine temporarily to set up the engine mounts. The front suspension has been replaced with a 1976 Mustang II independent suspension.

nois. The frame work was done by The Roadster Shop in Elgin, Illinois.

The rear end features frame rails that were entirely rebuilt. The original rails were cut off at the area to the rear of the cab. The original width of the stock 1940 frame rails were kept, but inside the truck these narrower frame rails were installed. These continue on the rear of the truck. A special suspension for drag racing, using a traction bar mounted to the axle housing (next to the differential) and a four-link suspension with adjustable coil-over shocks, allow for great flexibility in adjusting the rear suspension. By moving the links, the location and stiffness of the rear axle can be adjusted. The coil-over shocks provide additional flexibility. These can also be adjusted by turning the cylinder at the bottom to shorten or lengthen them.

Close-up of front suspension shows how brackets were welded to original frame. The strut rod is a unique item custom made by Heidt's Hot Rod shop in Illinois, to provide additional control and stability.

This photo shows the top control arm and coil spring. Also, the engine mount is visible. It was welded to original frame rail.

While the original frame rails were kept in the front and under the cab, behind the cab and dual rail setup was fabricated. The narrow rear end needed narrower rails. These run through and inside the stock frame rails under the cab for extra strength and rigidity.

The rear end uses a traction bar on the axle for stability, and four links, two on each side of the axle. These links can be adjusted to change the stiffness of the rear axle.

Rear view shows the nine-inch Ford rear end, narrowed, and coil-over shock absorbers. The bottom of the coil mount can be tightened or loosened to tighten up either side of the rear end.

View of the right side shows coil-over shocks and traction bar mount.

Mickey Thompson Sportsman tires are mounted on Center Line 15×15 wheels.

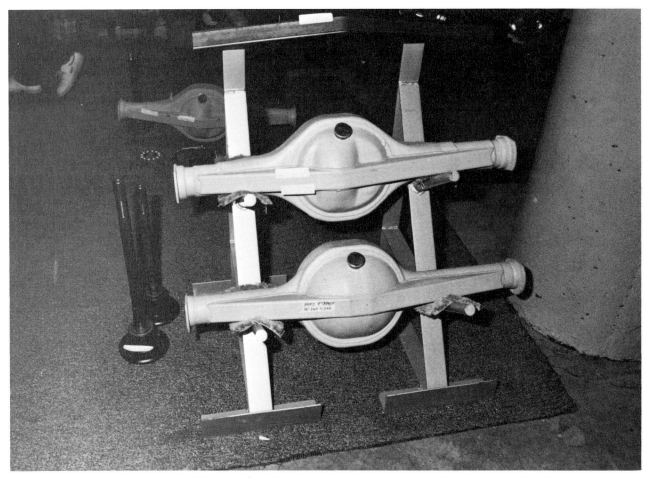

At a swap meet, some narrowed Ford rear ends are displayed for sale. These are 38 inches wide, with short- *ened axle shafts. For race trucks the rear axles are usually well below 40 inches in width.*

Restoration parts, supplies and equipment

There are several outstanding suppliers of parts for older pickups. They usually specialize in Chevrolet or Ford parts. This is primarily because of the enormous inventories of parts required to do a good job: Golden State Pickup Parts stocks over 3,500 parts for the 1947 to 1972 Chevy pickups! Other suppliers of Chevy parts include the following:

Arizona F-100
5230 W. Luke #2
Glendale, AZ 85301
    All pickups 1953-56

Bruce Horkey Cabinetry
R.R. 4 Box 188
Windom, MN 56101
    Ford 1932-88, Chevy 1940-88,
Dodge 1951-88

Eastwood Company
Malvern, PA 19355
    Restoration materials

Fairlane Company
210 E. Walker Street
St. Johns, MI 48879
    Ford parts 1938-56

Fiberglass & Wood Company
Route #3 Box 891
Nashville, GA 31639
    Chevrolet 1931-72

Grumpy's Truck Parts
Box 4721
New River Stage
Phoenix, AZ 85027
    Chevrolet/GMC 1947-66

Mar-K Specialized Mfg. Company
8022 N. Wilshire Center
Oklahoma City, OK 73132
    Chevrolet tailgates 1941-87

Obsolete Chevrolet Parts Company, Inc.
524 Hazel Avenue
Nashville, GA 31639
    Chevrolet 1929-59 and 1960-72

Roberts Motor Parts
17 Prospect Street
Newbury, MA 01985
    Chevrolet and GMC, 1927-72

Ron Francis' Wire Works
167 Keystone Road
Chester, PA 19013
    Complete wiring kit and accessories

Sacramento Vintage Ford, Inc.
4675 Aldona Lane
Sacramento, CA 95841
    Ford pickup parts

The Filling Station
6929 Power Inn Road
Sacramento, CA 95828
    Chevrolet 1929-66

Vern Sell
P.O. Box 650
Siloam Springs, AR 72761
    Heavy-Chevy truck parts

Manufacturers

Accent Distributing
6502 Elmwood Ave.
Suite 121
Indianapolis, IN 46203

Air Sensors
708 Industry Dr.
Seattle, WA 98188
   Electronic fuel injection system

Bell Super Tech
152 M St.
Fresno, CA 93721
   Lowering spindles for Chevy

Bill's Custom Louvering
623 Shady Ln.
Windber, PA 15963
   Louvered tailgates, roll pans and
other parts

Bushwacker
9200 N. Decatur St.
Portland, OR 97203
   Ground effects, other accessories

C&A Control Systems, Inc.
7117 Commercial Park Dr.
Knoxville, TN 37918
   LA-Z-START and Startguard remote starting systems

Conversion Components, Inc.
P.O. Box 429
Elkhart, IN 46515
   Seats, tonneau covers, ground
effects and more

Custom Wheel Emporium
5656 Auburn Blvd.
Sacramento, CA 95841

East Coast Customs
11335 Middlesettlements Rd.
Maryville, TN 37801
   Ground effects

Eastwood Company
580 Lancaster Ave.
Box 296
Malvern, PA 19355
   Restoration tools and equipment

Extang Corporation
2298 S. Industrial Hwy.
Ann Arbor, MI 48104
   Euro Lens headlight covers, Tuff
Tonno covers

GMC Truck Motorsports
Truck Center of L.A.
6901 S. Almeda St.
Los Angeles, CA 90001
   Corvette TPI engines and parts,
other custom accessories for GMC
sport trucks

General Systems Research
Box 604
Dearborn, MI 48121
   Electronic fuel injection system

Helder Manufacturing
11043-C Oroville Hwy.
Marysville, CA 95901
   Hydraulic parts, custom parts

Holley
Replacement Parts Division
11955 E. Nine Mile Rd.
Warren, MI 48089

HoTTops
1425 E. University
Suite 4
Tempe, AZ 85281
   Convertible conversions for most
minis and other pickups, neons,
ground effects

John Baker Performance
P.O. Box 329
Hwy. 35 & County Rd. D
Webster, WI 54893-0329

L.C. Engineering
2978 First St.
Unit G
LaVerne, CA 91750

Leigenfelter Racing
Decatur, IN
   TPI engine parts, modified high
performance TPI

Low Rider Hydraulics and Custom
Accessories
962 E. Santa Clara St.
San Jose, CA 95116
   Bed lift kits, hydraulic parts

Main Street Graphics
5508 Elmwood
Suite 318
Indianapolis, IN 46203
   Billy the Kid custom graphics artist

MaxiGuard of America
2700 Touhy Ave.
Elk Grove Village, IL 60007
   Vehicle security systems

Perfection Upholstery
542 W. Colfax
Palatine, IL 60067
   Custom interiors

190

Performance Covers
140-K Mason Cir.
Concord, CA 94520
  Seat covers

Pop Top Minis
31200 La Baya Dr.
Suite 303
Westlake Village, CA 91362
  Convertible truck conversions

Quarter Mile Competition Engines,
Inc.
10001 S. Harlem Ave.
Chicago Ridge, IL 60415
  Dyer blowers, parts, high performance engine rebuilding

Quickor Ground Effects
Warn Industries
13270 SE Pheasant Ct.
Milwaukie, OR 97222
  Ground effects kits

Racecar Painting, Lettering & Decals
Attn: Accent Distributing
5602 Elmwood Ave.
Suite 121
Indianapolis, IN 46203
  Vinyl graphics decals

Rancho Suspension
6925 Atlantic Ave.
Long Beach, CA 90805
  Lowering kits

Ron Francis' Wire Works
167 Keyston Rd.
Chester, PA 19013
  Replacement wiring, Component Panel

Rugged Trail Suspensions
237 W. National Pike
Uniontown, PA 15401

Sanderson Headers
202 Ryan Way
South San Francisco, CA 94080

Spring-Align
2312 Rand Rd.
Palatine, IL 60074
  Custom suspension work, lowering

Stillen Sportparts, Inc.
1627 South Boyd
Santa Ana, CA 92705
  Replacement grilles, other aerodynamic parts

Street Neon
P.O. Box 95488
Houston, TX 77213

Trail Master Suspensions
649 E. Chicago Rd.
Coldwater, MI 49036

Turbo City
1201 W. Katella
Orange, CA 92667
  Replacement chips

Weiand
P.O. Box 65977
Dept. #5
Los Angeles, CA 90065
  Blowers, accessories, high performance engine parts

Index